THE
WOODVILLE WOMEN

To my mother, that I wish I'd known

To my daughter, that I'll always love

And to all the women who went before us, in whose footsteps we walk

THE
WOODVILLE WOMEN

100 YEARS OF PLANTAGENET AND TUDOR HISTORY

SARAH J. HODDER

PEN & SWORD
HISTORY

AN IMPRINT OF PEN & SWORD BOOKS LTD.
YORKSHIRE - PHILADELPHIA

First published in Great Britain in 2022 by
PEN AND SWORD HISTORY
An imprint of
Pen & Sword Books Ltd
Yorkshire – Philadelphia

ISBN 978 1 39909 456 6

Typeset in Times New Roman 11.5/14 by SJmagic DESIGN SERVICES, India.
Printed and bound in the UK by CPI Group (UK) Ltd.

Pen & Sword Books Limited incorporates the imprints of Atlas, Archaeology,
Aviation, Discovery, Family History, Fiction, History, Maritime, Military, Military
Classics, Politics, Select, Transport, True Crime, Air World, Frontline Publishing,
Leo Cooper, Remember When, Seaforth Publishing, The Praetorian Press,
Wharncliffe Local History, Wharncliffe Transport, Wharncliffe True Crime and
White Owl.

For a complete list of Pen & Sword titles please contact
PEN & SWORD BOOKS LIMITED
47 Church Street, Barnsley, South Yorkshire, S70 2AS, England
E-mail: enquiries@pen-and-sword.co.uk
Website: www.pen-and-sword.co.uk

Or
PEN AND SWORD BOOKS
1950 Lawrence Rd, Havertown, PA 19083, USA
E-mail: Uspen-and-sword@casematepublishers.com
Website: www.penandswordbooks.com

Contents

Acknowledgements

I would like to thank Jonathan Feakin who very generously lent me his time and assistance with images from the Grafton Regis village website. Also to Sarah-Beth Watkins and Claire Hopkins who are always at the end of an email with support and advice and to my family, who allow me to indulge my passion for the past and to spend time walking alongside the ghosts of those women who feature in this book.

Introduction

The rule of the Plantagenets began in England in 1154, when Henry II, the son of Matilda and Geoffrey Plantagenet, Count of Anjou, succeeded to the English throne. This great dynasty would continue to rule for the next 300 years, their magnificent reign ending on a battlefield in the heart of England in 1485. The battle on Bosworth field, fought by men and with the kingdom of England at stake, bought a crushing end to the line of great Plantagenet kings and heralded the birth of a new dynasty, that of the Tudors. As the victor on that day, Henry Tudor would become the first-ever king of perhaps England's most famous dynasty of kings and queens, a dynasty which itself would end a comparatively small 100 years later with the death of Henry's granddaughter, the glorious and strong-willed Elizabeth I.

This book tells the tale of three women, just over 100 years in time span also, that begins in the Plantagenet era and ends during the reign of the Tudors. The protagonists are also named Elizabeth and they are all related – mother, daughter and granddaughter. Between them, these women lived through the Wars of the Roses and the rule of seven different kings, with our last Elizabeth dying early into the reign of Edward VI. Due to their sex, these women did not make take their place on the battlefield, nor could they make major decisions on England's fate, or even at times about their own destinies. But that did not make them powerless. Through their lives and the decisions they made, they could and did forge their own paths in a world dominated by men, sometimes with quite dramatic consequences. Through their stories and their involvement with the royal court, we can get a glimpse of an age of knights and chivalry, kings and queens, love and life.

Our first Elizabeth is Elizabeth Woodville, the young widow who one day crossed paths with England's king, Edward IV, and captivated him to the extent that he made her his wife and queen. In that one small act of marriage, she became a heroine to many and a villain in the eyes of many more who resented the meteoric rise of the Woodville family. Together, Elizabeth and Edward had ten children and the eldest, Princess Elizabeth of York, is our second Elizabeth. After the disappearance of her brothers, the rightful heirs to her father's throne, Princess Elizabeth became Queen of England after marrying Henry Tudor. But her path to the throne was not a straightforward one. Indeed, it was a plan concocted from a sanctuary building between mothers and its success was by no means guaranteed. But the hard-won union of Elizabeth of York and Henry Tudor bought an end to the conflicts of York and Lancaster once and for all, uniting the red rose and the white into the new Tudor rose.

Our last Elizabeth was not a queen, but a countess. The granddaughter of Elizabeth Woodville, and the niece of Elizabeth of York, she was Elizabeth Grey, the daughter of Thomas Grey and his wife Cecily Bonville. Thomas Grey, also known as the Marquis of Dorset, was Elizabeth's son from her first marriage to Sir John Grey of Groby. Elizabeth Grey led an eventful life, entwined with her cousins Mary Tudor and Henry VIII and through her marriage to Gerald Fitzgerald in or around 1520, she became Countess of Kildare. She died a year after her famous cousin Henry, in the reign of his much longed-for son, Edward VI.

All our Elizabeth's led extraordinary lives. Products of their time and circumstances, they were living in a man's world but all fought fiercely for themselves and their families and through courage, perseverance and resilience they survived and thrived. Through their stories, we can travel through 100 years of history.

Chapter 1

Before the Wars

Sometime between the years 1437 to 1440, in the sleepy village of Grafton in Northamptonshire, a girl named Elizabeth was born. No heralds announced her birth, and none other than her parents and close family celebrated her arrival into the world. So insignificant was she to the outside world that in the days before parish records had begun, her birth date was not even recorded. As her parents rocked her cradle and rejoiced in her safe arrival, not even they would have dreamt that their firstborn daughter would one day be Queen of England. Or that her grandson would become one of England's most infamous kings, making his way through six wives, dispatching two of them by way of the executioners' block. Or that a great-great-great-grandson of hers would rule over England's Witch Trials leading to the death of hundreds of women, accused of sorcery and black magic. But that was the future. For now, all that mattered was that mother and baby had survived the birth and that all was well in the world.

Baby Elizabeth's parents, who welcomed her into the world, were Richard Woodville and Jacquetta, his wife of six years. Whether Elizabeth was their firstborn child or just their firstborn girl is a matter of debate. Her brother, Anthony Woodville was their eldest son and both Anthony and Elizabeth were born somewhere between 1437 and 1440. It is also likely that another son, named Richard, was also born during this three-year period. A later note written in the 1580s by Robert Glover, Somerset Herald, has been cited in several works and gives a highly probable scenario of the birth order of the Woodville children.[1] If the note is factually correct then Elizabeth was Richard and Jacquetta's third child.

That she was a child born into a marriage based on love may have shaped Elizabeth Woodville's views on family from an early age. In the days when many marriages were contracts made between families, there would certainly have been no expectations that parents would love or in

1

some cases even like each other. But Richard and Jacquetta had married for love and as she grew up and their family expanded, the love and loyalty between Elizabeth and her parents and siblings would be clear to see throughout her life.

An accusation thrown at the whole Woodville clan, both during their lifetime, as they and their eldest daughter climbed to the upper echelons of society, and which has followed them throughout the centuries, is that the family were upstarts and social climbers. But in reality, they were never the small insignificant family that they were made out to be. That Elizabeth would reach the position of queen was certainly never on the horizon but only a few short years before Elizabeth's birth, her mother, Jacquetta, had been one of the foremost ladies in England, second only to the king's mother. But to first understand how Richard and Jacquetta ended up raising their family and a future queen in the quiet yet beautiful backwaters of Grafton, we must first go back and tell their tale.

Elizabeth's mother, Jacquetta, was descended from one of the leading families in northern Europe – the House of Luxembourg. Born c.1415/16, she was the eldest daughter of Peter of Luxembourg and his wife Margaret. Peter had inherited the title Count of Brienne upon the death of his father, John of Luxembourg, sometime around 1397 and in 1430 he succeeded his aunt, Jeanne of Luxembourg, Countess of Saint-Pol to become the new Count of Saint-Pol. Jacquetta's ancestry was therefore considerably rich, both in fact and, interestingly, in myth. In Phillipa Gregory's *The White Queen*, we are introduced to Melusine, the water goddess, and ancestress of Elizabeth Woodville through her mother's lineage. Although *The White Queen* is fiction based on fact, Melusine was not invented by Gregory, she is a mythical creature that actually features heavily in Jacquetta's real-life family tree.

During the Middle Ages throughout northern France and the low countries, family genealogy was often littered with mythical ancestors. As the centuries come and go, facts and folklore often become intertwined, blurring the lines between the real and imagined. The tales of King Arthur and Camelot or Robin Hood and his band of merry men have become part of our English folklore – legendary figures who may or may not be based in fact. For medieval Europe, it was Melusine who emerged in popular culture, a legendary water goddess who took the form of a mermaid, serpent or dragon and who was considered a seductress of men.

As a daughter of Luxembourg, Jacquetta's ancestry, therefore, weaved right back through the Counts of Saint-Pol and the House of Luxembourg to Melusine, her legendary ancestress. The Melusine legend was especially connected to the royal house of Luxembourg and the French Lusignan Royal House that ruled Cyprus from 1192–1489 and Jacquetta would certainly have learned of her ancestry as she grew up.

One of the most famous Melusine tales was written by Jean D'Arras, a bookbinder or librarian writing under the patronage of Jean, Duke of Berry. Completed in 1393, the book was published in print in Geneva in 1478. The duke's mother was Bonne of Luxembourg, daughter of Jean of Luxembourg and he was obviously aware of the widespread belief that the House of Luxembourg descended from Melusine.

As with all myths, several versions of the Melusine story exist, although they all have the same root at the heart of the tale – that of a promise made and subsequently broken. The book that Jean D'Arras wrote was titled *Melusine; or the Noble History of Lusignan* and was written to tell the story of this noble house for his patron.

The Melusine story generally begins the same way, as we learn the details of Melusine's parentage. Her father was said to be a human named Elinas, King of Scotland. Elinas married a beautiful fairy named Presine and made a vow to her before their wedding that he would never see her in childbirth. But one day, Elinas broke his promise and had to deal with the consequences. Presine left him, taking with her their three newborn daughters: Melusine, Melior and Palestine. Many years later, his grown-up daughters learnt of their father's broken promise and in anger at his betrayal of their mother, they imprisoned him inside a mountain where he would remain for eternity. But this action only earned them their mother's wrath, for she knew that without their father, the girls would never live their lives as mortals. In her anger, she assigned each of them a punishment. In Jean D'Arras' version, Melusine's sentence was that each Saturday she would be transformed into a serpent from the waist down. If she married, she would have to keep her secret from her husband, for this would surely shock and disgust a human man.

One day Melusine did meet a man she wanted to marry – a young nobleman named Raymondin. Raymondin had fled his native Brittany and whilst wandering through a forest, he came across a natural water source and there he met Melusine. The pair fell in love and agreed to marry. Once more a deal was struck. Melusine agreed to marry him on one condition – that he agreed to give her privacy every Saturday. She in turn promised to make him the most noble man of his lineage. The pair married, and Melusine used her magic to fashion a sumptuous wedding feast. After their marriage, she created a realm for them to inhabit, a world where springs appeared overnight and castles appeared out of nowhere. The fortress she revealed for them to live in was, in this version of the tale, named Lusignan.

To raise their status, Melusine named herself as a beautiful daughter of a powerful king and at the same time sought Raymondin's father's estates in Brittany and restored his good name. For a while, the couple lived an idyllic life together, bearing many sons, two of whom, Urian and Guyon, became Kings of Cyprus. Their son Antoine became Duke of Luxembourg and Renaud became King of Bohemia. This is where fact and fiction meet as in fact, Guy of Lusignan was indeed ruler of Cyprus. But one day, in a repeat of her mother's fate, Raymondin allowed himself to be persuaded by his brother to spy on Melusine. Cautioned that his wife's disappearance one day a week was suspicious, he peered in on her as she took her Saturday bath, thus breaking his vow. What he saw was that his beautiful wife was half-fairy and half-demon. With her secret revealed, Melusine fled never to be seen again.[2]

Jacquetta's ancestral connection to this mythical water goddess took a similar course. For the House of Luxembourg, the progenitor of the story was her actual ancestor, Siegfried, the first Count of Luxembourg who ruled from 922 to 988. In the mid-tenth century, he acquired the rocky promontory of Lucilinburhuc, where in 963 he built a castle. Siegfried actually married a woman named Hedwig of Nordgau around 950 but in legend, it is told that he took a first wife, a beautiful water goddess who he met one day in the forest near a stream. He was captivated by her and promised to marry her, agreeing to the condition that on one day a week, his wife would be allowed her privacy and she would not see him that day. It was Melusine who is said to have created the castle on the rocky outcrop that they lived in and their marriage was happy until Siegfried broke his vow and spied on her one Saturday whilst she was bathing. In this version of the tale, he discovers her secret – that she was half-human, half-mermaid. Realising her husband had broken his vow to her, Melusine gave an anguished cry and the bath immediately sunk into the rock and she was lost to him forever.

If I should be your wife, you must not seek
To know of anything that I may do
In secret on the last day of the week;
Upon that day I shall be lost to you.
But on the other six a consort meek,
Devoted, frank, affectionate and true.
If this shall be a bargain, so declare,
If not, ride off, and leave me in despair[3]

Jacquetta owned a rare copy of a manuscript with the story of Melusine in later life and perhaps read the tale of this mythical ancestor to her own children as they grew up.[4]

As a daughter of the House of Luxembourg, Jacquetta herself was raised in the beautiful castles and fortresses of northern France. She would have expected a good marriage to have been made for her and at the age of around seventeen or eighteen that marriage took place. The groom chosen for her was John, Duke of Bedford, the Regent of France and the uncle of the English king.

England's ruling monarch at the time of Jacquetta's marriage was Henry VI. He had ascended the throne in 1422, when he was just nine months old, after his father Henry V died. Due to his youthful age, a regency council was formed to rule in the king's name until he was old enough to do so himself. The council was headed up by his uncles, John, Duke of Bedford and Humphrey, Duke of Gloucester. From 1422 until 1437, during Henry VI's minority, England remained under their protectorate. The Duke of Gloucester was the king's representative in England and Bedford, Jacquetta's new husband, had been overseeing English territories in northern France.

Jacquetta was the duke's second wife; his first was Anne, Duchess of Burgundy. Anne was the sister of the Duke of Burgundy, England's great ally in the ongoing wars between the English and the French over huge swathes of land that both sides claimed as their own. But in late 1432, at the Hotel of Tournelles in Paris, Anne had died of what was described by the French chronicler, Monstrelet, as 'a lingering disorder'.[5]

Jacquetta's introduction to her charming new husband was made through her uncle, Louis de Luxembourg, who was one of the duke's closest advisors. Over twenty-five years older than Jacquetta, the duke was obviously enchanted by this lovely young woman and Louis quickly arranged the marriage between his English master and his young niece. The pair were married at the start of 1433, just a few short weeks after the death of the duke's first wife. The Duke of Burgundy was out of the country when the wedding took place, and learning of the marriage upon his return, he was incensed that his sister had been disrespected in this way. The usual accepted period of mourning was a year and the Duke of Burgundy took Bedford's second marriage as an insult to his sister and her family. From that moment on, relations quickly soured between England and Burgundy.

Jacquetta and Bedford were married in the town of Therouenne, with their sumptuous wedding feast celebrated in the episcopal palace there. The duke was so delighted with his new bride that he presented two magnificent bells of great value to the church, that had been made in England and transported across the channel at his own expense. The young Jacquetta, aged just eighteen or nineteen, was now the Duchess of Bedford.

After the wedding, Jacquetta would have left her family home to set up home in Paris in the duke's residence at the Hotel du Bourbon. Having been a new Duchess for just a few months, Jacquetta was soon to make her first trip to England. It must have been with excitement and some trepidation that she set sail from Calais across the English Channel to what would eventually become her new adopted homeland. As a duchess and the wife of the king's uncle, she was second in the land only to the king's mother, Catherine of Valois. Catherine had also made the same journey as a young bride, when she had married Henry V back in 1420, in a treaty negotiated by her father, the French king, Charles VI. In what became known as the Treaty of Troyes, Henry V took Catherine as his bride, and Charles agreed to name Henry as heir apparent to the French throne. But Henry V had not lived long enough to see that come to fruition, and Catherine was now the mother of the new young King of England.

Arriving through the gates into the city of London, the duke would have been greeted as a returning hero by the citizens of London, all lining the streets keen to catch a glimpse of him and his new duchess. When they presented themselves before the king, Henry and the council were so pleased with the duke's service in France that they offered him the option of remaining in England and taking retirement. Perhaps looking forward to a quieter life and settling down with his new wife, the duke accepted their offer. Leaving London, Bedford and Jacquetta travelled to the duke's home of Penshurst Place in Kent, just half a day's ride from London, where they would remain living for the next year.

For her first experience of living in England, Jacquetta could have done worse than the beautiful Penshurst Estate. Penshurst was a picturesque Kentish manor, acquired by Sir John Pultenay, a rich wool merchant, in around 1338. In 1340, he built the great hall that still survives today, a spectacular structure with high windows providing light and a beautiful chestnut timbered roof, the beams supported on grotesque wooden figures. Stairs from the main hall led up to the solar, a private apartment of the house, where the duke and duchess could enjoy their privacy.[6] The rest of the manor house was completed by 1341. Bedford acquired the house around 1430 and in later years it would pass through several hands before becoming Crown property in the time of Henry VIII, eventually becoming synonymous with the Sidney family who was gifted it by Edward VI in 1552.

Although vastly different from the castles of her homeland, Jacquetta's first year in England was spent in comparative luxury. A later member of the Sidney family, the poet Phillip Sidney, described the beauty of Penshurst in his literary work 'The Countess of Pembroke's Arcadia', written in the late sixteenth century.

> The house itself was built of fair and strong stone, not affecting so much any extraordinary kind of fineness, as an honorable representing of firm stateliness; the lights, doors and stairs, rather directed to the use of the guest than to the eye of the artificer, and yet, as the one chiefly heeded, so the other not neglected; each place handsome without curiosity, and homely without loathsomeness, not so dainty as not to be trod on, nor yet slubbered up with good fellowship— all more lasting than beautiful (but that the consideration of the exceeding lastingness made the eye believe it was exceeding beautiful)[7]

During her first year in England, Jacquetta would no doubt have met her brother-in-law Humphrey, Duke of Gloucester and his wife, Eleanor Cobham, the Duchess of Gloucester, who had made a scandalous marriage in 1428. Eleanor had once been a lady-in-waiting to the duke's

7

first wife, Jacqueline of Hainault, and it is thought that she had become the duke's mistress sometime around 1425. Eleanor was reportedly exceptionally beautiful, exceedingly clever and hugely ambitious[8] and Gloucester fell head over heels for her, so much so that he managed to get his marriage to his first wife annulled so he could marry Eleanor. Together they made a fine couple, with Eleanor's intelligence and loveliness complimenting her husband's cultivated and pleasure-loving character. During their marriage, they developed a manor at Greenwich into a pleasure garden. Known as La Pleasaunce, the manor was encircled by a wall with walks bordering the Thames, a tower, and a conduit. Sociable, well-known and admired, the Gloucesters formed their own miniature court here, attracting poets, musicians, scholars and physicians amongst their friends. Jacquetta and Bedford may also have moved in this sphere for a while and Jacquetta's later love of literature and learning, a trait that she shared with her eldest son Anthony, may well have been developed during these early days of mingling with some of these great and intellectual minds.

Bedford and Jacquetta remained in England at Penshurst for just over a year but in July 1434, the duke was persuaded to return to France to once again oversee the disorder that was taking place. The couple returned to a troubled Paris, where law and order were collapsing. Since their departure just over a year ago, the Duke of Burgundy had switched sides and was now assisting the French, who were reclaiming territory at speed and Louis of Luxembourg was pleased to have his old master back to assist him in defending English interests. He was also no doubt pleased to see his niece again. Bedford attempted to control the damage that had been done in his absence, and part of this involved bringing in reinforcements to strengthen the garrison at Calais. One of the men he brought in was a young man named Richard Woodville, who was assigned the position of captain of the garrison. But sadly Bedford's health was failing and fourteen months after arriving back in France, he died aged just forty-four. He was buried in Rouen, and Jacquetta, just into her early twenties, found herself a widow.

Presumably during her second sojourn in France, Jacquetta and Richard Woodville crossed paths and at some point, an attraction was born. As a duchess of England, she was a subject of the English king and therefore any future marriage she undertook could only be decided by him. Awarded her dower by Henry VI in February 1436, she was summoned to return to England. But after the death of Bedford, Jacquetta and Richard became close and sometime during 1436 they married in secret. They presumably stayed in Calais as long as they could, enjoying the first few weeks of wedded bliss. But they knew they could not remain in France forever, and eventually had to return to England to face their king. Returning to English shores in late 1436/early 1437, they had to confess their actions to King Henry. Their decision to return when they did may have been in some part due to Jacquetta finding herself pregnant around this time, and realising that with a child on the way, they had little choice but to return to England and face the consequences.

The marriage was not popular with either Henry VI or Jacquetta's family, who would have hoped for a husband of higher status for their daughter than a lowly soldier. According to Monstrelet: 'In this year, the duchess of Bedford, sister to the count de St. Pol, married, from inclination, an English knight called Sir Richard Woodville, a young man, very handsome and well made, but, in regard to birth, inferior to her first husband, the regent, and to herself. Louis de Luxembourg, archbishop of Rouen, and her other relations, were very angry at this match, but they could not prevent it'.[9]

Richard and Jacquetta were eventually forgiven by King Henry and received his pardon in October 1437, although the pair were still fined £1,000 by the king for marrying without his permission. They retired to Grafton, a Woodville family property, where Jacquetta presumably gave birth to her first child.

Richard Woodville's ancestry was not as illustrious as his wife's but the Woodville family had owned and inhabited properties in and around Grafton for centuries and were well established in the area, although Richard had been born not in Northamptonshire but in his family home of The Mote in Kent. The Woodville name can be traced back to at least the thirteenth century, although the original variant of the name was Wydeville or Widville, and Woodville is a later spelling that would not have been used by the family, although it is being used in this book as the most commonly recognised version of the surname today.

The small yet perfectly formed manor of Grafton lies just ten miles south of Northampton and four miles north-west of Stony Stratford. Situated high at the top of the hill overlooking a river valley, in 1086 only one household was recorded there, and by 1301 there were still only sixty-two people assessed to the lay subsidy.[10] From around 1100, the church and manor house (presumably the manor house was the building that stood there in 1086 to the west of the church) passed into the hands of a Norman monastery – Notre Dame de Grestain. The monastery retained possession until 1348 and the abbot of Grestain appears as the tenant-in-chief of Grafton in the early twelfth-century Northamptonshire survey and as lord of Grafton in 1166.

The connection between the abbey of Notre Dame de Grestain and the small English parish of Grafton came about through Robert, Count of Mortain, the half-brother of William the Conqueror. Located just a few kilometres from Honfleur, the abbey was founded by a Herluin de Conteville, according to legend, after he was encouraged to do so in a visitation from the Virgin Mary.

William the Conqueror was brought up by Herluin, who married his mother when William was a young boy. William's mother, the daughter of a tanner from Falaise, was named Arlette. Reportedly when William's father, Robert the Magnificent (the future Duke of Normandy), saw Arlette washing clothes in a fountain, he immediately fell head over heels in love with her. Robert and Arlette married according to the pagan tradition of the Vikings which meant their union was not recognised by the Church.

When William was just seven years old, his father decided to make a pilgrimage to the Holy Land. In the event that he died on the way, he asked Herluin to marry Arlette to protect her and their young son. As he feared, Robert never returned. Together Herluin and Arlette had several more children, including Robert, who would become the Count of Mortain.

When William invaded England, his half-brother Robert accompanied him. Through Robert's marriage to Mathilde de Montgomery, the daughter of Roger de Montgomery, the Earl of Shrewsbury, he obtained Grafton. It was they who gifted the abbey with 'A house in London, twenty-nine towns in the counties of Dorset, Sussex, Worchester, Northampton, Buckingham, Hertfordshire and Cornwall, the manor of Grafton (or "Grastone"), and the patronage of ten churches'.[11]

Grafton remained the property of the abbey until 1348, when it sold to Sir Michael de la Pole, a wealthy Hull merchant, for the remainder of the term of a thousand years. The manor house remained in the possession of the de la Pole family for the next three generations, and if the Woodvilles lived in the manor house during this period, it would have been as tenants of the de la Poles.

We know that as far back as the early fourteenth century, a Richard Wydeville lived at Grafton. He was born c.1310 and was a Knight of the Shire. Upon his death, sometime after 1378, his eldest son, John Wydeville (born c.1341) inherited the family seat at Grafton.[12] John Wydeville married a lady named Katherine Frembaud, who by their marriage bought into the family an impressive number of lands in Northamptonshire, Bedfordshire and Buckinghamshire and the couple obtained a royal charter enabling them to enjoy rights of free warren on the demesne lands. They had at least three sons and three daughters together, and it was their eldest son, Thomas, who became his father's heir to the Grafton properties in the fifteenth century.

When John Wydeville's wife Katherine died, he took as his second wife a lady named Isabel Passelow and they had one son together whom they named Richard. During his lifetime, John held various important offices in Bedfordshire, Buckinghamshire and Northamptonshire, including three terms as sheriff. In 1386, he sued Alice Perrers, the widow of William, Lord Windsor, and sometime mistress of Edward III, for possession of a messuage and three shops in Northampton. John Wydeville died sometime between 1399 and February 1401, when his eldest son Thomas Woodville (1364–1435) inherited all his father's estates, including presumably the tenancy at the manor house.

Thomas's half-brother, Richard, the product of the union between his father and Isabel, was not in line to inherit any lands or properties. As the youngest son, he made his own way in the world, serving as chamberlain to John, Duke of Bedford in 1422, and eventually earning himself enough money to buy The Mote at Maidstone in Kent. It was here at the Mote that our Richard Woodville would be born, in 1405. His mother was a lady named Joan Bittlesgate and Richard had two siblings – Elizabeth and Joan. Richard then followed in his father's footsteps in the service of John, Duke of Bedford.

It was only after the death of Thomas Wydeville, that the manor of Grafton came into the possession of the senior Richard Woodville. His mother, Isabel, had fought hard for some sort of inheritance for her only son and when Thomas Wydeville drew up his will on 12 October 1434, both his wives, Elizabeth and Alice had predeceased him. His next heirs were his sister, Elizabeth and the descendants of his other sister, Agnes, who between them shared the bulk of his estates. But it was the manor of Grafton that was finally settled on Richard Woodville senior by his half-brother, Thomas. So, when the newly married Richard and Jacquetta returned to England in 1437, presumably the tenancy of the Grafton manor house was offered to them by Richard Woodville senior, who was still living at The Mote. By 1440, the Poles had sold the manor of Grafton to Richard and Jacquetta, and they used it as security for two loans totalling 900 marks from two London merchants. Named 'The Bury', Richard and Jacquetta had a place they could call their own and they made it their family home.[13]

By the early 1440s when Richard and Jacquetta purchased the manor house, they were already a family of five with Anthony, another son called Richard (no doubt after his father) and Elizabeth. Richard Woodville continued to serve in the Calais Garrison, and it is likely that Jacquetta travelled with him on occasions, leaving the children behind in the care of a nurse. Presumably still very much in love, the couple were living a good life with their increasing brood.

Whether Jacquetta stayed connected with her former in-laws from her first marriage is unknown but in 1441, she would have received shocking news of the fate that had befallen her former sister-in-law. After the Duke of Bedford's death, his brother, Gloucester, became the heir apparent to the throne as during the mid-1430s, King Henry was neither married nor had any heirs of his own. A hugely popular figure, Gloucester had reached the height of his influence in the late 1430s and as his wife, Eleanor was also in a powerful position. It seems she exercised some influence over the young king and it is alleged that after Bedford's death, she became obsessed with the possibility of her husband succeeding the unmarried Henry VI.[14]

Reportedly obsessed as to whether this scenario would ever come about, she consulted horoscopes to predict the likelihood of there ever being a King Humphrey. The reading of horoscopes in itself was not a crime but unwisely her associates, Roger Bolingbroke and Thomas Southwell, her physician, made a somewhat foolish prediction that the king would indeed die. Predicting the death of a king was treason and the authorities hauled them in for questioning, whilst hurriedly commissioning an alternative horoscope to reassure the king that all was well. Southwell and Bolingbroke were indicted for sorcery, felony, and treason and Eleanor was charged with heresy and witchcraft as an accessory. A second woman was also caught up in the plot – Margery Jourdemayne, also known as the Witch of Eye. Eleanor tried to defend them both, claiming she only consulted Margery in order to receive potions to aid her in becoming pregnant but to no avail – Margery was tried as a witch and burnt at the stake.

Eleanor escaped with her life but was ordered to do penance by walking barefoot through London, dressed only in her kirtle and carrying a taper – a punishment usually meted out to harlots. She was then thrown into prison. To make matters worse, her husband, who had loved her enough to leave his first wife for her, completely disowned her. Her fall from grace was total. Forcibly divorced, she spent the rest of her life in prison, dying whilst still incarcerated on 7 July 1452.

The treatment of her ex-sister-in-law would have been a shock to Jacquetta, but perhaps not a surprise. The belief in superstition and magic was widespread in the Middle Ages. From the local wise woman who healed through potions, to the folklore that dictated the festivals and traditions, this connection to nature and mystical beliefs were very much a part of life. But there was also a darker side to this and many were scared of the power of magic and the existence of the witch. Although England had not yet reached the darkest days of witch trials, being accused of being a witch was still a very real fear. The accusation was often levelled against women and was a powerful weapon. Once accused, it was exceedingly difficult to prove your innocence. Both Jacquetta and Elizabeth to a lesser extent would face that accusation later in their lives, but in 1441 Jacquetta received first-hand experience of how it could destroy a woman's life as she witnessed the downfall of her sister-in-law.

A few years after this incident, a very much alive King Henry prepared to take a wife. In an agreement that formed part of a truce with France, his intended bride was Margaret of Anjou, the daughter of René, Duke of Anjou. A proxy marriage took place in March 1445, and shortly after Margaret arrived in Paris, where she was handed over by her brother into the care of the Dukes of York and Suffolk, who had travelled to France to escort her to England. The Duke of York, with 600 archers, welcomed her on behalf of King Henry and gave her a palfrey decked out in a crimson and gold velvet cloth embroidered with gold roses as a gift from her husband. Jacquetta and Richard were also part of the party that went to collect her and escort her to England. Margaret was accompanied all the way through Normandy to the coast, where she readied herself to board the ship to England. Having made the same journey herself as a young bride, Jacquetta may have been a good support to Margaret and the two women later became good friends, a bond that may have been formed during this voyage. When the party did set sail, the ship was buffeted by the wind of a terrible storm and during this rough sea crossing the ship lost both its masts. Almost certainly this was Margaret's first sea journey, and she was exhausted and ill by the time she landed at Portchester on 9 April 1445. Much to the disappointment of the townspeople who had planned a great welcome to their new queen, she could only stagger her way to a small cottage where she promptly fainted. It is reported that shortly after her arrival, the king visited her in disguise, dressed as a squire delivering a letter. She dismissed him without acknowledging his identity and whether she realised it was him or not is impossible to say.

Once fully established at court, Jacquetta was chosen to serve as one of Margaret's ladies and their friendship blossomed. She was often rewarded by Margaret for both her service and companionship and on 1 January 1446, Jacquetta's servants were to receive a new year's gift of 53s 4d.[15] Jacquetta herself also received gifts from the queen on many occasions.

As for the young Elizabeth, sadly these first early years of her life are pretty much lost to us. With her parents involved in the Lancastrian court, Elizabeth and her siblings would have remained at home in Grafton under the care of a nurse, or occasionally travelled with their parents as they got older. Maybe the young Elizabeth caught an early glimpse of court life, perhaps visiting with her mother on occasion. Their day-to-day activities are unavailable to us, but certainly as young children, they would have lived a carefree life, growing up in the beautiful Northamptonshire countryside. Their manor house was surrounded by three large parks of around a total of 1000 acres of land, ideal for Elizabeth and her siblings to run around and play in. As she became older, Elizabeth would have been taught much of what she needed to know to manage her own estates and family later in life, watching and helping with household chores such as drawing water and sweeping floors. She and her female siblings would have learnt the skills of sewing, spinning and weaving, whilst her brothers would have learnt to ride and played with small wooden swords or bows and arrows. Given her mother's love of literature, it is likely that Elizabeth and all her siblings were taught to read by either their mother, or by a tutor.

They would have become accustomed to their parent's absence, and perhaps listened out for the approach of horses with excitement when they knew that one or both was due home. Throughout the 1440s, Richard continued to travel backwards and forwards to Calais and Jacquetta would have spent much time with the queen, returning home for breaks or when she needed to enter confinement for the birth of her next child.

On 29 May 1448, Richard Woodville was honoured by the king for his loyal service when he was created Baron Rivers, an event that was important enough to be mentioned in the Paston letters.[16] As he grew in status, his family was also growing and by the end of the 1440s, there may have been as many as eight Woodville children living at Grafton. Following on from Anthony, Elizabeth and Richard, by 1448 Jacquetta had given birth to a further three sons, Lowys born c.1440–44 who also did not survive into adulthood, another son who they named Richard born during the same period (presumably their earlier son named Richard had died by that time) and John Woodville, born c.1445. Jacquetta, it seems was proving highly fertile as she had also given birth to three more daughters by the end of the decade: Jacquetta, named after her mother, who was born in c.1446, Anne born c.1447 and Mary born sometime between 1447 and the early 1450s.

With an ever-expanding family and the expectation that more children would follow, it was time for Richard and Jacquetta to plan for the future of their children. As the 1440s drew to a close, the Woodvilles came together to celebrate the first wedding of one of their own. But the first of the girls to be married was not Elizabeth as may have been expected, but Jacquetta, their second eldest daughter. Why Jacquetta's marriage was arranged before her elder sister's is unknown. It may be simply that due to the proximity in ages of the young Jacquetta and her intended husband, she was considered the more suitable. Jacquetta's chosen spouse, John Lestrange, was born on 20 May 1444 and Elizabeth would have been eight or nine years John's senior. Jacquetta, born two years after John, was most likely deemed a more suitable match.

The exact date of the marriage is unknown but it had certainly taken place by 1450, when an entry in the calendar of patent rolls, dated 27 March 1450, grants the manor of Midlyngton (now known as Middleton Stoney) 'to John Lestraunge and Jacquetta his wife and the heirs of their bodies'.[17] The young bride and groom would only have been about four and six years old at the time of their marriage and why it was arranged when they were so young is unclear, although not uncommon. In today's culture, a marriage between children would be unacceptable, but it was once a perfectly normal custom of the time, when alliances between families were forged by the marriage of their children, particularly as marriages nearly always involved a financial settlement. In canon law, marriage was legal when the individuals came of age which was usually considered twelve for girls and fourteen for boys. However, a marriage ceremony could be performed at an earlier age, usually when the child had reached seven or more, but on occasion, children were married even younger than this.

The connection between the two families may have been forged many years earlier. John's father was Richard Lestrange and John was the product of his father's second marriage to Elizabeth Cobham in 1439. Elizabeth was Eleanor Cobham's sister and this perhaps explains how the new young groom came to be known to the Woodville family. John Lestrange was just five years old when he succeeded his father, Richard Lestrange, to the title of the 8th Baron Strange of Knockyn and he was clearly considered a suitable candidate for one of their daughters.

Having concluded the marriage arrangements of one of his daughters, in 1450 Baron Rivers was ordered to Plymouth to assemble an army ready to set sail to France to defend the citizens of Bordeaux. Arriving in the southern coastal town, he soon found that there was no money forthcoming from the king to pay his men and Richard found himself stuck in Plymouth for almost a year, attempting to retain control of a group of unhappy soldiers. Jacquetta may have been with him for some of that time. Richard never made it across the sea and by July 1451, the town of Bordeaux had surrendered and Rivers returned home, where he was soon to make plans that would affect Elizabeth's future.

In 1451, Elizabeth was around twelve years old and it was now her turn to be found a husband. The man chosen for her was a Sir John Grey of Groby. Sir John was the eldest son of Elizabeth Ferrers, 6th Baroness Ferrers of Groby and her husband Edward Grey. Born in 1432, he was around seven or eight years older than Elizabeth. The date of their marriage is unknown, but it likely happened sometime before 1452. Elizabeth was given a dowry of 500 marks and John's parents, Lord and Lady Ferrers, agreed to enfeoff several manors for their use.

After her wedding, it would have been time for Elizabeth to leave her family home to go and live with her new husband. It was likely with some trepidation but with fond memories of her childhood that Elizabeth set off from Grafton, waving goodbye to her younger siblings and setting off to a new chapter in her life. It is often believed that she went to live at the Grey family seat at Groby Hall and it is probable that she did reside with her parents-in-law for a few years until she reached an age where she would manage her own household and affairs. However, a 2010 Time Team dig at Groby Hall and later investigations by historian David Ramsey suggest that she most likely lived with her new husband at Astley Castle, another Grey family property. Ramsey's findings point to Groby Hall being inhabited by Elizabeth Ferrers and her husband between 1430 and 1446, before they moved to London between 1446 and 1455 in service to the king.[18] It is not beyond the realms of possibility that she lived with her in-laws in London for a few years, before travelling to Astley. Either way, Elizabeth was now into the next stage of her life, as a married woman and no doubt looking forward to raising a loving and happy family as successfully as her own parents had done.

Chapter 2

A Troubled Land

Astley Castle was some twenty-five miles away from Groby, in the beautiful Warwickshire countryside. As Elizabeth and John approached the property that would become their new home, they would have been greeted by a stunning rectangular red-brick house surrounded by a moat. The house had originally belonged to the Astley family until the last of the male line, Sir William Astley, died in 1420. It then passed in marriage to the Grey family, through his daughter Joan Astley who was married to Reynold, Lord Grey of Ruthin.

Joan was Reynold's second wife and when he died, the bulk of the Grey estates passed to his heirs from his first marriage. But Astley was left to Edward Grey, Joan and Reynold's eldest son and Sir John Grey's father. Edward Grey had married Elizabeth Ferrers sometime around 1430 when she was just twelve years old and they had had four children together: three sons, John, Edward and Reginald, and a daughter, Anne.[1] Astley was clearly deemed a suitable family home for their eldest son and at some point in the mid-1450s, he and Elizabeth arrived at Astley ready to start their own family.

As a young woman now in charge of her own household, it was time for Elizabeth to draw on the skills she had learnt from her mother as she grew into adulthood. A woman of gentry status, Elizabeth was expected to run her estates alongside her husband and more importantly be able to run them on her own in his absence. To give us some idea of the life she would have expected to lead, we can turn to Christine Pisan (1365–1430), who was a celebrated fourteenth-century author, and even more impressively the first professional female writer of her time. Christine's writing was full of practical and moral advice to her fellow women. To those of Elizabeth's status, Christine informs us that barons, knights, squires and gentlemen were bound to travel and go off to the wars, it was part of their role in life, so their wives should be 'wise and sound administrators and manage their affairs well'.[2]

To be good administrators, Christine advises women to ascertain how much their annual income is and how much revenue their land will provide by persuading their husbands to share this information. The mistress of an estate, she recommends, should be knowledgeable about all laws relating to fiefs, rents, taxes and anything else that would normally come under the jurisdiction of her husband so that she will never be tricked by anyone.

As for day-to-day living, the lady of the house is instructed to get up early, as lying in bed until late will adversely affect the smooth running of the household. After hearing Mass and saying her devotions, she should busy herself around the house, giving orders as required. To issue correct orders, an oversight of the running of the estate was needed, so the mistress could ensure the animals were kept clean, protected from the weather and well-fed and that her household staff were gainfully employed no matter what the season. In the summer, her young lads could be instructed to work the fields and, in the winter, they should occupy their time cutting wood for the heating of the house. Her women and chambermaids should be kept busy at all times attending the livestock, feeding the workmen, weeding the courtyards and working in the herb garden.

Following Christine's guidance to keep herself and her household busy, Elizabeth and her women would certainly have spent some of their time spinning, weaving and making clothes and linen tablecloths and napkins, which would be kept neatly folded in a chest. A duty of a good wife was also to keep her husband's garments clean for him so he could present himself well-groomed at all times. A wise mistress of the house would also be familiar with the preparation of food, so she may know best how to organise it and give orders to those serving her. Her home should be kept clean and organised at all times in case her husband brought home visitors, and any children she had should be well taught and disciplined as they grew up. Elizabeth may or may not have been aware of Christine's writing, but during her years at Astley, Elizabeth's life would have been fairly similar to that described above.

Towards the middle of the 1450s, most probably sometime around 1454 if we accept a birth date for Elizabeth of around 1439/40, Elizabeth found herself expecting her first child. With no accurate way of detecting pregnancy, she would have suspected that she was pregnant when she had missed the first few of her courses and had it confirmed when she felt what was known as a quickening, the first flutters of the foetus within her, sometime around five months.

This news would no doubt have been received with joy by John and Elizabeth and their wider family. Her mother, Jacquetta, had proved herself fertile and Elizabeth would no doubt have hoped that she too would be able to provide her husband with sons and heirs. As the months went by, Elizabeth would have prepared herself for the birth of her first child with huge excitement, perhaps tempered with slight anxiety or fear. Childbirth was a necessary and wonderful part of life, but it always carries its risks, and in the fifteenth century, compared to today, they were incredibly high. Even by the sixteenth and seventeenth century, as medicine progressed in England, one in every forty women were still dying in childbirth.[3]

As Elizabeth's due date drew near, she would have retired from normal everyday life into what was known as her confinement. A few weeks before the birth, her chosen room would have been prepared and she would have entered this room where she remained until after the birth. The room itself would have been kept in semi-darkness, with tapestries hung over windows, and only a single window left open to provide a small amount of air. A summer birth must at times have been almost unbearable being confined within a hot and stuffy room. But the idea of this dark and warm space was designed to recreate the womb, to provide a welcoming environment to the newborn child.

As this was Elizabeth's first birth, she would no doubt have had the company of some of her female relatives – her mother and perhaps one or more or her sisters, and maybe even her mother-in-law would have made the journey to Astley to be with her and help her through the birth. Childbirth was a solely female affair with only women allowed into the birthing chamber. Known as gossips, which was not at all derogatory, just simply her childbirth companions, the pregnant woman would have her closest female family and attendants nearby to chat with her and keep her spirits up during the days and weeks leading up to the birth.

The experience of childbirth in Elizabeth's time was surrounded by a real mix of spiritual beliefs, superstition and folklore. The chosen room would have contained crucifixes and religious items to comfort the expectant mother and in a time where there was no pain relief, women would recite religious prayers and chants during labour, often while clutching holy relics in the hope their devotion would ease the pain and bring forth an easy birth. Birth girdles were also sometimes worn – strips of parchment bearing charms and prayers that women would wear around their stomach. St Margaret, the patron saint of pregnant women and childbirth would also be called upon to ease the pains of labour.

During labour, other more superstitious methods could be used. Amulets and amber could be placed upon the mother's stomach to help contractions and ease pain. Within the room drawers and cupboard doors would be opened, knots untied and the mother's hair loosened, symbolically removing any barriers that may prevent an easy passage for the baby.[4] This last custom may have originated in ancient Greece where they believed knots could prevent or delay a birth. In real-time, the midwife who attended the birth would anoint her hands with wild thyme oil, lily oil or oil of musk to massage the stomach and she would also turn or rearrange the baby if it were considered necessary.

Whatever religious or superstitious customs Elizabeth bought into her birthing chamber, she had a successful first birth and produced a healthy boy, whom they named Thomas. His exact birth date is unknown but 1455 appears to be the generally accepted date and once again accepting a birth date of 1439–40 for Elizabeth, it seems a sensible guess. Thomas would have been baptised shortly after his birth, although Elizabeth would not have attended. Custom dictated she should remain in her confinement room until approximately a month after the birth, when she would have then been churched and allowed to return to normal life. The churching ceremony was a time for purification when new mothers' offered gifts of candles before the altar dedicated to our lady. Attended by friends and family, it would have been a joyous occasion, in effect a celebration of the safe arrival into the world of the newborn child and that mother and child had made it through the ordeal safely.[5]

With a new baby in the cradle, 1455 should have been a happy year for Elizabeth and John and it may well have been. But there is also a chance that it was a stressful time for Elizabeth, due to the troubles that were brewing in the wider world. How much her husband was involved in political affairs at this point is unclear, but there is a chance she spent some of her pregnancy without her husband by her side.

By the early 1450s, King Henry had been on the throne for over a quarter of a century, but he had not proved himself a strong leader. Living no doubt in the shadow of his father Henry V, the great warrior king, Henry VI was his antithesis in every way. Where his father had marched into French lands, earning himself glory by defeating the French army at Agincourt, Henry VI was a peacemaker, and fulfilled the role of a kind father to his subjects, their mentor rather than their champion. Admirable qualities though these may be, they were not the desired qualities for a great ruler.

In the spring of 1450, the men of Kent had risen in rebellion, frustrated by the king's weak leadership and heavy taxation. Their leader, Jack Cade, presented the king with a list of demands entitled the 'Complaint of the Poor Commons of Kent'. The rebellion had been quashed, and Jack Cade had died sometime after his arrest, but it demonstrated a growing unease throughout the land around the king's leadership.

Around two years before Elizabeth gave birth to Thomas, Queen Margaret had given birth to a son. Born in 1453, he was their much-wanted heir to the throne and they named him Edward. However, just before his birth, King Henry had fallen into a strange state of depression, that royal physicians were unable to diagnose. It came on suddenly and rendered him into what can only be described as a living coma – awake but completely unresponsive. When his only son and heir was born, Henry had not even been able to recognise him, despite the attempts of the Duke of Buckingham and the queen, who presented the prince to him at Windsor, begging the king to bless the prince, thereby giving official recognition to his son. Glancing upon the tiny baby boy, he lowered his eyes to the floor, showing no reaction. His illness began to cause concern and questions began to be raised as to who should be in charge of the country until he had recovered. By January 1454, with the king seemingly not making any recovery, Queen Margaret, keen to safeguard herself and her baby son, made a case for her to act as regent until her husband was fully recovered. Her case was rejected. Instead, the council elected to name a protector, someone who would act as a caretaker of the realm until the king was well again. The man they chose for the role was Richard Plantagenet, the Duke of York, who was then the foremost duke in the land.

The duke was supported in his position of protector, by his brother-in-law the Earl of Salisbury, and his nephew, Salisbury's son, Richard Neville, the Earl of Warwick. Concerned about some of the corrupt advisors who surrounded the king, the first thing they did was remove them from positions of power. Their main target, a man they believed was having a corrupting effect on government, was Edmund

Beaufort, the Duke of Somerset. He was immediately thrown into prison. With Beaufort said to be a great favourite of the queen (there were even rumours of an affair, albeit unfounded) this immediately set York and the queen on a warring path.

By early 1455, the king seemed to have recovered well enough to resume his duties. Taking back the reins of government, this meant York's time as protector was over. Back on the throne, Henry was persuaded by the queen to drop the charges against Somerset and release him from prison. But tensions had been bubbling away under the surface over the last few years and with Somerset back in a position of power, York suspected he would exact revenge and attempt to bring charges against him and his supporters. On 22 May 1455, the first armed battle of the conflict that would eventually become known as The Wars of the Roses took place. Gathering a retinue of men together, the duke along with Salisbury and Warwick marched to meet the king and Somerset. The two armies – the Yorkists and the Lancastrians as they would become known – met near St Albans. The duke and his supporters were keen to make it clear they were the king's true subjects but were concerned about some of the king's advisors, particularly Somerset. Messages were passed backwards and forwards between the two camps, but eventually, negotiations failed and the fighting began. The poor residents of St Albans were witness to pitched battles through the streets of their town. As the two groups met, there was fierce fighting in the marketplace and town square and the frightened townspeople barricaded themselves in their homes. The actual combat lasted just an hour, during which time Henry VI was wounded and the Lancastrian leaders, Northumberland, Clifford and most importantly Somerset were killed. According to an old legend, the Duke of Somerset apparently refused to ever enter a castle as it had once been foretold that he would meet his death in one. In the end, although he met his death in the streets of St Albans, he was killed in one of the small streets inside an inn. Bizarrely the name of this inn was 'The Castle'. As the battle came to an end, King Henry was found taking refuge in St Albans church. York made it clear he still considered himself a loyal subject and the king was taken back to London where at a meeting of Parliament, York persuaded the council to promote his supporters into offices of state.[6]

During the 1450s, Elizabeth's family were all Lancastrian supporters. Her mother had a friendship with Queen Margaret and her father,

Lord Rivers, was one of the Duke of Somerset's lieutenants in Calais. Lord Rivers was not involved in the Battle of St Albans but it is quite possible that John Grey and his father could have been there. If he had gone off to battle it would have been a highly stressful time for Elizabeth, as she may have been heavily pregnant, or a new mother in May 1455, with the now added concern for the safety of her husband.

For the next four years after the two sides met at St Albans, there was an uneasy truce between them. By 1456, the queen, angry at the loss of her favourite, had caused York and his supporters to lose their positions and King Henry had remained well enough to continue governance of the realm. It was at some point during those truce years that Elizabeth gave birth to her second child, another son whom they named Richard. Once again, his actual birthdate is unknown but it is generally believed to have been around 1457/8.

But by 1459, the scarcely contained animosity between the two sides broke down again when a Yorkist army led by Salisbury was ambushed by the queen's army at Blore Heath on 23 September of that year. Salisbury and his men had been on their way to meet York's party, whilst simultaneously Warwick and his group of men were marching north from Calais, also intending to meet up with the York camp. Salisbury and his men engaged in battle and were victorious, continuing their march to Ludlow to meet up with the Duke of York and Earl of Warwick. By October 1459, all three men were at Ludlow. On the night of 12 October, they took up a defensive position at Ludford Bridge on the River Teme in the shadow of Ludlow Castle. But during the night many of their men defected, fearful of taking on the king's advancing army and committing treason. Knowing they had too few men to defeat the Lancastrian army, the men fled; York across the sea to Ireland and Warwick, Salisbury and York's eldest son, Edward, Earl of March, escaped across the channel to Calais.

The men spent Christmas 1459 in exile, and in January 1460, a noteworthy incident took place that must have been reflected on in later years by all those involved. Aware that the men in Calais still proved a danger to him, King Henry had ordered Elizabeth's father Lord Rivers, and her brother, Anthony Woodville (who was aged about twenty-three at the time) to muster forces at Sandwich on the Kent coast. This they did and on the night of 15 January 1460, the Yorkists based in Calais made a daring raid across the channel, and captured Rivers and Anthony, allegedly dragging them from their beds and taking them back across the sea to Calais as prisoners. It is possible that Elizabeth's mother, Jacquetta was also with her husband and son in Sandwich, and although she was not taken to Calais, the nighttime raid and witnessing her son and husband dragged away must have been terrifying for her. William Paston mentioned the incident, in a letter to his brother, John, dated 28 January 1460:

> As for tydyngs, my Lord Ryvers was brougth to Caleys, and by for the Lords with viij$^{xx.}$ [*eight score*] torches, and there my Lord of Salesbury reheted [*rated*] hym, callyng hym knaves son, that he schuld be so rude to calle hym and these other Lords traytors, for they schall be found the Kyngs treue liege men, whan he schuld be found a traytour, &c. And my Lord of Warrewyk rehetyd hym, and seyd that his fader was but a squyer, and broute up with Kyng Herry the V^{te,} and sethen hymself made by maryage, and also made Lord, and that it was not his parte to have swyche langage of Lords, beyng of the Kyngs blood. And my Lord of Marche reheted hym in lyke wyse. And Sir Antony was reheted for his langage of all iij. Lords in lyke wyse[7]

It seems on arrival in Calais, Rivers and Anthony were dragged before Salisbury, Warwick and Edward and all three harangued and insulted them calling Lord Rivers a knave and that his father was but a squire. Neither side could have known that less than five years later, Lord Rivers would be Edward's father-in-law and Anthony his brother-in-law. One can't help but wonder if this incident was ever discussed between them at a future date.

The news of the fate of her father and brother must have dearly worried Elizabeth when it reached her back in Warwickshire. A shocked and shaken Jacquetta may have returned to Grafton to await further news and perhaps Elizabeth even visited her there to comfort her mother. The two men were kept in Calais as prisoners for the next six months.

The Yorkist leaders finally returned to England's shores in the middle of 1460, when an army led by Warwick and Edward met the Lancastrian army at Northampton on 10 July. They emerged victorious and King Henry was captured and held for three days in Delapre Abbey by

Warwick, before returning with him to London. Hearing news of their victory, the Duke of York returned from Ireland and headed to London where York and Warwick assembled a parliament and York now made it clear that he was no longer declaring allegiance to the king but was ready to take the throne himself. This was not a random grab for power, his lineage could be traced back to Edward III, albeit through a lesser line than Henry's. Although his move to take the throne was rejected by Parliament, an agreement was made that York would become king on the death of King Henry VI. It was around this time that Elizabeth's father and brother were released and presumably returned home to Grafton, much to the relief of Elizabeth and her mother.

The queen, who had fled to Scotland after the loss at Northampton was furious at this bypassing of her son. She gathered an army and began marching back towards the capital. As her men began pillaging Yorkist estates in the north, the Duke of York gathered his men and marched north to confront her, spending Christmas at Sandal Castle. Queen Margaret's army surrounded him there. From his position within the castle, the duke could see he was outnumbered. He could have remained within the safety of the castle walls until further support arrived, but for some reason, York decided to emerge from the castle after the Christmas festivities to face the Lancastrian army. With his son, Edward, Earl of March hurrying from the Welsh borders with reinforcements, the duke engaged with the Lancastrians in a battle that ended in disaster when he was killed, alongside another of his sons, Edmund. His ally and brother-in-law, Salisbury, was also executed after the battle. In her victory, Queen Margaret ordered York's head to be displayed upon the Micklegate of York, with a paper crown placed upon it. The death of the duke could have heralded the end of the wars, but his son, Edward, upon hearing the news of the deaths of his father and brother, was now angrier than ever and determined to exact revenge.

Edward and his men immediately changed direction and headed for London. En route, his army defeated a Lancastrian army led by Jasper Tudor at Mortimer's Cross on 2 February 1461, before continuing their advance towards the capital. Just over two weeks later, on Shrove Tuesday, St Albans was once again the site of pitched battle where the Lancastrians defeated Warwick's men. Once again, the residents of St Albans woke at dawn to the noise of the fighting that started in the town and marketplace before flooding out onto Barnards Heath.[8] This time the Lancastrians had the upper hand and Warwick and his supporters fled once it was clear they were facing a loss. The king, who they had brought with them from London, was found by the queen sheltering in a tent.

So far Elizabeth and her family had only been briefly touched by this ongoing conflict, but this battle was to spell disaster for her. This time her husband, Sir John Grey, was certainly on the battlefield, fighting for the Lancastrian cause, and he was one of the men killed that day. The news would have filtered back to Elizabeth at Astley perhaps a few days later, and needless to say, she would have been devastated. Still only in her early twenties, she was now a widow with two young children to support.

Whilst Warwick was fighting in St Albans, Edward arrived in London and had himself proclaimed king on 4 March at Westminster. His victory was finally sealed once and for all on a wintry battlefield at Towton. On 29 March 1461, in blizzard conditions, the Lancastrians met a resounding defeat. Henry, Margaret and her son fled to Scotland and England had a new king, Edward IV.

Both Elizabeth's father and brother, Earl Rivers and Anthony, were part of the Lancastrian army at Towton and coming so soon after the death of her husband, Elizabeth must have been terrified that the same fate would befall them. In the end, both men escaped unharmed, although they were captured and held after the battle, only to be released in June that year. The Woodville family had been staunch Lancastrians from the start, but with a new king on the throne, the reality of their situation was that they were going to have to now transfer their allegiance. In June they were pardoned by Edward who wrote to London to say he had 'pardoned and remitted and forgiven unto Richard Woodville, knight, lord rivers, all manner of offences and trespasses of him done against us'.[9] According to John Ashdown-Hill, who has compiled a comprehensive itinerary of Edward's movements throughout his reign, Edward was at Stony Stratford from 10 to 12 June 1461, which is near to the Woodville home at Grafton, so it is possible he visited Grafton or summoned the family to Stony Stratford where they pledged their allegiance to him and he officially forgave them.[10] The possibility exists that this may even have been the first time he set eyes on Elizabeth, although no evidence to prove or disprove that exists.

After her husband's death, Elizabeth had to look to providing for herself and her two young sons. Many women after they had been widowed would have remained in the family home in the expectation that her husband's inheritance would pass to her and her children. But after John's death, Elizabeth found herself in a difficult position. Back in 1456, Lady Ferrers, John's mother, had given Elizabeth and John three manors which were conveyed to a group of trustees to provide an annual income of 100 marks for the couple. These manors were Newbottle and Brington in Northamptonshire and Woodham Ferrers in Essex. These should have been provided to Elizabeth in her widowhood as part of her jointure, as well as forming part of her sons' inheritance. But Sir John Grey's father, Edward Grey, had died in 1457 and his mother had remarried. She and her new husband, Sir John Bourchier, for reasons unknown, tried to recover the manors after John's death. The dispute over these manors and Elizabeth's right to the income from them became ugly enough that the matter was taken to the courts of chancery, and Elizabeth made the decision to return with her sons to her family home at Grafton.[11] To make matters worse, Lady Ferrers also claimed that Elizabeth's full dowry of 500 marks had not been paid by Elizabeth's father. Earl Rivers disputed this and this also went to litigation through the chancery courts.[12]

When Elizabeth arrived back at her family home of Grafton, she would have been met by a slightly fuller household than the one she had left. Her parents had at least twelve children together and possibly fourteen or fifteen in total when you count those whom we believe did not live to adulthood. As well as her elder brother Anthony, Elizabeth had four other surviving brothers: Richard born c.1440, John c,1445, Lionel c,1453 and Edward c.1456–7. She also had six surviving sisters: Jacquetta as mentioned previously who was closest in age to Elizabeth as well as Anne, born c.1447, Mary c.1447–51, Margaret c.1454, Jane c.1455–56 and the youngest Katherine, c.1458. There may also have been another sister, Martha, although evidence is scarce as to whether she existed or not.[13] By the time she returned to Grafton, most of her siblings would still have been living at home with the exception perhaps of Jacquetta, who may already have been living with her husband (although she may not have actually moved to her later home of Colham in Middlesex until September 1462 when her husband was given licence to enter into all his possessions when he came of age). During her years away, her brother Anthony was the only other sibling to have married; his bride was Elizabeth, Baroness Scales and the pair had been married at some point between July 1460 and March 1461. Returning home to a full house, she would no doubt have been welcomed with plenty of love and comfort and also young playmates in the form of the younger Woodville siblings for Elizabeth's two boys, Thomas and Richard.

What the plan was now for Elizabeth, or if indeed she even had a plan we cannot possibly know. For the next two years, she remained at Grafton, raising her boys and perhaps waiting to see what the future held for her. Some research by her biographer, David Baldwin, recounts a story that was first mentioned by a gentleman named Henry Coore, and published in 1845. Coore tells us that in the autumn of 1461 after Sir John's death, Elizabeth had intentions to marry a man named Jocelyn de Hardwycke. The Hardwyckes of Hardwick Hall in Derbyshire were related to the Grey family. Roger de Hardwycke was Elizabeth Ferrers cousin and supposedly his nephew, Jocelyn, the son of Sir John de Hardwycke had 'for a long time ardently admired Elizabeth'. Elizabeth is alleged to have visited Hardwick Hall in the Autumn of 1461 and was even apparently betrothed to Jocelyn for a time, although of course they never married. Jocelyn was said to have remained devoted to Elizabeth throughout his life. Having 'sworn never to marry but to devote his life to the queen', he allegedly shared Edward IV's exile in later years and eventually died fighting for Henry Tudor.[14]

Whether this story is of a real event in Elizabeth's life or whether it is simply a mistake or even pure fiction, is impossible to know with the evidence available. The Hardwick family did live in Hardwick Hall of course, with perhaps its most well-known figure being Bess of Hardwick in the next century. But the existence of Jocelyn de Hardwycke remains a mystery and his place in the Hardwick family has so far never been traced. Just because there is a lack of evidence for this story does not of course mean it should be simply discounted – the old adage 'there is no smoke without fire' often proves itself to be true. However, without any further evidence becoming known, it is also highly possible that this was not a real event in Elizabeth's life and that somewhere in the re-telling of a story, people and places have become mixed up and that there was never a romantic connection between Elizabeth Woodville and a member of the Hardwick family.

What we do know is that Elizabeth did make it home to Grafton and in her wish to claim what was rightfully hers from her mother-in-law, she eventually turned to a Leicestershire gentleman named William Hastings for help. Her reasons for approaching him are unclear; he may have been a friend or acquaintance as his home at Kirby Muxloe in Leicestershire was just a short distance away from the Grey family home at Groby. At that time, he may just have been the most powerful person she knew who she felt she could approach for help.

William Hastings was Lord Chamberlain to King Edward IV. A retainer of the Duke of York from a young age, he had fought with the king at Towton and had been knighted on the field after the battle as a reward for his support to Edward and his family. As well as his official role in serving the king, Edward and Hastings were also close friends. When Elizabeth approached him for assistance, Hastings agreed – but it came at a price. Elizabeth had to agree to a future marriage between her son Thomas and any daughter of Hastings that was born or, if he did not father any daughters, one of his nieces. Furthermore, until Thomas was twelve years old, Hastings would have a share in any monies they could get from Lady Ferrers.[15] Elizabeth agreed and in April 1464, an indenture was drawn up for a marriage between Thomas Grey and any daughter born to Hastings or if he did not have any daughter, then any daughter born to his brother Ralph in the next five years.

But then something extraordinary happened that would change the course of Elizabeth and her family's life forever. The date of their first meeting has never been determined, but at some point, Elizabeth herself had crossed paths with the king. As stated earlier, it may even have been as early as 1461 that they first met, but if that was the case, it raises the question as to why she did not ask him to help with her financial troubles rather than Hastings. Perhaps they had crossed paths before 1464 but nothing had ever come of it. There is also a compelling case that it may even have been Hastings who introduced Elizabeth to the king.

Events leading up to their marriage are, like most tales, entwined with hearsay, assumption and mystery. The writer of the Danzig Chronicle reports that Edward fell in love with Elizabeth when he dined with her frequently.[16] Perhaps Edward was a constant visitor to the manor of Grafton and the more time they spent together, the closer they became.

But the most well-known and accepted version of how they met is that Elizabeth, knowing that the king was due to pass by, waited under an oak tree with her two boys so she could catch his attention and request his help with her boys' inheritance. The oak tree, now known as The Queen's

Oak, was situated in a field which is today in the parish of Potterspury, just east of Potterspury Lodge off the A5; it survived all the way to 1994 when it sadly burnt down in a fire. The king, riding by with his men, was said to have stopped when he caught sight of a beautiful young woman on the side of the road, and this was their first encounter.

But one meeting at the side of a road under an old oak does not in itself lead to marriage. What happened next, according to the chronicler Edward Hall writing over half a century later, is that the king became so enchanted with Elizabeth, that he wanted her to become his lover. But she, unwilling to risk her reputation, refused.

Hall believed that their meeting was written in the stars and asks the reader to consider 'that if one considers the old proverb to be true then marriage is destiny'. According to Hall, the king was hunting in the nearby forest when he arrived at Grafton. He tells us that Elizabeth pleaded her suit to the king and that the king not only favoured her suit but was enamoured with her person, for she was lovely looking with a feminine smile. He found her to be eloquent with a great wit and womanly demeanour and was determined that she should become his lover and mistress. But Elizabeth withheld from him, refusing to enter into a romantic engagement with him as anything other than his wife as her honour would not allow her to become his mistress. According to Hall, her refusal made Edward even keener to have her, and struck as he was by the 'darte of Cupido', he determined that he would marry her.[17]

However they met, the one certainty is that they did meet and not only that, before too long, Elizabeth was Edward's wife and in all but name the new Queen of England.

The popular date given for their wedding, which was held in secret, is 1 May 1464. If we accept the theory that when Elizabeth signed the indenture with Hastings in April 1464 she did so because she was not at that point associated with the king and able to therefore ask for his help instead, it would mean that the speed at which they met (or perhaps became re-acquainted) and then married was fast indeed. The date of 1 May is mentioned by the chronicler, Fabyan, and has become the generally accepted date of their union:

> In suche passe tyme, in moste secrete maner, vpon the
> firste claye of May, kynge Edwarde sponsyd Elizabeth, late
> the wyfe of sir Iolm x Graye, knyght, whiche before tyme

> was slayne at Toweton or Yorke feklc, wliiche spowsayles
> were solenipnyzed erely in y mornynge at a towne named
> Graston[18]

The first of May was a day of celebration in England. Known as May Day, it was a sign that spring had finally arrived and heralded the oncoming of summer. The populace could look forward to a warmer season, as days grew longer, and the world became a brighter, more fruitful place after what may have been a hard winter. Tradition had it that if a girl washed her face in the early morning dew, her beauty would be enhanced and this, in turn, would enable her to attract a good husband. It was a day of magic and beauty, bringing with it an optimism for the forthcoming months. Later detractors of Elizabeth would claim that she used sorcery this day, to enchant and entrap the king into marriage. Later romantics would say this was the perfect day for a young couple in love to tie the knot.

May Day 1464 may well have dawned fine and would have been welcomed by the English who were emerging from a particularly hard winter of 1463. The cold weather of that year was clearly widespread as Monstrelet tells that in France 'In this year, the frost was so severe that wine was not only frozen in the cellars but at table: even some wells were frozen, and this weather lasted from the 10th of December to the 15th of February. The frost was so sharp for seven or eight days that many persons died in the fields; and the old people said that then had not he so very severe a winter since the year 1407. Much snow also fell and the rivers Seine and Oise were frozen so that waggons passed over them'.[19] The chronicler, John Warkworth, also found the weather in England at that time notable enough to record, telling us that the winter of 1463/4 brought a fervent frost through England and much snow. Warkworth also reports that Edward and Elizabeth were indeed married on this date: 'the weddynge was prevely in a secrete place, the fyrst day of Maye'.[20]

The location for this most secret of royal weddings was believed to have been a small hermitage on the Woodville lands at Grafton, that around this time was most probably being used as their private chapel. The hermitage had been in existence from at least 1180, when Helias, the hermit of Grafton, had witnessed a charter of Walkelin, the Abbot of St. James's Abbey, near Northampton.[21] The building came into the possession of the Woodville family from about 1370. The house seems to have gone into decline after 1370 and is not heard of again until

32

Thomas Woodville in his will of 1434 directed his trustees to convey the hermitage to St. James' for a term of fifty years.

It seems the abbey never really took charge of the hermitage and the Woodvilles took over the chantry again and undertook a major reconstruction of the building. Floor tiles within the hermitage were said to have been decorated with the arms of Woodville and the house of York, a feature that seems to back up the story that the chapel was the location of the marriage between Edward IV and Elizabeth Woodville in 1464.[22]

On that May Day morning, Elizabeth was said to have quietly left the house and made her way to the hermitage, alongside her mother, Jacquetta, who was the only other person in her family aware of this huge step she was about to take in marrying the King of England. According to Fabyan, the only others present at this smallest of royal weddings were two gentlewomen, the priest and a young man to help the priest sing. After the service, Fabyan tells us that the couple went to bed, where they remained for three or four hours, before Edward returned to nearby Stony Stratford telling his men he had been hunting. Supposedly the king then sent to Lord Rivers to say he was coming to lodge with him for a few days, and he was received with all honour and stayed at Grafton for four days, during which time Elizabeth was brought secretly to his room each night by her mother and kept a secret from all the other members of the family.[23]

According to John Ashdown-Hill's itinerary, Edward was in Northampton on 2 May, which was a Wednesday, and then there is a gap between 3 and 6 May where quite feasibly he could have spent some time staying at Grafton and spending time with his secret new bride before he then set off on his progress north, arriving at Leicester Castle on 7 May.[24]

Edward did not return from his northern progress until the end of August, four long months after their wedding, during which Elizabeth must have been suspended in time, a wife and yet not a wife, a queen and yet not a queen, and wondering perhaps at times what on earth she had done and whether, in fact, she had been made a fool of.

Chapter 3

Elizabeth the Queen, Elizabeth the Princess

According to John Ashdown-Hill, Edward arrived in Reading around 14 September 1464. His wedding to Elizabeth had been kept secret all of this time, and by then Elizabeth may have been having severe doubts as to whether the king would renounce her and deny the wedding had ever taken place. What contact they had with each other between May and September is unknown. It is reasonable to conclude they had some contact, and in messages to her, he may have been reassuring of his love and that he would reveal their union when the time was right. But she would have to be patient. He presumably knew what sort of reaction his announcement would receive, thus keeping it a secret for so long. His cousin, Warwick, had been in France, attempting to secure a foreign marriage for the king with Bona of Savoy – a union that would bring an alliance with a foreign kingdom and a queen for England of suitable birth. Instead, Edward had married a widow with no large dowry and a father who was 'but the son of a Squire'. She was also not a virgin, an undisputed fact given that she was already a mother of two sons, yet a quality that was deemed particularly important when choosing a wife for a king. Both Edward and Elizabeth would have been aware that their union would not be received with joy by all. Elizabeth may also have heard rumours of Edward's womanising nature and it would be only natural for her to wonder if she had just been taken in by a charming and velvet-tongued suitor who had no intention of actually making her his queen. The popular view is that they married for love but as each day passed and her marriage remained a secret, Elizabeth must have worried that perhaps the king had indeed married only for lust. Perhaps Edward at times even considered this too?

However, whatever internal processes the king may or may not have gone through, he held true to the vows that he had made and at a meeting of the council in Reading Abbey in September 1464, Edward finally announced to those councillors gathered that he had married. No official chroniclers were on hand to record the scene but the reactions of the group of councillors gathered there were said to be somewhere between shocked and furious. The writer of the Danzig Chronicle reported the news of their marriage when it reached him that 'although royal custom in England demands that a king should marry a virgin, whoever she may be, legitimately born and not a widow, yet the king took this one against the wish of all his lords'.[1] Monstrelet tells us that it was not just the men gathered at Reading that disapproved of Edward's announcement, but that as the news filtered out across the land, it was widely considered an unsuitable marriage. Referencing Elizabeth's renowned beauty, he writes in relation to Elizabeth's mother, Jacquetta, that 'She [Jacquetta] had several children by lord Rivers, and among them was a daughter of prodigious beauty, who, by her charms, so captivated King Edward that he married her, to the great discontent of several of the higher nobility, who would, if possible, have prevented the marriage from taking place'.[2]

Perhaps the angriest of all at the revelations was the king's cousin, Warwick. Warwick had played a huge role in Edward's path to the throne, and it was not for nothing that his name of 'kingmaker' has travelled down the centuries. He not only would have been furious at being kept in the dark and excluded from Edward's confidence, but he seemingly felt very strongly that this marriage was a mistake. Warwick knew that Edward, relatively new on his throne, was not yet safe and secure and that an alliance with a powerful country would have brought an added layer of support to Edward if he ever needed it. He also, as is human nature, probably felt annoyed that all his efforts of the last few months in seeking a suitable bride for Edward would now amount to nothing. Bona of Savoy was clearly not the only candidate Warwick had been considering; a later letter from Isabella of Castille to Richard III shows that she had also been approached. She informed Richard that 'Edward the Fourth had committed a most unkingly act in making a real love match', and Isabella 'was turned in her heart from England for his refusing of her and taking to his wife a widow of England'.[3] How different our history books would have been if this union had been achieved. Isabella, only thirteen years old to Edward's twenty-two years in 1464, would later go on to marry Ferdinand of Aragon and they would become a phenomenal partnership in Spain, ruling together as joint monarchs for over thirty years. They were also the parents of Katherine of Aragon, who would later eventually bring about a Spanish-Anglo alliance through her marriages to two grandsons of Elizabeth and Edward: Prince Arthur and of course Henry VIII.

Once Edward had broken the news, Elizabeth and her family were sent for and it must have been with a huge excitement coupled with much apprehension that Elizabeth set out on the sixty-mile journey from her home at Grafton to the abbey at Reading. After a private reunion with her husband, Elizabeth was formally introduced to the court and acknowledged as Queen of England at the abbey on Michaelmas day, 29 September 1464. An oil painting in the possession of Reading Museum depicts the possible scene (see illustrations). Edward greets his wife, before she proceeds to the chair of estate in the chancel of Reading Abbey.

Elizabeth was escorted into the abbey by Edward's younger brother, a twenty-four-year-old George, Duke of Clarence, and the Earl of Warwick, a role that Warwick presumably undertook through gritted teeth. It was in this stately abbey of Reading that she was publicly declared queen, although her official coronation would not take place until the following year. One can only imagine what must have been going on in her mind during this first official recognition of her queenship; most certainly she must have marvelled at her meteoric rise from young gentry widow to Queen of England. After what must have felt like four long and tedious months whilst she was waiting on Edward, it must now have felt like no time at all.

Edward and Elizabeth remained at the abbey for several weeks, during which time arrangements were made for the betrothal of one of Elizabeth's sisters, Margaret Woodville, to Thomas Fitzalan, Lord Maltravers, son and heir of William Fitzalan, the Earl of Arundel. It is reported that the ceremony was held at Reading Abbey. The arrangements must have proceeded at pace if they were married at the abbey, with presumably Edward and Elizabeth and the rest of the Woodvilles in attendance. John Ashdown-Hill places Edward in Reading until at least 21 November, so it is possible that the wedding of Elizabeth's sister and Lord Maltravers did take place here between September and November 1464. Whenever and wherever it occurred, it was certainly by February 1465 when a gentleman named John Wykes sent a letter to John Paston, written 'at London, the Monday next after Saint Valentine' (17 February 1465) which detailed: Item, the Earl of Arundel's son hath wedded the queen's sister.

The marriages of Elizabeth's many siblings which took place after she became queen are the source of much of the criticism thrown at Elizabeth and her family, both by their contemporaries and even those today who consider them social climbers, who somehow contrived to better themselves. In this, they did themselves no favours when in January 1465, Elizabeth's twenty-year-old brother John was married to the Dowager Duchess of Norfolk, Katherine Neville, who was Warwick's aunt and aged sixty-five. The union was branded a 'maritagium diabolicum' by the chronicler William Worcester, and it is hard to argue that this union was not made for financial gain (although the Duchess had the last laugh when she outlived her young husband by at least fourteen or fifteen years). But this faux pas aside, the marriage of the rest of her female siblings in particular would always have been arranged for them once they came of age, whether Elizabeth was queen or not. But with the increase in her status, their pool of suitable matches naturally widened. Edward, still relatively new to his throne, needed to forge allegiances wherever he could, and the decisions on who the Woodville girls married would not have been Elizabeth's alone. By marrying Elizabeth's sisters into some of the great families in the land, the king managed to form a tight group of families around him, bound together by marriage.

When Elizabeth married Edward in 1464, only two of her siblings were already married, Jacquetta and Anthony. After Margaret's marriage in late 1464, and John's in early 1465, the next of her siblings to be matched was actually the youngest Woodville daughter, Katherine. Katherine was born around 1458 and her wedding to the ten-year-old Duke of Buckingham also took place in early 1465, as she was titled the Duchess of Buckingham at Elizabeth's coronation a few months later. Her husband, Henry Stafford, was the eldest of two Stafford brothers who had been made wards of court after their grandfather had been killed fighting on the side of the Lancastrians in the Battle of Northampton. The Buckingham lands were confiscated and both Katherine and her young husband and brother-in-law would be raised at Edward and Elizabeth's court during their young years.

Elizabeth had three more brothers who reached adulthood, Richard, Edward and Lionel who did not follow their brother John's example, and in fact, all three remained unmarried for life. Elizabeth's remaining sisters were not found husbands until the following year, 1466, when in or around February of that year the nineteen-year-old Anne Woodville was wed to William Bourchier, a cousin and close ally of the king. William's mother, Isabel of Cambridge, was the elder sister of Richard Plantagenet, Duke of York, and thus Edward's aunt. Her husband, William's father, was Henry Bourchier. Henry had been created Earl of Essex by Edward IV after fighting alongside the Yorkists in the battles of Towton and the second battle of St Albans. At around the same time another of her sister's, Jane Woodville, was matched with Anthony Grey, eldest son of Edmund, Lord Grey of Ruthin. Jane would have been about eleven years old and although Anthony's birth date is not recorded, his younger brother, George Grey was said to have been born c.1455 so it is safe to assume that Anthony was probably born in the early 1450s and was of a similar age to Jane.[4]

Seven months later, in September 1466, her remaining unmarried sister, Mary, was wed to the Earl of Pembroke's eldest son, William, in a ceremony that took place at Windsor Castle. William's father, also named William, was a powerful Welsh magnate and as one of Edward's most loyal supporters, he maintained a huge Yorkist power base covering most of Wales from his home of Raglan Castle. Two years later, in 1468, Edward would reward him for his support by creating him Earl of Pembroke. Prior to his wedding to Mary, William junior had been knighted by the king at Windsor and given the title Lord Dunster.

When Edward and Elizabeth eventually departed from Reading in November 1464, they made a short stop at Windsor before arriving at Edward's favourite palace of Eltham in time for Christmas. Once a grand manor house, Eltham came into the Crown's possession in 1305, gifted by Anthony Bek, Bishop of Durham to the future Edward II. A moated property, access was across a timber drawbridge. Later in the mid-1300s, a new drawbridge and service buildings were added by Edward III as well as new royal lodgings, which featured a bathroom for the king with a tiled floor and glazed windows.[5] The property also possessed chapels for the king and queen and vined gardens.

The ivy-walled palace of Eltham was in an elevated position, with commanding views of Blackheath, Greenwich Park and in the far distance the Surrey hills. The spire of St Paul's was also viewable from the palace and the surrounding parkland around the palace had long since been enclosed and was known as the Great Park. Nearby Shooter's Hill was the only place on higher ground in the locality.[6]

Upon her arrival at Eltham, Edward commanded the Exchequer to pay £466 13s 4d 'to our right entirely well-beloved wife, the queen, for the expenses of her chamber, wardrobe, and stable against this feast of Christmas next coming'. Provision was also made for her in lands worth 4000 marks a year.[7] Less than a year before, Elizabeth had been a young widow, worried about the future and how she would support her two young sons. But as she celebrated Christmas in 1464, in the beautiful palace of Eltham, she must surely have taken a few moments to contemplate the events of the past year and how far she had come.

As early 1465 dawned, plans for Elizabeth's coronation began in earnest. Many of those who disagreed with Edward's choice of queen argued that her lowly birth was a factor in their opinion of her suitability. To counteract this, Edward sent a message to Jacquetta's family in Luxembourg, asking them to send a representative to the coronation, thus illustrating that she did have the credentials needed to be Queen of England. Monstrelet recorded that: 'to satisfy them that the lady's birth was not inferior to theirs, King Edward sent letters to the count de Charolois, to entreat that he would send him some lord of the family of the lady to be present at her wedding. The count sent him Sir James de St. Pol, her uncle, grandly accompanied by knights and gentlemen, to the number of more than 100 horse, who, on their arrival at London, put an end to the murmurings on this marriage, and gave great satisfaction to the king. After the feasts, when they were about to return home, the king presented Sir James de St. Pol with 300 nobles; and to each knight and gentleman of his company he gave fifty nobles, besides most handsome entertainment'.[8]

Elizabeth's coronation date was set for Sunday 26 May and on 7 April, the king sent formal notification to the mayor of London and all the other officials of the date so they had time to prepare. Elizabeth would make her official entry into the city two days before, on Friday 24 May, across old London bridge, and the accounts of the expenses incurred by the Bridge House, the administration which ran London Bridge, give us a fascinating insight into the work that went into receiving and greeting their new queen as she entered her capital city for the first time.

All along the route that Elizabeth was to take, she was to be met by choirs and pageants, lifelike statues and real-life Londoners, cheering for their new queen. The nobility may have resented her sudden rise in status but the common people of London were prepared to accept their new queen whatever her lineage. Mary of Cleophas was one of the saints represented in the pageants; the half-sister of the Virgin Mary she had been married twice, as Elizabeth Woodville had. The citizens of London loyally celebrated this as a compliment, realistically appreciating that life was fickle and that it was common to be married more than once.[9]

Payments listed in the bridge house accounts list the names and amounts given to many of those involved in the elaborate preparations. Tailors William Parys and Richard Westmyll received 6.5d for preparing and making the clothes for some of the figures that would greet the queen at the Staples of the Bridge and at the Drawbridge. This work took them three and a half days. A John Genycote was paid 3.5d for writing six ballads which were to be presented to the queen at her approach and John Thomson also earned 8d for writing the said six ballads on boards fixed to the pageants at the Bridge.

Within the accounts are orders recorded for one ounce of saffron used for dying the flax to make the hair for the angels and maidens as well as for three pounds of flax bought and used for their hair. Nine hundred peacock's feathers were also required to make the angels' wings. All those involved in the preparatory works required refreshments and 46s. 10d was paid in expenses to the workers, incurred by them in an alehouse called the Crown, situated next to the Bridge House.[10]

Where Elizabeth departed from on the morning of the 24th is unclear. The king had left Eltham in early January and returned to Westminster to be ready to open parliament. They may have travelled between several of the London palaces during early 1465, with Edward introducing her to her new homes of Westminster Palace, Greenwich and Sheen. With Eltham's proximity to Shooters Hill, it is likely that Elizabeth was there on the morning of Friday 24 May. As the day dawned, Elizabeth, although now eight months into her life as queen, must have been mentally preparing herself for what would perhaps be the most surreal few days of her life thus far. Coronations are and always have been a magnificent affair, heaped in tradition, pomp and pageantry and to those watching a coronation, the proceedings are awe-inspiring and spectacular. To those relatively few people throughout history who have been crowned, the scale of emotions that they must feel to be part of such a display can only be guessed at.

As her journey to the city began, the queen was met at Shooters Hill by the mayor, Ralph Josselyn, his two sheriffs and other officers of the city, all finely decked out in their blue and blue-grey parted gowns and hoods. Riders from the many livery companies accompanied them, dressed in gowns of murrey. From Shooters' Hill, they conducted her to Southwark where she would cross the great bridge into the city.

The great stone bridge, known as old London bridge, had been completed about 1209 and was the only bridge into the city at the time. The entire bridge was almost like a small village itself, with houses, shops and even a chapel lining the route, some of the buildings three storeys high, a living, breathing and crowded thoroughfare across the River Thames, As Elizabeth approached the Southwark end of the bridge, she would have started her journey across the Thames through the bridge foot, which comprised all the buildings on the bridge up to the Stonegate, a great drawbridge that could be closed to bar entry to the bridge if necessary.

All across the bridge, the householders hung out the best arms and cloths of silk and cloth of gold. Many also let out their upper rooms to friends and associates to watch the procession. A citizen of London, Peter Johnson, a well-to-do shoemaker, originally from the Low Countries, had a prime property at the Staples of the Bridge and was paid handsomely for letting out a room for clerks to sing at the approach of the queen.

One of the main tasks that had to be completed just before Elizabeth's arrival was the cleaning of the bridge. Forty-five loads of sand were strewn across the bridge as she approached. As Elizabeth made her way across the Thames, the sounds of choirs filled the air all along the route. Once she had passed the Staples, she was met by the clerk of the church of St Magnus and his boys, the master of the Society of Clerks and twenty-five others sang for her at the drawbridge and another male choir stood at the door of the chapel on the bridge to sing as the queen approached. The sights and sounds as she crossed the river must have been spectacular; the Londoners had certainly put on a show for their new queen.

When she finally reached the city side of the bridge, Queen Elizabeth proceeded due north up Bridge Street and Fish Street, no doubt experiencing more of the same from the residents that lived there. The procession ended that day at the Tower where the queen was conducted to her apartments to prepare for the next day's vigil procession to Westminster.

Edward was at the tower to greet Elizabeth and that day in her honour he created nearly fifty knights of the Bath, including two of Elizabeth's brothers, Richard and John Woodville, two of her new brother-in-laws, Thomas Maltravers, married to Margaret Woodville and the young Duke of Buckingham, Harry Stafford, newly married to young Katherine Woodville. Anthony Grey was also knighted that day, who would later be matched with Jane Woodville. These new knights, dressed in blue gowns with white hoods, all accompanied Elizabeth the next day as she travelled by litter to Westminster Palace where she would spend the eve of her coronation.

Then on Whit Sunday, 26 May, Elizabeth was finally anointed Queen of England with great solemnity in Westminster Abbey. Clothed in a mantle of purple (the colour of royalty), with a coronal upon her head, Elizabeth entered the hall walking under a canopy. Ahead of her the king's brother, George, Duke of Clarence, accompanied by the Earl of Arundel and the Duke of Norfolk rode around the hall on horseback clearing a path through the gathered crowds. She carried the Sceptre of St Edward in her right hand and the Sceptre of the Realm in her left and was escorted by the Bishop of Durham on her right and the Bishop of Salisbury on her left. Behind them followed the Abbot of Westminster.[11] As she neared the lower steps of the abbey, Elizabeth removed her shoes and walked barefoot upon the ray cloth into the building. The two dukes and the earl had now dismounted and proceeded before her into the abbey. Once inside, the Archbishop of Canterbury greeted her.

Following behind Elizabeth were her ladies and attendants, including two of Edward's sisters and Elizabeth's mother Jacquetta. The young Katherine Woodville and her husband, the Duke of Buckingham were reportedly carried upon the shoulders of squires. Notable absences from the coronation procession were Warwick and the king's mother, Cecily Neville, who were deemed to have been showing their disapproval at the king's choice of wife by staying away. The king was also not present, but that was tradition, so as not to steal the limelight from the queen's celebrations which were designed to be hers alone.

When she reached the high altar, Elizabeth knelt while the Archbishop of Canterbury read aloud the solemnities before she then prostrated herself in front of the altar as was required. Once the required supplications had been said, Elizabeth was anointed and crowned before being led to her throne. The service continued with further rituals and after the Te Deum had been sung, the procession retraced its steps back out of the abbey and through the great hall.

After the formal proceedings, the queen returned to her chamber where she may have found a few moments respite to take a breath. In her chambers, she 'was new revested in a surcoat of purple' before being led to a grand state banquet held in her honour in Westminster Hall.[12]

In the great hall, Elizabeth took her place at the high table. The Archbishop of Canterbury sat to her right and the Duchess of Suffolk on her left. Kneeling to the left of the queen were the young countesses of Shrewsbury and Kent, who held a veil in front of Elizabeth as she ate. Elizabeth removed her crown as she ate and replaced it in between courses.

The rest of the hall was filled with three other long tables of guests. Each of the courses served began with elaborate ceremony. Clarence, Norfolk and Arundel, back on their horses 'richly trapped to the ground' rode into the hall to the sounds of trumpets, and the earls, barons and knights entered on foot. The newly created knights of the bath served the first course of seventeen dishes to the hundreds of diners gathered. Anthony Woodville had the honour of cupbearer, serving hippocras (spiced wine) to those gathered. Similar processions followed the second course of nineteen dishes and the third course of fifteen dishes. Throughout the banquet, the king's minstrels and others played music for the entertainment of the guests. As the banquet drew to a close, the Earl of Oxford carried in the basin for the queen to wash before she was escorted back to her chamber once more by the Bishops of Durham and Salisbury.[13] The whole three days must have been an exhausting but exhilarating experience for Elizabeth and as she retired to be bed on the Sunday evening, we can only but wonder what sort of thoughts were going through her head.

The following day, the coronation festivities reached their conclusion when a grand tournament was held on the green next to Westminster Abbey. It was perhaps the least spectacular of the events for those involved but was a chance for some of London's citizens to attend and share in the celebrations by watching the jousting and the games.

Once the formal celebrations were over, it was now time for Elizabeth to really begin her life as queen. Anointed in the sight of God, no matter who disapproved of her, she could be certain in her position as queen and wife of the king. As head of her own household, she would have numerous staff around her most of the time, and they would travel with her between royal palaces, including her own townhouse at Ormond's Inn in Smithfield which was gifted to her for her use after her coronation. In John Strype's *Survey of the City of London and Westminster* in 1720, he recorded:

> Over against Ipres Inn in Knight-riders street, at the corner towards St. James at Garlickhithe, was some time a great house builded of stone, and called Ormond place, for that it some time belonged to the Earls of Ormond. King Edward IV. in the fifth of his Reign, gave to Elizabeth his Wife, the Manor Greenwich, with the Town and Park, in the County of Kent. He also gave this Tenement called Ormond place, with all the appurtenenaces to the same, situate in the Parish of S. Trinity in Knight-riders Street in London. This house is now lately taken down, and divers fair Tenements are builded there, the corner house whereof is a Tavern.

The head of Elizabeth's household was her chamberlain, Lord Berners, who was paid forty pounds a year for his service. Several posts, unsurprisingly, were granted to her family members. Her brother, John, became her master of the horse, also on a salary of forty pounds a year and her sister, Anne Woodville became one of her ladies-in-waiting on the same salary. Her other ladies-in-waiting included her sister-in-law, Elizabeth, Lady Scales, married to Anthony Woodville, Lady Alice Fogge who was married to Sir John Fogge, Treasurer of the King's Household, Joanna Norris and Elizabeth Uvedale.[14]

Other members of the queen's household included her confessor, Edward Story, her accountant, John Forster, her physician, Domenico de Sirego, and her apothecary, John Pykenham. She also rewarded an old ally, Robert Iseham, who was appointed as her solicitor and later the queen's attorney. Iseham was one of the feoffees given the responsibility of looking after the manors of Newbottle and Brington in Northamptonshire and Woodham Ferrers in Essex during her marriage to Sir John Grey. After Sir John's death, when ownership of these lands was disputed by her mother-in-law, Iseham seems to have been one of the only trustees to have done his best to help her case.[15]

Living within her household was her youngest sister, Katherine, and the two Buckingham boys and she received 500 marks yearly for their maintenance. A schoolmaster, John Giles, was hired to teach the boys grammar on a comparatively tiny salary of just six pounds over a near two-year service.[16]

A few months after her coronation took place, good news was to reach the court when old King Henry was captured hiding out at Waddington Hall, in Yorkshire. Edward and Elizabeth were on a pilgrimage to Canterbury when they received the word of his capture, arriving there on Saturday 13 July and remaining in the city until Tuesday 23 July.[17] A Lancashire monk was dispatched to Canterbury to break the news to them, and they immediately went in celebration to Canterbury cathedral to announce the news to the people. Arriving back in London on 25 July, they were informed that Henry had arrived in London as a prisoner the day before, 24 July, and had been arrested in Edward's name by the Earl of Warwick who had just returned from Calais. Henry was thrown into the tower where he would remain for the next few years, although reportedly Edward treated him kindly and 'gave orders that he was to be supplied with all necessaries and treated with respect and as much kindness as was consistent with his safe custody'.[18]

During her trip to Canterbury, Elizabeth may have suspected or been aware that she was in the early stages of pregnancy; as a mother of two already she would have been able to recognise the signs. She may have even offered up a little prayer at the Canterbury shrine of St Thomas a Beckett to assist her with many successful future pregnancies so she could provide the king with a whole court of healthy children. Whether St Thomas had any influence or not, Elizabeth was indeed pregnant and on 11 February 1466, just under nine months after her coronation, she gave birth to her first child with Edward IV, a daughter whom they named Elizabeth. Not long after her birth, the young princess was baptised in St Stephens Chapel, Westminster, by Archbishop George Neville, a brother of the Earl of Warwick. Although she was a girl, and not the much longed-for son and heir that every king desired, she was, according to Agnes Strickland, baptised 'with as much pomp as if she had been the heir apparent of England; indeed the attention Edward IV bestowed upon her was extraordinary'.[19] Ever the proud father, Edward rewarded his wife for delivering him a beautiful daughter with a gift of a jewelled ornament, purportedly worth over £60,000 in today's currency to mark the occasion.

Elizabeth had been through two births before so she understood what the experience entailed. But this time the rituals surrounding the birth were on a far grander scale than when she gave birth to Thomas and Richard some ten years previously. Her confinement would have been within her apartments in the Palace of Westminster, relatively new rooms in the old palace which Edward had begun building for her after their marriage in 1464. Comparatively, this would not have been too different to before, apart from perhaps the grander location and of course more servants on hand to provide for her needs. But now she was queen, her churching ceremony, which took place a month after the Princess Elizabeth's birth, was on a significantly grander scale than what Elizabeth would have experienced with her two boys.

Details of her churching were recorded by a gentleman named Gabriel Tetzel of Nuremberg, who had recently arrived in England with his master, Leo, Lord of Rozmital, brother of the Queen of Bohemia. Arriving at Westminster, as honoured guests of the king, they were provided with the most comfortable lodgings and welcomed with a fifty-course banquet. Tetzel wrote much of Elizabeth's beauty and was on hand to witness her churching ceremony as it took place.

The queen was helped to rise from her bed by her ladies, who also assisted her in dressing. She was then led from the palace to the abbey in a large procession headed up by ecclesiastics, followed by scholars bearing lighted candles, singing as they walked. Behind them came noble ladies from across the land, then trumpeters, pipers and players of stringed instruments, the king's minstrels and then the heralds and pursuivants. These were then closely followed by the lords and the knights and lastly, under a canopy, came the queen, supported by two dukes and followed by her mother and her ladies. Tetzel did not witness the service in the abbey, or if he did, he did not record it. After the abbey service was over, the whole procession retraced their steps back to the palace where all those present dined together – their number apparently so great that they filled four great rooms. Lord Rozmital dined with the Earl of Warwick and afterwards, Warwick took him into the hall where the queen was seated in solitary grandeur on a golden chair.

It is from the rest of Tetzel's report that Elizabeth has perhaps earned some of her haughty reputation. According to Tetzel, even the king's sister and the queen's mother were required to keep their distance from Elizabeth and that they had to kneel if spoken to. He writes that not until the first course was served and the queen had drunk water were her sister-in-law and mother allowed to sit, and that for the next three hours, all the while dinner lasted, the other ladies in the room remained on their knees and not a word was spoken. He records that once the meal was over and the tables removed, the dancing began and that Elizabeth watched from her golden chair, her mother kneeling at her side, only standing up to stretch her tired muscles.[20]

Assuming Tetzel's report to be first-hand and therefore fairly accurate, it would be easy to see how a reputation of being arrogant and superior could be applied to Elizabeth if this were taken at face value. Perhaps it is even true, and that she did demand this of those around her and that her newly acquired power had, using a modern phrase, 'gone to her head'. Looking back at an event like this, it would be foolish to assume from both the distance of time and our modern viewpoint that we knew what Elizabeth's character was.

However, we must also consider that of course she was superior to the others at the festivities. She was the Queen of England, and therefore the most important person in the land, bar the king himself. And at the royal court, the show of grandeur was designed to present a picture of excellence, of opulence and of power. Social etiquette was at play, and traditions and the trappings of wealth were paramount to maintaining that show of power. And as A.R. Myers discusses in his introduction to *The Household of Edward IV*, this show of power was needed to keep your affinity base strong which was of the utmost importance to a king retaining his throne.[21] Elizabeth may have had little option other than to fulfil her role exactly as was required of her.

Lastly, when looking at what Tetzel recorded of that day, it is possible that some of it was hearsay or came to him second-hand. As he and his master were seated in another room, would they have witnessed the first course being served or all three hours of the meal? The portrayal of Jacquetta kneeling at Elizabeth's side during the dancing, may not have been one of superiority from Elizabeth over her mother, but simply that formalities forbade Jacquetta from pulling up a chair to sit near her daughter, so she knelt by her side to be near her. Elizabeth and Jacquetta reportedly had a loving relationship, and Jacquetta, no stranger to the royal court, would have understood exactly what was required of them both.

Once their esteemed visitors had left court, it was time for the royal family of three to settle into daily life. Edward had now been on the throne for nearly five years and was a hugely popular king with the common touch. As Thomas More tells us: 'he [Edward] was a godly personage, and very princely to behold; of heart courageous, politic in counsel; in adversity nothing abashed, in prosperity rather joyful than proud; in peace just and merciful, in war sharp and fierce; in the field bold and hardy, and nevertheless no farther than wisdom would adventurous'.

Eighteen months after the birth of their first child, the king and queen were delivered of their second daughter, Mary, on 11 August 1467 at Windsor Castle. Her christening took place the next day, 12 August and the infant Mary was sent to join her elder sister, Elizabeth, in the nursery at Sheen under the care of their nurse, Margaret Lady Berners. On 9 October that year, the queen was granted £400 per year for their upkeep.

As royal children, Elizabeth and Mary would have been brought up to learn manners and decorum, as well as the skills they would need to make good wives and mothers. Religion would have played a hugely significant role in their upbringing and if their household followed that of their later brother, Edward's, whose household routine has been passed down to us in a set of ordinances, they would have been bidden to rise early to attend matins. If you arrived late, you would spend the day on bread and water. After morning prayer, they would breakfast followed by morning lessons. Dinner would be taken at 10 am, followed by an afternoon of recreation and/or further learning. Supper would be at 4 pm and the girls would then have some leisure time, before retiring to bed by 8 pm. After they had gone to bed, only their attendants were permitted to enter their chambers. The outer gates to the palace would be closed at 9 or 10 pm dependant on the season, and night watchmen would patrol several times throughout the night to ensure their safety.

In the summer of 1467, the court was treated to a visit from the Bastard of Burgundy, the son of the Duke of Burgundy. He visited Edward's court to put the case for the marriage of his elder brother, Charles, Earl of Charolais to the king's sister, Margaret. Described by Holinshed as 'a lady of excellent beauty, with so many worthy gifts of nature, grace and fortune', Margaret was Edward's younger sister.[22] The king agreed to the union although the contracts were not signed until the following year. Whilst in England, the Bastard challenged Anthony Woodville, Elizabeth's brother, to a joust. His challenge was accepted, and the two men, both keen sportsmen, put on a fine show over several days. The lists were prepared at Smithfield with 'verie faire and costlie galleries for the ladies' to watch the sport. On the first day of the tournament, both men were equal in their prowess, then on the second day, the proceedings were brought to a sudden halt when Anthony's spear pierced the nostrils of his rival's horse. On the third day, the two men fought hand-to-hand combat and took part in other challenges, once again to the delight of the king and spectators. The celebrations ended when the Bastard received the news of the death of his father and had to journey home to support his brother, the new Duke of Burgundy.

Marriage contracts were finally signed in early February 1468 and the new Duchess of Burgundy left London for her new home, setting out on 18 June. After making an offering at St Paul's, she rode through the city with the Earl of Warwick riding before her. Margaret lodged that night at the Abbey of Stratford, where the king and queen were staying, before travelling onto Canterbury, and eventually Margate. The ship awaiting her was *The Ellen of London* and Margaret was accompanied on board by Anthony and John Woodville amongst others who sailed with her to Flanders.

With old King Henry in captivity, his queen Margaret of Anjou in exile and with two children already in the royal nursery, this should have been a happy settled time for Edward and Elizabeth. But as they neared the end of the decade, the disgruntled Earl of Warwick began causing trouble. He and Edward had been on a collision course since the mid-1460s, and certainly, Edward's choice of bride could be considered as one of the catalysts in the deterioration of their relationship. Warwick had been hugely influential in Edward's path to the throne, but not as influential as he had perhaps imagined he would be during Edward's reign. Edward's middle brother George, Duke of Clarence, was also falling under Warwick's influence, causing a rift to form between the two brothers. Handsome and full of charm, George was also spoilt and easily influenced and was somewhat indulged by his older brother. As early as 1467, Warwick had broached the idea of a marriage between George and his eldest daughter, Isabel Neville. Sensing collusion between his wayward brother and the powerful Warwick was a dangerous idea, Edward flatly refused to even consider the notion.

On 20 March 1469, into what was becoming a seriously unsettled time for the Yorkist royal family, a third daughter was born to the king and queen. Princess Cecily of York was born at Westminster and her arrival would have been a welcome distraction from the rumblings of trouble that were seemingly ever-present in spring of that year. Likely named in honour of Edward's mother, Cecily Neville, to celebrate her christening, two barrels of hippocras and a pipe of Gascon wine were delivered into the king's cellar.[23] Shortly after Cecily's birth, Edward and Elizabeth set out on planned progress to East Anglia, accompanied by the king's youngest brother, Richard, Duke of Gloucester, and Elizabeth's brothers, Anthony and John Woodville. The two eldest York girls, three-year-old Elizabeth and two-year-old Mary also travelled with their parents. The royal visit to the county of Norfolk was reported by the Paston family in a letter from John Paston, dated June 1469:

> The Kyng hathe ben in this contre, and worchepfully receyvyd in to Norwyche, and had ryght good cher and gret gyftys in thys contre, wherwythe he holdyth hym so well content that he wyll hastyly be her agayn, and the Qwen allso, with whom, by my power avyse, ye shall com, if so be that the terme be do by that tym that she com in to this contre[24]

By the end of June, reports of skirmishes in the north were not abating, and Edward realised he had little choice but to deal directly with the troubles. Edward was unaware that on 11 July, in a direct violation of his ruling, Clarence and Warwick had travelled to France and in a ceremony held in the port of Calais, Clarence wed Isabelle Neville. But this was no love match. With Edward having not yet sired a son, if anything happened to Edward, they both knew that Clarence would be next in line to be king with Warwick's daughter as his queen. Warwick's motives were clear, he was trying his hand at kingmaking again. Clarence, seeing a route to great wealth and power and likely bored of being an underdog to his elder brother, went along with the plan.

Edward, gathering his men, left Elizabeth to continue their progress and fulfil their commitments in Norwich whilst he travelled north to investigate the reported troubles. The city had gone to great expense to welcome the royal family and Elizabeth and her daughters, arriving through the Westwick Gate on 18 July, were greeted by a stage covered in red and green fabric, atop of which were angels and giants, with crests of glittering gold leaf. The royal entourage was treated to a pageant entitled 'Salutation of Mary and Elizabeth', presumably in honour of the queen's daughters, before proceeding to the Friars Preachers, where another stage had been constructed and another performance was put on for them. This second performance was bought to an untimely finish when a deluge of rain sent the royal family scurrying to their lodgings.[25]

As Edward and his men headed towards Fotheringhay, he issued a demand for Warwick and Clarence to join him, still completely unaware that they were in Calais. The men did not heed his call, instead Edward would receive what could only be described as a rebel manifesto sent by Warwick, which had been signed by himself, Clarence and Archbishop George Neville. The manifesto pledged their support to the northern rebels and accused members of the queen's family as well as others around the king of allowing the realm to 'fall in great poverty of misery … Only intending to their own promotion and enriching'. Clarence and Warwick then returned from France and began marching north with the intention of joining the rebels.

Edward was at Newark when he received notification of Warwick and Clarence's treachery, presumably with shock and disappointment. He sent word out for support and the Earls of Pembroke and Devon answered his call. On Wednesday 26 July, the armies of Pembroke and Devon were ambushed by Warwick's men and in what became known as the Battle of Edgecote, the Yorkist forces were routed. In a horrific turn of events for the Woodville family, Earl Rivers and John Woodville, the queen's father and brother, were captured and beheaded at Kenilworth, on the orders the Clarence and Warwick.

As news of the death of her brother and father reached the shocked queen a few days later, she and the two young princesses were hurriedly escorted back to London by her brother Anthony, who had left Edward, presumably on the king's orders, and returned to Norwich at speed, avoiding Warwick's men, to ensure her safe journey back to the capital. In what must have been an arduous and emotional journey back to London, it must surely have crossed their minds that it was only by the grace of God that Anthony too had escaped a similar fate.

As the queen and her two girls hurried back to London, they arrived back to the capital keeping such 'scant state' that the mayor and alderman voted to give her some wine ten days later.[26] Reunited with her youngest daughter, Cecily, Elizabeth would have no doubt hugged her tight, grieving for her family, worrying about Edward's whereabouts and with a fierce desire to keep her girls close against the danger that faced them.

Elizabeth may also have been reunited with her mother at this point, both women comforting each other in their grief.

Hearing the news of Edgecote, many of Edward's men fled, and Warwick was able to capture the king at Olney. He subsequently took him back to his home of Warwick Castle as his prisoner.

What a turn of events this was, two cousins, once the best of friends and allies, now one a prisoner and one his captor. News would have quickly filtered down to the women in London that Warwick had succeeded in capturing Edward and alone in London for the next few months, it would have been a hugely worrying time for them. But things were about to get worse. A follower of Warwick named Thomas Wake produced some lead images that he claimed Jacquetta had made for the purposes of witchcraft and sorcery, supposedly using them to bring about the marriage of Edward to her daughter. Jacquetta was well aware of the seriousness of this charge, having witnessed the downfall of Eleanor Cobham. But despite the shock of the murder of her husband and son, or perhaps because of it, Jacquetta stood strong and refused to be cowed by the accusations. She wrote an impassioned letter to the mayor and the aldermen of London for their assistance, reminding them of a favour she had done them in 1461, when she had persuaded her one-time friend, Margaret of Anjou, to spare the city from Lancastrian destruction. The council agreed to come to her aid.

With Edward and Warwick still shut up in Warwick castle, it soon became clear to the Earl that he could not raise enough supporters to remove Edward from the throne. Without their king, the country was descending into chaos and Warwick found himself without a recognisable authority to regain control. Unable to bring himself to commit cold-blooded murder on his king and one-time close ally at this time, he embarrassingly had to let Edward go. Edward returned to London at the end of 1469 and a shocked Elizabeth must have been relieved to have him back. Edward 'in peace just and merciful' forgave Clarence and Warwick and they returned temporarily to the fold. Back in charge again, Edward had to make a demonstration of following the law and deal with the charges of witchcraft that had been made against his mother-in-law. In January 1470, a proud, angry and determined Jacquetta went before the king's great council, where the witnesses back-pedalled, and she was acquitted. She wisely insisted that her exoneration be recorded in the official records so that it could not be levelled at her again in the future.

The fact that Edward had forgiven Warwick and Clarence must have been galling to Elizabeth and her mother and may have bought some tension into what up until then had seemed a perfect marriage. There are no reports that give us details of their relationship, but as a close-knit family Elizabeth would have been both horrified and upset at the death of her father and brother and to have the main perpetrators forgiven must have been hard to swallow. Suddenly Elizabeth's perfect fairytale scenario had taken a sinister turn.

Behind the scenes, Warwick and Clarence were still plotting however, and in March 1470, they chose to openly rebel again. A private feud between two Lincolnshire lords began to spill over, and Edward riding with his men to control the situation, discovered that once again some of the troublemakers were openly aligned with Clarence and Warwick. By May of that year, the pair realising that their treachery would not be forgiven so easily this time, fled to France, where the men of Calais, remaining loyal to their king, this time refused to allow them to dock. During this sea journey, Clarence's wife, Isabel, gave birth to a son, in what must have been horrendous conditions below deck. Eventually making shore further down the coast, Warwick, in a surprising turn of events, met with the Lancastrian Margaret of Anjou and made a deal that he would help restore her husband to the throne, if she agreed to a marriage between her son Edward and his youngest daughter Anne Neville who had also travelled with them, making Anne the next potential Queen of England. Margaret agreed and the marriage took place once again on French soil. Warwick then began preparations to sail to England with an army.

The vain and arrogant Clarence now began to suspect that his importance in these schemes was waning. The scheme he had agreed to had changed – Warwick was now fighting to put Henry back on the throne rather than Clarence and Isabel. He was also under pressure from his family to remain loyal to Edward, particularly from his two sisters and no doubt his mother. Whilst still appearing to support Warwick on the surface, the duke was 'quietly reconciled to the king by the mediation of [their] sisters, the Duchesses of Burgundy and Exeter'. The former, from outside the kingdom, had been encouraging the king, and the latter, from within, the duke, to make peace.[27]

Warwick, having made his pact with Margaret of Anjou, set sail back to England and headed for London, his mission to free Henry VI from the Tower of London. October 1470 found Edward trapped, surrounded by rebels in the north and Warwick's army marching up from the south. He was faced with no choice other than to flee abroad himself with his most loyal supporters, including his youngest brother, Richard, Duke of Gloucester and William Hastings, his trustworthy friend and Lord Chamberlain.

When the news reached the queen of Edward's departure, she was heavily pregnant with their fourth child. Understandably, she feared for her life. After what had happened to her father and brother, she did not trust that she or her family were safe and clutching her daughters and with her mother in tow, she took herself to her barge, and fled up the Thames to Westminster. Here in the precincts of the abbey, she took refuge in a strong, gloomy building called the sanctuary, which occupied a space at the end of St Margaret's churchyard. Entering the sanctuary, she registered herself, her mother, her three little daughters and an attendant, Lady Scrope, as sanctuary-women. Mary and Cecily were just toddlers, but for Princess Elizabeth, who was just a few months away from her fifth birthday, this must have been a scary time to see her mother so stressed, and one she may well have remembered later in life.

Their flight to safety was reported by John Paston to his mother, Margaret, in a letter dated 12 October 1470:

> To my right worshipful mother, Margaret Paston, be this delivered. The Queen that was, and the Duchess of Bedford, be in sanctuary at Westminster; the Bishop of Ely with other Bishops are in Saint Martins. When I hear more, I shall send you more. I prey God send you all your desires. Written at London on Saint Edwards Eve. Your son and humble servant.

The sanctuary is described by Agnes Strickland in her book as being located a short distance from Westminster Palace within the abbey grounds. It is described as a massive structure, of strength sufficient to stand a siege, with a church built over it, in the form of a cross. Strickland based her description on the account of the antiquarian Dr William Stukeley, who had seen it. He recalled that 'it was of vast strength, and only with much labour was it demolished'. The right of sanctuary here according to Stow extended not only to the church itself but to the churchyard and adjoining close. Stow also recorded that 'at the entrance of the Close there is a lane that leadeth towards the west, called Thieving Lane, for that thieves were led that way to the Gate House while the Sanctuary was in force'.[28] To the west of the sanctuary stood the almonry, where the alms of the abbey were distributed.

Shut away in this dark and probably damp building, Elizabeth must have been close to despair. Edward's flight from England's shores was fast and unexpected, and completely unpredictable even just a few weeks before, but when it happened it was absolutely necessary. Elizabeth would not have known whether he would return, although knowing his character, she must have believed that he would not abandon them there without a fight. But the situation was desperate; there was no guarantee that if Edward did return and fight, he would not be killed in the process. If Edward did die, she would have no claim to the throne and thus far she had only born daughters, who could not inherit after their father. Amongst all the bleakness, there was one tiny glimmer of hope. She was weeks away from giving birth and if she could produce a son, Edward would have the much-wanted son and heir and that may just make a difference.

With Edward in exile and Elizabeth in sanctuary, Warwick openly returned to London. In an illustration of just how bad their relationship had become, the king's once-loyal cousin who fought with Edward to gain the throne just a decade ago, called on his fellow countrymen to free 'our most dread sovereign Lord, King Henry the Sixth, very true and undoubted king of England and France' from the hands of 'his great rebel and enemy, Edward, late Earl of March, usurper, oppressor, and destroyer of our said sovereign lord and of the noble blood of all the realm of England and of the good, true commons of the same'.[29] In a period that became known as the re-adaption of Henry VI, Warwick proceeded to free Henry VI from captivity and restored the old king to the throne. For the next six months, the House of Lancaster was back in charge of the country.

Chapter 4

All's Well That Ends Well

It may have bought small comfort to Elizabeth that upon his return to London, Warwick issued a statement that sanctuary was not to be breached 'upon pain of death'. Although she appeared not to be in any immediate danger, she was eight months pregnant, surely tired and worried, and given his past behaviour towards her and her family, she had every reason to doubt his sincerity. The new government agreed to pay Lady Scrope to attend the queen in sanctuary, and reportedly a butcher, John Gould, supplied the women with a half of beef and two muttons every week to keep them fed.[1] But other than having a roof over their heads and a supply of food, the conditions they were now living in would have been dismal, a vast difference to life in the royal palaces.

For the three princesses in the sanctuary building with their mother and grandmother, only Princess Elizabeth may have been aware of the seriousness of their situation. Mary was just three years old, Cecily just over eighteen months and the innocence of childhood would have sheltered both. But Princess Elizabeth was just a few months away from her fifth birthday, and at an age where she would have understood some of the seriousness of the situation, and certainly at an age where she would have asked questions. As much as her mother and grandmother may have attempted to shelter her emotionally, the news that her father had gone away, coupled with their new living situation, however much they sugar-coated it, would have been unsettling for a small child. As the queen and her daughters waited for news and prayed for the safe return of their father, news would have reached them of his attainment and that of their uncle, Richard, Duke of Gloucester. The situation looked bleak.

Then on 1 November 1470, Elizabeth gave birth. It was a boy, the long-awaited heir to the house of York. Poignantly named Edward in honour of his absent father, this would have been an entirely different birthing experience than any Elizabeth had been through before, with none of the comforts that were available to her for the births of any

56

of her previous children. Although her physician was on hand to assist her if required, Elizabeth was supported during the birth by a local midwife, Mother Cobb, and presumably also by her mother. The little boy was baptised shortly after his birth, with Thomas Milling, abbot of Westminster, standing as godfather. Elizabeth's mother and Lady Scrope stood as his godmothers. His birth would have been a small glimmer of hope and joy amongst the despair that the sanctuary women must have been feeling.

Meanwhile, in sanctuaries across the city, many of Edward's friends and supporters had also taken refuge or were in hiding and Edward himself had found his way to The Hague. Edward's character dictated that he was never going to go down without a fight, but as news of the birth of his son reached his ears by the way of messengers loyal to the house of York, galloping on horseback to catch the next ship across the sea with the news, he now had even more of a reason to fight his way back to the kingdom he had ruled over for the last nine years.

When Edward had departed England's shores, the unexpectedness of the situation meant that he did not have a grand plan. According to Commynes, he made his escape 'by the assistance of a small vessel of his own and two Dutch merchantmen, attended only by 700 or 800 men, without any clothes but what they were to have fought in, no money in their pockets, and not one of them knew whither they were going'.[2] Before they left his chamberlain, William Hastings instructed all who remained behind to make peace with Warwick for their own safety but stay loyal to Edward. Presumably Edward may have thought that his best hope was to make his way to the court of his sister and brother-in-law, the Duke of Burgundy, but upon reaching shore, he was rescued and subsequently spent the winter of 1470 as honoured guests of Louis de Gruuthuse, governor of The Hague.

Lord de Gruuthuse dealt very honourably with Edward and his men during their stay and it was an honour that Edward would later repay. Conducting Edward and his party safely to The Hague, where they arrived on 11 October 1470, he then despatched the news of their arrival to the Duke of Burgundy, who, according to Commynes 'was much surprised when he heard it and would have been much better pleased if it had been news of his death; for he was in great apprehension of the Earl of Warwick, who was his enemy, and at that time absolute in England'. Although the duke may not have been entirely pleased to hear that Edward was alive, it seems that family ties won out and most likely under pressure from his wife, Edward's sister Margaret, the Duke of Burgundy provided him with 500 golden crowns per month for his support.

Having spent the winter at The Hague, Edward then continued his journey to the Duke of Burgundy's court at St. Polt, where he pleaded with the duke to give him supplies to enable him to recover his kingdom. He assured the duke 'of the great interest he had in England, and entreated him, for God's sake, not to abandon him, since he had married his sister, and they were besides brethren of the same orders'.[3] The duke it seems was torn between his loyalty to his wife and by extension her family, and his fear of upsetting Warwick. Eventually, he took the middle ground, publicly declaring he would not support Edward, but secretly supplying him with more money and three or four great ships, which he ordered to be equipped for him at La Veret in Holland. Edward gladly accepted and began his journey back across land towards his passage home. Commynes reports that the duke later 'received letters from the duchess, his wife, that the king of England was not at all satisfied with him; that the assistance he had given him was not done frankly and willingly, but as if for a very little cause he would have deserted him; and, to speak plainly, there was never great friendship between them afterwards',[4] although Edward it seems did personally write and thank the duke himself, in a letter sent on 28 May 1471, in which he thanked the duke for 'the valuable and brotherly assistance he had given him in his distress'.

Edward and his men finally landed back on England's shores six months after they departed. Landing at Ravenspur in the north of England in March 1471, several cities weary of trouble refused to admit him. With only his few loyal supporters with him, Edward knew he was not yet a match for his enemies and declared himself loyal to Henry VI, claiming he was only back in England to reclaim the York title that was rightfully his after the death of his father and brother. He then began a slow march down the country, collecting men in support along the way. Hastings had already ridden ahead to his homelands in the Midlands and by the time Edward had reached Leicester, Hastings had gathered an army of over three thousand 'stirred by his [Hastings] messages sent unto them, and by his servants, friends and lovers, such as were in the country'.[5]

Meanwhile, the Earl of Warwick was in Coventry and refusing to engage with Edward, so he bypassed him and continued his march south, meeting up with Clarence in Banbury, where George fell on his knees and begged forgiveness from his brother. Edward hugged him and immediately forgave him. The pair and their armies returned to Coventry where Warwick, who had been expecting Clarence to bring reinforcements to assist him, realised he had lost his son-in-law's support and still refused to engage. Edward's men left him there and began to march on London to reclaim the capital.

By Tuesday 9 April 1471, the City of London was aware that 'Edward late King of England was hastening towards the city with a powerful army'. At the same time, Warwick was writing and urging the city to remain steadfast in support of Henry VI. With the Aldermen of the City in confusion and unsure of what they were supposed to do, the mayor, John Stockton, allegedly retired to his bed due to the stress and could not be persuaded to leave it.

Archbishop George Neville who was in London at the time, made a last-ditch attempt to persuade the people of London to remain loyal to Henry, by parading him through the streets. But the difference between the two kings was striking – the old and fainthearted Henry VI, looking shabby in his old gown was no match when compared to the youthful, strong and popular Edward, and when Edward finally reached London, the gates were opened to admit him. Commynes believed there were three reasons why the gates of London were thrown open; firstly because of all Edward's friends in the sanctuaries around the city and the birth of his son; secondly due to the amount of money he had borrowed from the tradesmen of London who knew if they did not aid him in his quest he would be unable to pay them back and thirdly, that all the wives of the city with whom he had previously flirted or charmed persuaded their husbands to declare themselves on his side. Whatever the reason, he was allowed access and upon entering the city he rode straight to St Paul's to give thanks, before heading to the sanctuary to reunite with Elizabeth and meet his son for the very first time. Here he found Elizabeth 'sojourning in deep trouble, sorrow, and heaviness, which she sustained with all manner of patience belonging to any creature, and as constantly as ever was seen by any person of such high estate to endure'.[6] It must have been a great relief to her to have her husband back unharmed, especially given that this was never a guaranteed outcome by any means. For Princess Elizabeth too, seeing her father again must have been a moment of joy. Proudly showing her husband his newborn son, Elizabeth and her girls left sanctuary after a long six months, returning with Edward to Baynards Castle, the home of his mother, where they spent the night.

Without much resistance, Edward IV was back as King of England. In a face-to-face meeting with old King Henry, allegedly the frail and old man greeted him like a friend and cousin, without fear, and Edward dispatched him back into imprisonment in the Tower. But although Edward was back in London and reinstated as king, the danger was still very real and imminent as Warwick was still at large and as much as he was a formidable ally, he had also proved himself to be a dangerous foe. Edward had only one possible choice. Gathering his men, he set off to find his once-loyal cousin. On 14 April 1471, Edward and Warwick finally met on the battlefield at what would become known as the Battle of Barnet. Both men must have been aware that the battle had to be decisive. And it was. Warwick, one of the most powerful and influential men of his time was killed and Edward, this time with both of his brothers at his side, emerged victorious. But there was still one more fight to be had. On the same day that the Battle of Barnet was raging, Margaret of Anjou and her son had landed on English shores. Upon hearing the news, Edward once again gathered his men and headed off to meet her en route to London. The two armies met at Tewkesbury and Edward once more emerged victorious. Margaret's son, Edward of Lancaster, was killed and the defeated queen of Henry VI, broken with grief at the death of her son, was captured and taken to London where she would remain a prisoner for the next few years. Anne Neville, Warwick's youngest daughter who had been married to Edward of Lancaster in the deal struck by her father, was also with the party. She too was escorted back to London and placed into the care of her elder sister and brother-in-law, Isabel and Clarence. Not long after Tewkesbury, Henry VI was found dead in his room in the tower, supposedly of natural causes although undoubtedly few believed this official version of the story. For Edward and his family to be safe, the Lancastrian threat had to be removed once and for all.

With all their enemies disposed of, the reunited king and queen spent much of June and July 1471 at Westminster and Windsor, no doubt relieved that the turmoil of the last few months was over and that they had come through relatively unscathed. In a ceremony on 11 June 1471, Prince Edward, who was by then seven months old, was invested as Prince of Wales at Westminster abbey, and in early July at a council meeting he was formerly recognised as the heir to the throne and allegiance was pledged to him by all the great and noble magnates of the land. For the young Princess Elizabeth, she was back in the safety of the royal palaces, with her family back together and with peace and security restored. News that her mother was pregnant again, which would have been confirmed by the queen sometime around November of that year, would have brought joy to the whole family. The royal family ended 1471 at the Palace of Westminster, where Edward and Elizabeth took part in a second coronation on Christmas Day and Twelfth Night in the abbey. Elizabeth, who was certainly aware of the new life growing inside her at this point, was experiencing tiredness and did not wear her crown.[7] The re-crowning ceremonies were a time of celebration for all they had survived over the past year, for the beginnings of Edward's second reign and for the new child they were expecting in the spring; the new year of 1472 would have begun with optimism for the future.

Elizabeth's fifth child was born on 10 April 1472 at Windsor. The king and queen named her Margaret, and the news was reported in a letter, written by Sir John Paston to his brother, also called John, at the end of April who after greeting his brother, and giving him news of several prominent persons who had wedded or died, informed him that 'The Qween hadde chylde, a dowghter, but late at Wyndesor; ther off I trow ye hadde worde'.[8]

Whilst the king and queen were rejoicing over their new baby daughter, the dynamics of their family were changing again. Anne Neville, now a widow after the death of Edward of Lancaster, was seemingly having a miserable time living with Clarence and Isabel at their home at Coldharbour Place. And she had conveyed her unhappiness to Edward's youngest brother, Richard, Duke of Gloucester. How or where these discussions with Gloucester took place is unclear, but together they had formulated a plan. Rumours abound that Clarence became aware of his brother's intentions to marry Anne and tried to keep her out of his reach, one account telling of how on one occasion he sent her to the house of one of his retainers, disguising her as a kitchen maid so Gloucester was unable to locate her. This story may be fictional, but in truth, Clarence may have tried to limit their meetings as much as possible. The pair must have made contact at some point however and made plans, as on 16 February 1472, Gloucester enabled her to escape from Coldharbour into the sanctuary at the London Collegiate church of St Martin Le Grand until they could marry. Just twelve days after Princess Margaret's birth in April, a papal dispensation was issued permitting the marriage of Richard of Gloucester to Anne Neville. The dispensation arrived in England in June, although the marriage may almost certainly have taken place before then.

The reason Clarence would have been so keen to keep his younger brother away from Anne was financial and involved the vast Warwick estates. In 1472, Clarence held custody of the estates by right of his wife and was eager to keep them all for himself. Anne, as a 'guest' in their household had no power over any inheritance that was hers. Warwick's widow, the Countess of Warwick, was also written out of the equation; still living in 1472, she had taken refuge in Beaulieu Abbey during the troubles of the previous year. By rights, the Warwick estates should have been hers, but as punishment for the actions of her husband, she was refused her entitlement. A few years later it was taken a step further when parliament, in an appalling move, declared her legally dead when they divided up the Warwick estates, even though she did not actually die until the early 1490s.

Richard and Anne had known each other since childhood and much debate has been had over the motives behind their wedding. The romantics take the viewpoint that it was a love match, they had known each other for many years and the lovestruck couple plotted together to sneak Anne out of 'captivity' so they could be together. But with Clarence in possession of all the Warwick estates, a dispute arose between the two brothers with Gloucester demanding his share of the lands, which were worth a considerable amount and represented significant wealth and power. His demand for Anne's rightful share may have been a dutiful husband assisting his wife, or perhaps Anne was his route to the Warwick wealth? Either way, with Gloucester wanting his share, and his brother Clarence refusing to give them up, the brothers were set on a warring path, with King Edward having to act as mediator.

Once married the young couple went to live at Middleham, in the north of England, where they remained for the next ten years, with Richard supporting his brother in the management of the north. The matter of the Warwick estates would rumble on for another two years before parliament would pass an act dividing the lands equally between the two brothers.

Elizabeth, who came from such a close-knit family, may have found it challenging to deal with the dynamics of Edward's kin. Reportedly her mother-in-law was against her marriage from the start, although whether their relationship improved over time is unknown. With Clarence directly involved in the death of her father and brother this no doubt greatly clouded Elizabeth's relationship with him and with both her sisters-in-law daughters of Warwick, she cannot have felt much love toward them either. Family loyalty was definitely a trait that Edward's family could have learned from the Woodvilles; Elizabeth had remained close and surrounded herself with family members even after she became queen. Astonishingly this has been the cause of some criticism of her.

The close ties that Elizabeth kept with her family, meant that the sadness and grief she would have felt on 30 May 1472 when her mother died, would have been heartbreaking. Jacquetta had been a rock to Elizabeth throughout her life, a constant support through the good times and the bad and Elizabeth must have felt her death keenly. After all that had happened over the last decade, Elizabeth was undoubtedly devastated with grief at the loss of her biggest confidante. No details survive of Jacquetta's funeral and burial, and Elizabeth may have taken some time away from public duties to mourn. But as was expected of her, she had to resume her duties in the autumn of 1472, when alongside her husband they prepared to greet Edward's saviour during his exile, Louis de Gruuthuse, during his trip to England.

Gruuthuse was accompanied to England by his entourage which included his son and a manservant named Bluemantle Pursuivant, who left a detailed account of the visit. The royal family were staying at Windsor Castle when their esteemed guest arrived. The king's Lord Chamberlain, William Hastings, met the party upon their arrival at Windsor and escorted him to meet the king and queen. The Burgundian party were allocated three richly hung chambers to sleep in during their stay and that evening, the king accompanied Seigneur de Gruuthuse to Elizabeth's chamber, where she and her ladies were playing games and dancing. Princess Elizabeth also got to join in the fun, dancing with her father around the room.

After Mass the next morning, Edward gifted his visitor a gold cup, supposedly set with a piece of unicorn's horn, before presenting him to the Prince of Wales, who was not yet two years old. During the rest of his stay, Gruuthuse was treated to a hunt, a walk in the palace gardens and a visit to the vineyard before Elizabeth once again invited him to a banquet held in his honour in her chambers. The Gruuthuse's (father and son), sat with Elizabeth and Edward at the main table, together with Elizabeth's younger sister, Katherine, the Duchess of Buckingham and her young husband, the Duchess of Exeter (the king's sister), and Princess Elizabeth. Courtiers and Gruuthuse's gentlemen sat at two other tables. Gruuthuse and his son were then taken to new and still more exquisitely furnished rooms, where they took a bath, Hastings bathing with them. The floor had been covered with warm towels, and the wooden tubs were placed under white canopies, a procession of servants needed to fill them with hot water from ewers. After bathing, the visitors were served with green ginger, comfits and spiced wine.[9] Before he left, Edward created him Earl of Winchester to thank him for his friendship. The visit was a huge success and sealed the friendship between Edward and Gruuthuse. Elizabeth no doubt was equally grateful for his support of her husband in his hour of need.

1472 had been a year of mixed emotions for Elizabeth, with real highs and lows, but as the family approached the Christmas season, another disaster occurred when in another heartbreaking turn of events, the young Margaret of York, whose birth had surely bought such joy to the family earlier on in the year, died on 11 December. Elizabeth was no stranger to loss, but this was very possibly the first child she had lost (barring any unrecorded miscarriages or stillbirths) and following so soon after the death of her mother, it would have brought her much sadness. Princess Margaret was laid to rest in Westminster Abbey; her tiny coffin placed in the chapel of St Edward the Confessor, where her small altar tomb, now without inscription, can still be seen. As she said a sad goodbye to her young daughter, Elizabeth may have been in the first few weeks of her next pregnancy, that of her second son with Edward, Richard, who would be born in August the following year. As the royal family ended 1472, and passed into the new year of 1473, they must have hoped for a more peaceful time to come.

With Edward now firmly settled on the throne of England, it was time for Elizabeth and Edward to not only look to their future, but also to that of their children. In 1473, negotiations were begun to arrange a marriage for Cecily, their third eldest daughter. An agreement was reached between Edward IV and King James III of Scotland that Cecily would wed James' young son, James IV when they both came of age. Seemingly, Cecily was the first of Edward's daughters that he had started marriage discussions for; perhaps she was deemed the most suitable and the closest in age to her intended spouse, (Cecily was four in 1473, the infant Prince of Scots just a year old) or perhaps Edward already had his sights on an even greater match for her two elder sisters. A formal betrothal took place in October the following year in Edinburgh, as part of a treaty between the two countries and on 26 December 1474, a ceremony took place in Edinburgh with a deputation standing in for Cecily. From then on, the young Princess was styled Princess of Scots.[10]

Also in 1474, Elizabeth's eldest son from her first marriage to Sir John Grey was married. This was not his first marriage. After Elizabeth became queen, her agreement that she had made with William Hastings back in 1464 before her marriage to the king was broken off. Instead, a marriage had been arranged between Thomas Grey and Anne Holland, the daughter of Anne of York, Edward IV's sister. The marriage between Thomas and Anne had taken place in Greenwich in 1466 when Anne was around five years old and Thomas aged around twelve. But when Anne Holland died in 1474, a match was proposed between Thomas Grey and Cecily Bonville. Cecily was the stepdaughter of William Hastings; her mother was Katherine Neville, a younger sister of the Earl of Warwick, and after the death of Cecily's father, William Bonville, in 1462, a marriage had been made between Katherine and Hastings.

Cecily Bonville was a rich woman, as the only heir to the Bonville estates, and Queen Elizabeth agreed to pay Hastings 2500 marks for the marriage of his stepdaughter and an agreement was reached that the queen would receive income from all of Cecily's estates until she reached sixteen years of age. Her marriage contract to Thomas was dated 18 July 1474 and their required dispensation (due to their joint descendance from one Reginald Grey), was received on 5 September 1474.[11] Cecily was around fourteen or fifteen at the time of their marriage, and Thomas was around the age of nineteen. A year later, Thomas, who clearly had a good relationship with the king, was given the title of Marquis of Dorset. Cecily, as his wife, was made Marchioness of Dorset.

Arrangements for Princess Elizabeth's marriage would also begin in 1475, when she was betrothed to the Dauphin of France, with the expectation that she would one day be Queen of France. Her father had travelled to France on a military exercise in August of that year with the aim of repeating the success of past kings and taking French lands back under English rule. Things had not gone according to plan, however. Abandoned by his allies, Edward's campaign resulted in him striking a peace deal with King Louis XI known as the Treaty of Picquigny.

As part of the treaty, an agreement was made that when they came of age, Elizabeth would marry Louis' son, the Dauphin Charles. From 1475 onwards, Princess Elizabeth became known as Madame la Dauphine with the arrangement made between the French and English royal houses that as soon as she reached the age of twelve, Princess Elizabeth would be sent to France to live at the French royal court. With one daughter a potential Queen of Scotland and one a potential Queen of France, Elizabeth must have been pleased with these arrangements for her daughters, hopefully securing their positions in life. No arrangements were made at this stage for her second eldest, Mary, although perhaps her father had ideas of a good match in mind that never came to fruition.

By the middle of the 1470s, the court of Elizabeth and Edward was a much more peaceful place than during the early days of their marriage. Edward remained a popular king; as Polydore Vergil, an Italian Scholar who settled in England in the early 1500s noted: 'his kindness (which was very innate in him) [meant] that he existed on more familiar terms with the common run of humanity than the honor of his majesty dictated'. Vergil was commissioned to write a history of England by Henry VII and in it, he describes Edward as 'tall and lofty of stature, so that he towered above everybody else. He had an honest face, happy eyes, a steadfast heart, a great mind, and a memory that retained whatever he had absorbed. He was circumspect in his actions, ready amidst dangers, harsh and fearsome towards his enemies, liberal towards his friends and guests, and very fortunate in fighting his wars'. More gives a similar description of Edward 'He was a goodly personage, and very princely to behold: of heart, courageous; politic in counsel; in adversity nothing abashed; in prosperity, rather joyful than proud; in peace, just and merciful; in war, sharp and fierce; in the field, bold and hardy, and nevertheless, no further than wisdom would, adventurous'.[12]

There is no substantial contemporary description of Elizabeth's character however, mainly because she was female and women were just not written about in detail. Historians down the ages have made assumptions on her character, good and bad, based on their assessment of her reported actions. Contemporary mentions of Elizabeth generally allude to her appearance and historians have generally accepted that she was considered a beautiful woman. Portraits of her that have survived, such as the ones held by Queen's College Cambridge, of which she was a patron, generally back this up. With Edward also considered to be aesthetically blessed, she and Edward gifted their striking good looks to their children. Elizabeth's relationship with her husband is also generally accepted to have been a close one, but it seems that even marriage to his beautiful wife was not enough to prevent the king from seeking the company of other women.

Edward was undoubtedly a charmer and a ladies' man, a fact that Elizabeth must have known even from the start of their marriage, and presumably had to accept. Commynes tells us 'His thoughts were wholly employed upon the ladies (and far more than was reasonable), hunting, and adorning his person. In his summer-hunting, his custom was to have several tents set up for the ladies, where he treated them after a magnificent manner; and indeed his person was as well turned for love-intrigues as any man I ever saw in my life: for he was young, and the most handsome man of his time'.[13]

It was around the mid-1470s that Edward began what was perhaps his most recognised liaison with a young woman named Jane Shore. Born Elizabeth Lambert sometime around 1450, Jane was the daughter of a London mercer, John Lambert and his wife Amy.[14] At some point in the mid to late 1460s, Jane was matched in marriage to another mercer, named William Shore. It seems that for whatever reason, the couple were incompatible, and within a few years of their wedding, Jane appealed to the Court of Arches, requesting a divorce and alleging that her marriage was unconsummated. This in itself was a courageous move for her to make, as women rarely initiated separation from their husbands. The appeal was denied, but Jane refused to give up. She took the matter to court more than once and was eventually granted a divorce on 1 March 1476, around about the same time she is thought to have become the king's mistress. How she met the king is unclear. Whether he assisted her in her divorce matter also went unrecorded, but it is not beyond the realms of possibility that the two were linked.

Edward was famously known to have had at least three mistresses, whom he allegedly categorised as 'the merriest, the wiliest and the holiest' women in the land. Jane is believed to have been the 'merriest' and the fact that she remained his mistress from the mid-1470s through to his death indicates that he obviously thought highly of her. But how did Elizabeth feel about having to share her husband?

There are of course many reasons why a woman chooses to turn a blind eye to her husband's extramarital affairs. He was not the first man to have a mistress and the position of women in the Middle Ages meant that once married, a woman became the property of her husband and women rarely initiated separation or divorce. That women had to accept that their husband may spend time in the company of other women was generally a given, although not all men, of course, chose to do so. There is no evidence that Elizabeth's father, for instance, was ever unfaithful to her mother.

Christine Pisan, a respected source on questions of morality, advises women on how to deal with their husband's adultery. Every married woman should respect their husband, she counsels, and live in peace with him. She points out that certainly not all men are deserving of their wives' love. Sometimes a man may behave rudely or stray into a love affair. But if the wife cannot remedy the situation, she must put up with this and dissimulate wisely, pretending she does not notice it. Because a prudent woman knows that speaking harshly to him will gain nothing. This advice is not given to take away a woman's pride, in fact, quite the opposite. By being pleasant and kind to her husband whilst he is behaving so badly, she will secure herself a moral victory. Christine counsels that if the man does not change his ways, the woman should take refuge in God and be resigned to the situation. For, at some point, the husband will feel remorse at how he has treated his faithful wife and eventually she will have won her cause through steadfast enduring.[15]

Elizabeth may or may not have been of this opinion, but whatever she felt about her husband's womanising ways, she knew that she had no choice but to accept it, along with countless other women who would have had to ignore their husband's infidelity. Certainly, as king, Edward would have had his pick of women and it seems his love for his wife did not prevent him from taking his pleasures elsewhere when he chose. And Elizabeth's love for him meant she had to ignore his extramarital liaisons, no matter what personal pain it caused her.

Elizabeth of course was now living the life of a queen, her role being to support her husband and provide heirs, which she did with poise and composure. Edward clearly trusted her implicitly; during his campaign to France in 1475, he had left her in charge of the country and named her as his 'derrest and moost entirely beloved wiff' as the main executor of his will. She now had her own household, separate from that of her husband, but it seems that even with his affairs they remained close as a couple.

Her daily life was now on a much grander scale than any she would have experienced before. Life at Grafton and as a wife at Astley Castle would have involved the understanding and management of a small household, but the royal palaces were on such a grand scale, they were almost like miniature towns. There were a vast number of departments, working together like clockwork, to keep the royal court functioning. From the treasury to the counting house, the royal wardrobe to the apothecary, each had its own role to play and bought with it its own costs. After his return from Burgundy in the early 1470s, Edward had been inspired by the grandeur of the Burgundian royal court, its opulence and majesty that presented an outward show of wealth and power. But there was also a real need to balance this grandeur with a requirement to economically balance the books. The court did not have a finite amount of money and finely tuned rules were called for on how the household should be run to strike the balance between affluence and economy. The Black Book of the Household of Edward IV, begun most likely early into Edward's second reign, was designed to do just that.

From details in the Black Book and the household ordinances of 1478, both of which have survived, we can get a real glimpse into the royal household during Edward and Elizabeth's reign. Food and drink obviously played a huge part in the running of the court, and with so many mouths to feed, mealtimes were well regulated. From these documents we learn that twenty-four squires were engaged to serve the king and queen, twelve who would serve the first course and dine themselves at the second and vice versa. During the fifteenth century, mealtimes were much earlier than nowadays and the ordinances instruct that 'every eting day the first dyner be redy upon IX of the clok and in likewiese the first souper begynne at IIII of the clok at the furthest, and on fasting dayes the first dyner to begynne at XI of the clok'.[16]

Although 9 am seems early for dinner, the populace generally rose much earlier than we do today, often rising at daybreak. The ordinances instruct that 'every eting day be ordeyned a large brekefast for the king to thentent that such lords, knyghtes, and squyers with other awaiting upon his person shal mowe breke their fastes with that remayneth of the same. And that for the quene be ordeyned in like wise'. They would also retire to bed much earlier – with only the richer households able to afford candles, many of the poorer population would rest and rise in accordance with the rising and setting of the sun. At the royal court, to get them through the lengthy period from their last meal at 4 pm, a meal known as 'all night' would be sent to the king and queen's chambers to provide them with refreshments throughout the night. Any food that was left over from mealtimes would be taken and distributed at the gates of the palace as alms. The food for the king and queen and the vast number of staff in the royal household would be provided by a multitude of different departments all working together: the pantry, the buttery, the bakehouse, the spicery, the confectionary, the Butelary of Ale and even an Office of Purveyors of Wine. The royal court was a finely tuned machine, and as queen, Elizabeth had her part to play within it.

During 1478, as the ordinances were being compiled, the first marriage of one of the York children took place when the four-year-old Richard of York was wed to Anne Mowbray, who was just five at the time of their nuptials. The wedding took place on 15 January 1478 in St Stephens Chapel, Westminster. Elizabeth and Edward, proud parents of the young groom, were seated under a gold canopy within the chapel alongside the eldest York princesses, their brother Edward and the king's mother. After the ceremony, Richard of Gloucester showered the waiting crowds with gold and silver coins before the wedding party went on to a banquet where the young Anne was announced as Duchess of York – her young husband had been created Duke of York when he was just nine months old. A few days later, a tournament was held at Westminster, followed by dancing in the king's chamber by the young Duchess and the royal princesses. Sadly, Anne would never fully live the life of a Duchess of York; she died at Greenwich a couple of weeks before her ninth birthday.

With the joy of the wedding celebrations still ringing in their ears, a family conflict that had been simmering for months was brought to a head just a few weeks later in February 1478, when in what some could say was the inevitable finale of their relationship, Edward sentenced his brother, Clarence, to death.

After Clarence's betrayal in the late 1460s when he sided with Warwick, Edward had welcomed him back into the fold. Clarence had celebrated along with his brothers after their victory at Tewkesbury and appeared to settle into family life for a while, electing to spend less time at court and more time with his wife, Isabel, and their young family. Apart from the disputes over the Warwick inheritance between Clarence and Gloucester, all seemed to be well and all three brothers displayed a show of unity in 1476, when they came together for the reburial of their father.

After the Duke of York and his son was killed at Wakefield in 1460 and the gruesome Lancastrian celebrations where their heads were displayed on the Micklegate Bar in York, mocking their defeat. Edward had vowed to make things right. Shortly after he became king in 1461, he had the heads removed and buried with their bodies in Pontefract but it was not until fifteen years later, when he was finally firmly established on his throne and financially able, that he was able to honour his father and brother as he wanted.

In a service attended by Elizabeth and the royal children, as well as Edward's family, the bodies of the duke and Edmund were exhumed from their burial place in Pontefract and brought to the family mausoleum at Fotheringhay. The duke's last journey had begun in Pontefract on Monday 22 July and the cortege arrived at their destination seven days later, between the hours of 2 pm and 3 pm. The bodies had been accompanied all the way by Richard, Duke of Gloucester, acting as chief mourner. Edward greeted the hearses carrying their bodies with tears in his eyes at the entrance to the cemetery; at his side were his brothers (Gloucester had ridden on ahead for the last part of the journey, to be able to greet his father) and other male family members, including the queen's brother, Anthony Woodville and her son, Thomas Grey. Edward was dressed in a dark blue habit and hood, the mourning colour for kings.

The following day the funeral took place which was attended by Elizabeth and her two eldest daughters; they were also dressed in blue. Afterwards, there was a great feast reportedly attended by around 20,000 people, held in the castle and in pavilions erected on the grounds.[17]

This reburial ceremony brought the York brothers back together but it was not to last; there remained in the background an undercurrent of discord. And the outward appearance of harmony was shattered when after giving birth to her fourth child in October 1476, Clarence's wife Isabel died. This sent Clarence, either through grief or some other disturbance of mind, off the rails again.

Immediately after Isabel's death, Clarence had cited witchcraft, blaming one of his wife's servants, Ankarette Twynyho for her death, and accusing her of poisoning his wife. Much to the horror of her family, Clarence had her arrested and summarily executed immediately after a trial, during which he heavily influenced the jurors to pronounce a guilty verdict. Her family complained to the king and Edward attempted to reel his unruly brother in.

Clarence then sought the hand of Mary, the only daughter of Charles, Duke of Burgundy, and the stepdaughter of his sister, Duchess Margaret. Edward refused, and according to Vergil, it was due to the obstruction of his marriage plans that 'the ancient hatred between these brothers (nothing stronger) manifested itself'. George took this rebuttal with ill grace and left court, refusing to dine with the king claiming he feared he would also be poisoned. In perhaps an illustration of the continued enmity between Elizabeth and Clarence, this empty accusation was directed mainly at her.

The troublesome chain of events continued when three men were arrested, accused of plotting Edward's death. One of the accused was a close associate of Clarence, and all three were found guilty at trial. Two of the three were then executed for treason, the third narrowly escaping with his life. This should have been a warning to Clarence, but he didn't take it. Instead, he elected to align himself with a preacher, who happened to be a notorious Lancastrian, and burst into parliament to protest the innocence of the condemned men, at the same time taking the opportunity to bad-mouth the king and disrespect the queen and her family. Edward could not let this continue and found himself with little choice but to arrest his troublesome brother and throw him into the tower.

During his trial on charges of treason, Edward elected to personally question his brother. With the two pitted against each other, the Croyland Chronicle reported that 'no one spoke against the Duke but the king, and no one answered but the Duke'. Clarence was convicted and despite desperate pleas for clemency by their mother, Cecily, for Edward to spare his life, on 18 February 1478, George, Duke of Clarence, was put to death. The method used to end his life is unknown, although the legend that has passed down to us is that given the choice of choosing his own means of execution, he chose to be drowned in a barrel of Malmesbury wine. His daughter, Margaret, reportedly wore a bracelet with a small barrel attached to it for the rest of her life in memory of her father. A portrait in the National Portrait Gallery of a woman who is yet to be fully identified but traditionally thought to be Margaret Pole, Countess of Salisbury (her later married name), shows a woman with a tiny barrel charm. George, Duke of Clarence, is buried in Tewkesbury Abbey alongside his wife, Isabel.

Whatever had occurred between the brothers in the late 1460s, this was still an ugly chapter in Edward's reign. An old legend tells of a prophecy that Edward had consulted around that time, which was something he was allegedly prone to do in times of doubt. The tale was first mentioned by John Rous in his *Historia Regum Angliae*, written between 1489 and 1491 and apparently foretold simply that G would follow E (which was understood to foretell that after Edward, G would reign).[18] It is unlikely that Edward had his brother put to death solely on a prophecy, but it is highly likely that he took it more seriously than perhaps we would today. Hall attributes their final clash and Clarence's ultimate demise as the rising of 'old grudges before time passed' and it is likely that Edward had just reached the end of his tolerance for his troubled and troublesome younger brother. Coupled with everything else that he had to consider whilst deciding George's fate, he may strongly have felt that to protect his young son Edward's inheritance, he needed to rid himself and his family from the threat of G.

Vergil also mentions this prophecy, asserting that a rumour had circulated at the time that Edward had become frightened by a soothsayer's prediction that after him would reign a man whose name began with the letter G. Ironically, the prophecy did come true, but the G turned out to be his younger brother, Gloucester. Vergil, noting the irony, wrote: 'Because devils are wont to play their pranks to inveigle the minds of folk who delight in such illusions, they said that this prediction was not untrue, since after Edward the Duke of Gloucester occupied the throne'.

The execution of Clarence has been on many occasions attributed to the influence of Elizabeth Woodville. Citing the animosity between Elizabeth and her brother-in-law, her detractors lay the death of Clarence right at her door – her ultimate revenge for his part in the deaths of her father and brother. But to award Elizabeth the credit for Clarence's death does Edward IV a disservice. His reputation as a strong leader is what ultimately gave him the advantage over his predecessor, so to presume he could be swayed to kill his own brother on the word of his vengeful wife is illogical. After her father and brother were killed by his command, it would be no surprise that Elizabeth disliked him as much as she disliked Warwick. If she called for revenge, it would likely have been immediately after the deaths of her father and brother and yet Edward did nothing. If he ignored her then, there is no reason to suggest he acted purely on her word all these years later. The decision to execute his brother, like so many others that the queen was blamed for over the years, was ultimately Edward's alone. Edward could not have made this decision lightly, even though George had been a thorn in his side for much of his reign. Although he ordered his brother's execution, he undoubtedly reflected on it later with sadness and possibly even regret. Their younger brother, Richard, Duke of Gloucester, who had always been loyal to Edward and had also had his disagreements with Clarence, was said to have been equally divided at this significant turn of events.

The news of Clarence's fate would have reverberated across the family. Princess Elizabeth would have heard the news at some point along with the rest of her siblings. Their reactions are of course not recorded, nor is their relationship with their uncle ever detailed. Whether they were close to him or not, it must be hard to reconcile that your father has judicially sentenced your uncle to death, even if your father is king. Perhaps for the twelve-year-old Elizabeth, it taught her an early lesson in ruling a kingdom and what actions may need to be taken to protect the line of succession and to protect your family and country.

After all the drama at the start of that year, Princess Elizabeth reached the age of twelve in 1478 and should have been excitedly getting ready to leave court and travel to her new home, to begin her life as a Queen of France in training. Having been styled as the French queen for the past few years, her father now called on King Louis to honour the deal. Her dowry was paid, and dresses were made for her in the French style so she could be appropriately dressed for the French court. But Louis stalled. According to Holinshed: 'Ambassadours were sent to and fro betwixt the king of England and France, and still the French king fed the king of England with faire words, putting him in hope to match his sonne and heire the Dolphin with the ladie Elizabeth daughter to the king of England, according to the conclusions of agreement had and made at Picquenie betwixt them, although in verie deed he meant nothing lesse. Thus the French king used to dallie with King Edward in the case of this marriage, onelie to keepe him still in amitie. And certeinelie the King of England, being a man of no suspicious nature, thought sooner that the sunne should have fallen from his circle, than that the French King would have dissembled or broken promise with him'.[19]

As the months went by and Princess Elizabeth remained at court, it was not at all clear when she might finally make the journey overseas. As the eldest child, she would have been schooled in what was expected of her and although twelve years of age seems impossibly young for a child to leave home, it was not an unusual occurrence for young ladies to leave home at that age to live with the families of their intended spouse. Queen Elizabeth too must have had pangs of motherly doubt about her eldest daughter leaving her, but she too knew what was expected of them both. She had already had to deal with the absence of her eldest son, Prince Edward, who had been sent to Ludlow Castle as a small child, to be established in his own household as the heir to the throne, away from the dangers of the English capital, so she was well aware that she had to be a mother second and a queen first. She still of course had plenty of other children with her as after the birth of Richard in 1473, she had since given birth to another princess, Anne, in 1475 and a third son in 1477, whom they named George.

Princess Elizabeth was still in England in early 1479 and was therefore present in March of that year when tragedy struck as two-year-old Prince George succumbed to 'an epidemic', as reported to his aunt in Burgundy and recorded by a Burgundian chronicler.[20] There was a serious outbreak of 'the great pestilence' in the spring of 1479 and George, it seems, became a tiny victim of the disease. He was buried on 22 March in St George's Chapel, Westminster in an elaborate ceremony befitting a prince of the realm. At the time of his death, Queen Elizabeth Woodville was four months into her eleventh pregnancy so once again she must have experienced a rollercoaster of emotions, grieving for George and then a mere five months later experiencing some joy and renewal of hope in life when in August 1479, she gave birth to a healthy baby girl. Their sixth daughter was born at Eltham Palace, and they named her Katherine.

The Princess Katherine took her place in the royal nursery along with the rest of her siblings under the care of a nurse called Joan Colson. Entries in the patent rolls for 1480 record an annuity of five pounds to Joan and her husband 'nurse to the King's daughter, Katherine' along with grants of land in Hitchin. As the king and queen and their family entered into the next decade, they had much to look forward to. They were still sure of Princess Elizabeth's destiny and they had a brood of healthy children in their ever-growing family. Life was good.

In early 1480, Princess Elizabeth took part in the annual feast of St George at Windsor Castle. During the 1480 celebrations, Elizabeth's younger sisters, Mary and Cecily, were both made Ladies of the Garter. The Order of the Garter, created by Edward III and embraced wholeheartedly by Edward IV, was inspired by the legends of King Arthur. The Order originally consisted of twenty-four trusty knights and was reserved as the highest award for loyalty and military prowess. The Ladies of the Garter were generally members of the royal family or closely associated with the order by marriage and were also allowed to wear the habit of the Order of the Garter on the feast days of St. George. The first Lady of the Garter was recorded in 1347 – the king's mother, Joan Plantagenet, mother of Richard II. Princess Elizabeth and her mother had been initiated into the order a couple of years before and in 1480, it was the turn of Cecily and Mary. The keeper of the Royal Wardrobe, Piers Courteys, had the care of the liveries of the brotherhood of St George and the Garter, for which he was paid a salary of £100 pa and in 1480, he organised for robes and hoods to be made for the queen and the three eldest York girls to attend the annual feast. As it turned out, Princess Mary did not attend the ceremony, due to ill health.

A few months after the St George's day celebrations, Duchess Margaret of Burgundy arrived back in London to visit her brother. Having left England at the age of twenty-two, she was now thirty-three years old and a widow (her husband had died three years previously) and she had become one of the most influential women in Europe. She was also extremely loyal to her York family and in later years would become a thorn in the side of Henry VII in her continued support of her brother Edward and his sons. After the death of her husband, Margaret, who had formed a close bond with her stepdaughter Mary, had been hugely instrumental in arranging Mary's marriage to Maximilian of Austria, future Holy Roman Emperor. Part of her return to her brother's court was to discuss the possibility of a marriage between Mary and Maximilian's eldest son, Philip and Princess Anne.

Edward Woodville, the queen's brother, was dispatched to escort Margaret home. Arriving in Calais in his ship named the *Falcon*, he collected Margaret and delivered her safely across the channel into the port of Gravesend. They then completed the journey into London by barge along the Thames.

Edward was no doubt delighted to see his younger sister again, and he made every effort to impress her on her visit, beginning with an elaborate procession to celebrate her arrival. The royal barge that sailed her up the river was rowed by the master and twenty-four oarsmen, all dressed in smart new jackets of murrey and blue, embellished with roses.

Once on dry land, she was transported to Greenwich by horses bedecked in harnesses of 'green velvet, garnished with aglets of silver gilt, bordered with spangels'.[21] Her homecoming was a real family reunion, as waiting to greet her was her brother the king and Queen Elizabeth, Margaret's mother Cecily Neville, her brother Richard of Gloucester and her elder sister Elizabeth, Duchess of Suffolk. The royal children were also there to welcome their exotic aunt, most of whom had never met her before. Whether George, Duke of Clarence was conspicuous by his absence or not we can only guess at.

Prior to her arrival, Edward had given instructions that Greenwich Palace and Coldharbour House were to be prepared for Margaret's stay, two of her favourite childhood residences. Her first stop was to be Greenwich where she was escorted to her opulent chambers, hung with intricately woven tapestries and a feather bed with a valence of velvet. Pieces of woven wool tapestry covered the table containing images of 'roses, sunnes and crowns'.[22] In her honour a banquet was held at Greenwich, hosted in their mother's name. Margaret was to remain in England until September 1480, during which time she and Edward had much to discuss, including her wish for England to support Burgundy against their troublesome neighbour France, and of course the terms of Anne's betrothal to Prince Philip of Austria.

During Margaret's visit, Elizabeth would have been heavily pregnant again and on 10 November 1480, she gave birth to what would be her and Edward's last child together. Princess Bridget of York made her entrance into the world at Eltham Palace in London, just like her sister Katherine had a little over fourteen months earlier. It is highly probable that her name was inspired by her paternal grandmother's devotion to Saint Birgitta.

Twenty-four hours later, on St Martin's Day, the young princess was christened at the chapel of Eltham by the Bishop of Chichester. Details of the occasion survive and were published in 'The Gentleman's Magazine' in 1831.[23] As was the custom, Elizabeth would still have been lying-in after the travails of childbirth and would not have attended the christening. Princess Elizabeth did get to play a key role however in the christening of her youngest sister. The newborn Princess was carried into the chapel by Margaret Beaufort, the Countess of Richmond, assisted by Thomas Grey, Elizabeth's son from her first marriage. Princess Elizabeth awaited at the font along with her grandmother, Cecily Neville, both honoured with the role of godmother alongside Margaret Woodville (lady Maltravers), sister to the queen.

> In the twentieth year of the reign of King Edward IV on St. Martin's Eve was born the Lady Bridget, and christened on the morning of St. Martin's Day in the Chapel of Eltham, by the Bishop of Chichester in order as ensueth:
>
> First a hundred torches borne by knights, esquires, and other honest persons.
>
> The Lord Maltravers, bearing the basin, having a towel about his neck.
>
> The Earl of Northumberland bearing a taper not lit.
>
> The Earl of Lincoln the salt.
>
> The canopy borne by three knights and a baron.
>
> My lady Maltravers did bear a rich crysom pinned over her left breast.
>
> The Countess of Richmond did bear the princess.
>
> My lord Marquess Dorset assisted her.
>
> My lady the king's mother, and my lady Elizabeth, were godmothers at the font.
>
> And when the said princess was christened, a squire held the basins to the gossips [the godmothers], and even by the font my Lady Maltravers was godmother to the confirmation.

But although Edward and Elizabeth were still producing healthy children, the marriage arrangements for their eldest girls were not going so well. Two years after Bridget's birth, Princess Elizabeth had still not been dispatched to France, and by 1482, now four years after she should have left, the young princess must have been wondering if her destiny as French queen was ever going to come to fruition. Unbeknownst to Edward, Louis had been in discussions with the King of Scotland, to forge an alliance by marrying the Dauphin Charles to James III's daughter Margaret. Nothing came of these discussions but then in 1482, the French king changed tact again and reached an agreement with Burgundy, known as the Treaty of Arras. In accordance with this treaty, the dauphin would marry Mary of Burgundy's daughter, the two-year-old Margaret. Edward did not discover this alliance until early

1483 and he was understandably furious. For Princess Elizabeth, she must have felt crushed and humiliated.

Cecily's arrangement with the King of Scots also fell through in 1482. James III was an unpopular ruler and the English alliance between his son and Cecily was not well liked. The Scottish king had also fallen out with his brothers and had them both arrested on charges of treason. In 1482, one of his brothers, Alexander Stewart, Duke of Albany managed to escape captivity and he turned up in England at the English court and persuaded Edward to switch allegiance to him. Edward agreed to support him and as part of the deal, he switched Cecily's betrothal from the young Scottish prince to the Duke of Albany. The duke was twenty-eight years old, fifteen years older than his intended bride.

Edward sent a small force north, headed by Albany and Richard, Duke of Gloucester. When they arrived in Scotland, Albany made peace with James, as did Gloucester, and with supposedly normal business resumed, Cecily was once again promised to the future James IV. A short while later an attempt was made on the Scottish king's life and once again, the Duke of Albany sought Edward's support and protection. Cecily found herself once again promised to the Duke of Albany. Finally, in October 1482, Edward called off her betrothal for the last time. But the king and queen soon had more to worry about when in May 1482 they lost their second eldest daughter, Mary, at the age of fifteen.

Having been absent from the Garter ceremony two years before, it seems that Mary may have been sick for a while. Whatever had ailed Mary, she sadly never recovered and she died at Greenwich Palace. The family had lost children before so were no strangers to grief, but this must have hit them particularly hard because Mary was no longer an infant, she had lived into her teenage years and they would have known and loved her dearly. There are two surviving accounts of Mary's death and burial, with the date of her passing given as either the Monday or Thursday before Whit Sunday. Both agree on her funeral dates as 27 and 28 May 'in the towne' of Greenwich.

Her funeral is described for us in great detail in *The Royal Funerals of the House of York at Windsor* by Anne F. Sutton and Livia Visser-Fuchs. On Monday 27 May, Mary's body was brought to the parish church of Greenwich. Four tapers were placed around the body and a dirge was sung by the Bishop of Norfolk, who also sang Mass the following morning. The chief mourner was not identified, but it was very possibly her aunt, Jane Woodville, who is listed first among the ladies. Also present in the funeral party was her cousin, Joan, Lady Stanley, daughter of her aunt Jacquetta Woodville and another cousin, Dame Katherine Grey. This Katherine may have been of a similar age to Mary and perhaps was a childhood companion.

Dinner was served to the women at the palace and the mourners then set off to accompany Mary's body from the church to a chariot, which was adorned in black cloth. The chariot and procession left the church, heading south across the Thames at Deptford, before turning west towards St George's bar, at the boundary of Southwark. The cortege then turned south, heading towards Kingston upon Thames.

As was custom, the procession was met a mile outside Kingston by local dignitaries. All parishes were required to send out a party to honour the cortege and accompany the funeral procession through their parish, until the next location took over. The bells of each town would also be rung as the cortege passed through. It appears on this occasion, the parish of Wandsworth failed in their duty as they are specifically mentioned as not having sent out a party to accompany the procession. One wonders what sort of a reprimand they would have received for this.

The night of 29 May was spent in All Saints Church in Kingston upon Thames. The following morning, they continued their journey to Windsor, accompanied by twenty to thirty poor men carrying torches. As they neared Windsor, they were met by the mayor and several other personages, who were accompanied by a group of young girls dressed in white linen and holding torches and white candles. On entering the town, they proceeded to the first gate of the castle, where they were greeted by the college of St George. At this point, all except the mourners departed and Mary's body was carried from the chariot to the hearse in the choir. In need of repast, the ladies took turns to stay with the body, while others ate in the Dean's House. After they had all eaten, a dirge was sung by the Bishop of Chichester, and Mary was then laid to rest next to her brother, George, who had died in 1479 aged just two years old.

The following day Masses were said for her soul and alms were distributed to the poor, as was customary – the prayers of the poor were considered hugely important for easing the passage of the soul through purgatory.

Her father had intended St George's Chapel to become the family mausoleum since the early 1470s and he loved Windsor Castle, lavishing plenty of money and attention on it. The chapel was the seat of his esteemed Order of the Garter and was dedicated to St George. Both of Mary's parents would join her here in their final resting places. Mary's coffin was discovered and opened during excavations in 1810 when a vault was under construction for the family of George III. Her body was well-preserved, enveloped in numerous folds of strong cerecloth, closely packed with cords. She was revealed to have long, pale blond hair, a family trait it appears, and blue eyes which were open but disintegrated immediately when exposed to the air. Observers could see that she had been beautiful, an attribute that has been showered upon all of the York princesses. Thanks to the chapel's redevelopment, begun by her father and completed by her nephew, Henry VIII, in the sixteenth century, Mary now rests regally in the company of a multitude of other royals who have been laid to rest there over the centuries.

As 1482 ended, the whole family came together at Eltham Palace to celebrate the Christmas period in celebrations that were so opulent, they were thought worthy to be recorded. Edward, in a display of his generosity, reportedly fed over 2000 people each day during the festivities. The Croyland Chronicle reported 'King Edward kept the following feast of the Nativity at his palace of Westminster, frequently appearing clad in a great variety of most costly garments, of quite a different cut to those which had been usually seen hitherto in our kingdom. The sleeves of the robes were very full and hanging, greatly resembling a monk's frock, and so lined within with most costly furs, and rolled over the shoulders, as to give that prince a new and distinguished air to beholders, he being a person of most elegant appearance, and remarkable beyond all others for the attractions of his person. You might have seen, in those days, the royal court presenting no other appearance than such as fully befits a most mighty kingdom, filled with riches and with people of almost all nations, and (a point in which it excelled all others) boasting of those most sweet and beautiful children, the issue of his marriage, which has been previously mentioned, with queen Elizabeth.'

As a family, they may have lived within the trappings of royalty but much as any other family, they experienced their fair share of troubles and heartaches. As they celebrated Christmas and New Year together at the palace that Elizabeth had first been introduced to eighteen years ago, it seems they had everything. Little did they know that the wheel of fortune was about to spin and that everything they knew and had would be taken and spun upon its head.

Chapter 5

The World Falls Apart

In March 1483, King Edward had been at Windsor. In his *Itinerary of Edward IV*, John Ashdown-Hill places Edward at Windsor from Tuesday 4 March, returning to Westminster around Tuesday 25 March, just before Easter Sunday. Upon his return to London, he was taken so violently ill that he retired to his sickbed. Remaining bedridden for the next few days, he retained a state of consciousness, but presumably realised how ill he was as he called to his bedside those whom he needed to instruct or speak with before he died. He also added several codicils to his will during that time. Then, on 9 April he died. He was not yet forty-one and his son, Edward, Prince of Wales, was just twelve.

What the illness was that eventually led to his death was a matter of speculation even then and remains so today. Dominic Mancini, an Italian poet who spent some time in England during early 1483 and recorded what he witnessed upon his return to his homeland later that year, believed that the king had caught a cold from a recent fishing trip. His death was also attributed by other sources at the time to an ague or fever or even a stroke.

Edward's death must have left Elizabeth distraught and in a state of shock. She had already lost one husband, so she knew too well the heartbreak that accompanied the death of a partner, but this was a man she had been married to for the last nineteen years. For their children as well, Edward's death, as with the death of any father, would have been a traumatic event. Most of the York children would have been in London, but for Edward's heir, and England's new king, he would have received the news at his home in Ludlow and would have had to prepare himself to make the long journey back to London to support his family and take over the leadership of the country. Although he had been raised as a future king, this must have been a huge amount to process for a young boy, not yet a teenager.

In the days before his death, one of those codicils that Edward added to his will was allegedly designed to heal a rift that had grown between

Elizabeth's eldest son Thomas Grey, Marquis of Dorset and Edward's best friend, William Hastings. Hastings had seemingly thought highly of Dorset at one point as he had approved the marriage between him and his stepdaughter, Cecily. But in later years it seems the pair had fallen out. The popular view of the enmity that by then existed between them, centred around the promiscuous behaviour of either one or both of these men, and in particular their love or infatuation towards Edward's mistress, Jane Shore.

Jane had remained Edward's mistress right up until his death and he was clearly fond of her. But it was rumoured that within the licentious court of Edward IV, the men had often shared mistresses and that perhaps Dorset, Hastings or even both men had also been enamoured with her. Whether they were also in a relationship with her, or whether they just held an affection for her, is unknown. According to Thomas More, 'when the king died, the Lord Chamberlain took her – which in the king's days, albeit he was sore enamored upon her, yet he forbare her, either for reverence or for a certain friendly faithfulness'. If this is true, Hastings may not have had a sexual relationship with Jane Shore during the king's lifetime. Mancini also wrote about their ongoing conflict, describing it as a jealousy 'as a result of the mistresses they had abducted or attempted to entice from each other'. What we do know though is that in the days before his death, Edward called the men to his bedside and pleaded with them to put aside their differences. According to More, in his description of Edward's last few days: 'in his last sickness when he perceived his natural strength so sore enfeebled that he despaired all recovery … he called some of them before him that were at variance, and in especial the Lord Marquis Dorset, the queen's son by her first husband, and Richard [William] the Lord Hastings, a nobleman then lord chamberlain, against whom the queen specially grudged for the great favor the king bare him and also for that she thought him secretly familiar with the king in wanton company'. More goes on to say that the king begged them [Dorset and Hastings] to reconcile 'for all the love that you have ever borne to me, for the love that I have ever borne to you' and that 'amongst much weeping they joined hands and forgave each other'.[1] Edward would have been well aware that at such a young age his son, now King Edward V, would need his close family and friends around him to support him, and would need the support of both of these men to ensure a smooth transition of power and to guide his young son in the early months and years of his kingship.

In the early days, a friendly countenance had existed between Hastings and Elizabeth Woodville, indeed he was the man that she turned to when she needed help to obtain her sons' inheritance. But by the time of Edward's death, their relationship had also deteriorated and the queen no longer had high regard for her husband's best friend. It was alleged she blamed him for his part in Edward's extramarital affairs, as over the years he was apparently often found with Edward in pursuit of 'wanton company'. The discord between them was apparent in a council meeting that took place shortly after Edward's death, when plans were being made for Elizabeth's son, and England's new king, to hasten to London. At the meeting, Elizabeth reportedly proposed that the young king should be escorted to London with a powerful army. According to Strickland, Hastings vetoed the idea asking her insolently against whom the young sovereign was to be protected?[2] Many on the council were rightly or wrongly unhappy for the new king to be solely under the power of the Woodville family. According to the writer of the Croyland Chronicle, Hastings won the argument and Elizabeth 'most beneficently tried to extinguish every spark of murmuring and disturbance', and wrote to her son, requesting him, on his road to London not to exceed an escort of two thousand men. The chronicler references Elizabeth's ongoing friction with Hastings, reporting that his reticence towards a Woodville dominance of the new king was 'For he was afraid lest, if the supreme power should fall into the hands of the queen's relations, they would exact a most signal vengeance for the injuries which had been formerly inflicted on them by that same lord; in consequence of which, there had long existed extreme ill-will between the said lord Hastings and the Quene'.[3]

As well as informing Edward in Ludlow, Hastings had also written to the king's younger brother, Richard, Duke of Gloucester who was at his home in the north. Gloucester replied from his home in Middleham by sending 'loving letters to Elyzabeth the Quene, comforting hir with many woords and promising his allegiance and to increase the credit of his carefulness and natural affection towards his brother's children'.[4] He also commanded all his men to swear obedience to Prince Edward. It seems at this point that all was going well and according to plan.

Edward IV's funeral took place ten days after his death, on Friday 19 April. On Wednesday 17 April, the king's body had been conveyed to Westminster Abbey from St Stephens Chapel where he had lain since his passing. The coffin was draped with a pall of cloth of gold with a cross of white cloth of gold. Within forty-eight hours of the king's death, letters were sent across the country proclaiming Edward V the new king and announcing a coronation date of 4 May. Although Prince Edward had begun making his way to London from Ludlow, he was not expected to arrive in time for the funeral. The funeral also went ahead without Gloucester's presence, as he was also not expected to arrive in time. Out of Edward's relatives who were in London, the first of those in the line of precedence was the king's eldest nephew, the Earl of Lincoln, the son of Edward's sister Elizabeth. Although the chief mourner was not specifically recorded, it was presumably Lincoln who took on the role, walking directly behind the coffin in its procession from St Stephens to the Abbey.[5] Also in the procession were Hastings and Dorset. As a king's funeral was primarily a male affair, neither Elizabeth nor her daughters would have attended.

After the service in the abbey, the coffin was loaded upon a chariot for Edward's last journey to Windsor. Six horses were ready to pull the chariot, each in trappings of black velvet. The procession then set off on Edward's last journey, spending the night of the 17th at Syon Abbey where the Bishop of Durham conducted a late service, as the cortege did not arrive until after dark.

The following day, Thursday 18 April, the procession set off again, arriving at Windsor later that day. Edward's final destination was St George's Chapel, the place he had been rebuilding since the early 1470s as his family mausoleum. By the time of his burial there, it was not yet finished but it was roofed with timber and the vault of the aisle near the king's tomb and chantry were complete. His tomb of black touchstone was only partially built – he surely did not think he would be in need of it as soon as he did.[6] Then with great ceremony the following day, Edward IV was laid to rest. His young son, and England's new king, was on his way to the capital and what should have happened next was a simple transition of the crown.

But what did happen next, and the events of the next few weeks and months are amongst the most debated and intriguing in history and led to Richard, Duke of Gloucester becoming one of our most notorious historical figures. Whilst Elizabeth and her daughters waited in London for the arrival of her eldest son, Gloucester had also set out on the long journey down from his home in the north of England to London. The new king was being escorted to the capital by his older brother Richard Grey, and his uncle, Anthony Woodville, Earl Rivers, both of whom had been with the young prince at Ludlow. The Duke of Buckingham, who had grown into a young man in Elizabeth Woodville's household and was married to Katherine Woodville, the queen's sister, met up with Gloucester along his route and on 29 April they spent the evening in Northampton, sharing a friendly meal with Rivers and Richard Grey who had ridden to meet them there. The new young king did not join them for the meal but remained behind at Stony Stratford. By all accounts all four men enjoyed each other's company that evening. However, the next day, 30 April, they began their journey together to meet up with the new king at Stony Stratford, eighteen miles south of Northampton. But before they reached the town, Gloucester and Buckingham pulled up their horses and informed Rivers and Richard Grey that they were under arrest. The two dukes then rode off to meet Edward to escort him to London themselves, ordering Rivers and Grey be taken to one of Gloucester's northern castles as prisoners.[7]

What instigated this unexpected turn of events is unclear. As the prince was still a minor, Edward IV had added a codicil to his will, naming his brother, Gloucester, as Lord Protector until his son came of age, so Gloucester already had the legal powers to oversee the new king's rule. His decision to arrest the queen's brother and son was clearly designed to separate Edward from his mother's family. When news of their arrest reached Elizabeth back in London, she realised something was terribly wrong. For the second time in her life, believing herself and her family to be in danger, she gathered her belongings and fled into sanctuary with her daughters and her younger son Prince Richard. Dorset, appreciating the danger to himself after the arrest of his brother and uncle, also took sanctuary alongside his mother.

This time Elizabeth's place of sanctuary was the abbot's house on the grounds of Westminster Abbey. The abbot at the time was John Esteney and seeing her distress, he allowed her to take refuge in the abbots' dining hall. In her haste to get her family to safety from what she clearly perceived to be a threat from her brother-in-law Gloucester, it is reported that her servants broke down walls to hurriedly get all her personal possessions to safety with her. Agnes Strickland in her *Lives of The Queens of England* paints a mournful image of the widowed queen 'sat alone on the rushes all desolate and dismayed. Her long fair hair, so renowned for its beauty, escaped from its confinement and streaming over her person, swept the ground'.[8]

During the nineteenth century when Strickland was writing, the hall was in use as a dining room for the Westminster college students, and she gives us a description of the place that was to be Elizabeth and her family's home for the next few months during perhaps the most turbulent period of her life:

> Still may be seen the circular hearth in the midst of the hall, and the remains of a louvre in the roof, at which such portions of smoke as chose to leave the room departed. But the merry month of May was entered when Elizabeth took refuge there, and round about the hearth were arranged branches and flowers, while the stone-floor was strewn with green rushes. At the end of the hall is oak panelling, latticed at top, with doors leading by winding stone-stairs to the most curious nest of little rooms that the eye of antiquary ever looked upon. These were, and still are, the private apartments of one of the dignitaries of the abbey, where all offices of buttery, kitchen, and laundry are performed under many a quaint gothic arch, in some places (even at present) rich with antique corbel and foliage. This range, so interesting as a specimen of the domestic usages of the middle ages, terminates in the abbot's own private sitting room, which still looks down on his little quiet flower-garden. Nor must the passage be forgotten leading from this room to the corridor, furnished with lattices, still remaining, where the abbot might, unseen, be witness of the conduct of his monks[9]

The right of sanctuary that Elizabeth called upon twice in her life was written into English common law and was based upon the fact that a church or holy building was a consecrated place, offering a haven to all. As any type of violence was forbidden within the walls, the sanctuary claimant could not be removed by force. It is thought that after the Battle of Tewkesbury, King Edward and his supporters had broken the rule of sanctuary by entering Tewkesbury Abbey and dragging the Lancastrians who had taken shelter within, back outside to their deaths.

87

By taking the privilege of sanctuary, the claimant, by law, was allowed to remain there for up to forty days after which they had to either turn up at court or elect to leave the country forever. However, some large sanctuaries, such as Westminster Abbey, could house a huge number of people and had the facilities for those claiming sanctuary to stay indefinitely. Inevitably, some criminals abused the right of sanctuary and continued their activities from within the sanctuary walls, and in the sixteenth century Henry VIII began to limit the right of sanctuary and it was eventually abolished in the seventeenth century.

Still grieving for her husband and also most likely in a state of shock and anxiety, Elizabeth must have been, by now, hugely worried for her young son. For the princesses too, now over ten years older than the last time they had entered sanctuary with their mother, this must have been an upsetting and potentially frightening time. Across London, as it became clear that trouble was in the air, people began to take sides. Uncertain of what was happening and who was going to emerge victorious, Croyland reports that some men collected their forces at Westminster in the name of the queen, others at London under the shadow of Lord Hastings, although many were ready to switch at a moment's notice depending on how events played out.

Upon hearing of the queen's plight, the archbishop reportedly took the great seal to her in the sanctuary confines, reportedly telling her to be of good cheer, for if they were to crown any other king than the rightful king Edward, then with the great seal in their possession they would 'on the morrow crown his brother, whom you have with you here'. Embarrassingly for him, he was later instructed to enter the sanctuary buildings and retrieve the seal from Elizabeth.

For the young princess Elizabeth, now seventeen years old, this was the second time she had seen her characteristically strong mother in distress and had fled with her into the abbey confines. But this time she would have felt the burden of responsibility to support her mother more keenly than the first time, when she was just a young child. During their first spell in sanctuary, the queen had been accompanied by her mother and the two women would have been a mutual support for each other. But Jacquetta was no longer here and as the eldest daughter, this time Elizabeth would need to be strong for her mother and her younger siblings.

When Prince Edward arrived in London, he was initially taken to the Bishop of Ely's palace, before being moved to apartments within the Tower to await his coronation. On the surface, things appeared to be proceeding as they should. But with one Yorkist heir in the Tower, Gloucester decided he needed to obtain custody of the other Prince before he could proceed any further, the ten-year-old Richard of York. Unlike in 1470 when Warwick issued a statement that sanctuary should not be broken upon pain of death, this time it was decided that sanctuary could be breached if necessary. After lengthy discussions amongst the gathered councillors, the Star Chamber decided that as children could commit no crime in which sanctuary may be needed, sanctuary, therefore, did not apply to them. Knowing that the queen may not release her other son willingly, Gloucester surrounded the building with troops. Once again, the archbishop was the messenger who conveyed this news to the women, warning them that the young prince could be taken by force if they could not be persuaded to hand him over into his care. The official story was that Prince Richard was required as a playmate and companion to his brother, Edward, whilst he awaited his coronation. Knowing they would attempt to take him by force if necessary, ultimately the queen had little choice but to hand him over as much as it must have pained her to hand over the little boy into the care of men she now considered their enemies.

Not long after Richard joined his brother, the boys were moved into apartments further within the tower. Mancini tells of how they were seen less frequently through bars and windows, and that all their servants were soon dismissed until eventually they were no longer seen at all. Mancini also alleges that Gloucester stopped wearing mourning and started wearing purple, the colour of royalty. One of the last attendants to see the boys was their physician, John Argentine, who according to Mancini reported that Prince Edward daily sought remission of his sins because he believed that death was facing him. Mancini was reporting this second or third hand so we cannot be sure that the statement that Edward was aware of his impending death is fact or embellishment. Whether the new king considered himself captive or just believed he was awaiting his coronation is unknown and may have changed as time went on. It is likely that in the first instance, he trusted his uncle and did believe he would be king. How quickly that changed, would depend on what their fate actually was and how soon he became aware of it and is part of the integral mystery of their disappearance.

Once Gloucester was in possession of both York boys, events then moved surprisingly quick. The council pronounced him Lord Protector and on 10 and 11 June he wrote to the City of York and to Lord Neville (his mother's family) asking them to bring troops 'to aid and assist us against the queen, her bloody adherents and affinity; which have intended and daily doth intend to murder and utterly destroy us and our cousin the Duke of Buckingham and the old royal blood of the realm'.[10]

Dropping all pretence, Gloucester was now on a collision course with the queen and her family that was not going to end well. On 13 June, he called a council meeting and according to Vergil, he invited some of the nobles to a meeting at the tower, and others to a meeting at Westminster, supposedly to discuss Edward's coronation. The meeting at the tower was attended by William Hastings and by all accounts, the meeting began congenially. However, a short while into proceedings, Gloucester allegedly requested that the Bishop of Ely who was also present, return to his garden at Holborn to pick them some of his excellent strawberries. The bishop agreed to send for some, and Gloucester excused himself and left the room. Returning shortly after, his earlier amiable mood had now turned sour. Demanding of the gathered men what punishment they thought should be meted out to any who threatened his life, it is reported that Hastings replied that anyone who threatened the life of the Protector should be treated as a traitor and punished accordingly. Gloucester then declared that the traitors he spoke of were 'the sorceress, my brother's wife and Jane Shore, his mistress, with others, their associates'. Citing witchcraft, he apparently revealed his arm to the group of men, which he claimed had been withered away by sorcery.

He then accused Hastings of colluding with the women and slamming his hand down upon the table, he gave a cry of treason, causing a retinue of armed men to storm into the room. Hastings was dragged from the room and out onto a patch of grass within the tower, where immediately, without trial, he was beheaded. To further emphasise the cold-heartedness of the situation, the Croyland Chronicle adds that the execution took place just 'before Gloucester's dinner was served'.[11] Three other men were also seized with Hastings that day: Lord Stanley and the Bishops of York and Ely. The two bishops were initially thrown into prison and Stanley was only released when his son arrived to rescue him. Later, Bishop Morton, Bishop of Ely was taken to Raglan as a prisoner of the Duke of Buckingham, and the Bishop of York was put into the care of Sir James Tyrell. The very same day that this took place,

Gloucester sent orders to Pontefract that the queen's other son, Richard Grey, and her brother Anthony, should be executed.

But was there any truth in Gloucester's allegations? Once again, the accusation of witchcraft and sorcery was present, an easy and inevitable accusation to throw at the women. But could Jane Shore and Elizabeth Woodville have been acting together to pass messages? Elizabeth undoubtedly would have known of Jane's existence and almost certainly would not have held her in high esteem. She may even have felt something akin to hatred towards the woman who was having an affair with her husband. Would Jane have felt the need to assist her lover's wife? Perhaps not. But Dorset was also within the sanctuary confines. If there was some sort of relationship between them and it was Dorset she was actually helping, this would be a more plausible reason for Jane's involvement. And for the sake of her son, Elizabeth may have accepted her help.

The reason for Hastings' murder has never been established. If he was also in a relationship with Jane, perhaps even sheltering her in his house after Edward's death as some believe, when he began to suspect that Gloucester's aim was not to see Edward's son safely onto the throne, perhaps he did use Jane as a go-between to pass messages to the queen. Hasting's loyalty was not to the queen, or even perhaps to Gloucester, but his love for his friend and master, Edward IV, meant that his loyalty was purely to see Edward's son and the rightful heir on the throne. Gloucester and Hastings had both given tireless loyalty to Edward IV during his reign and as a result, must have spent much time together. With a common cause, you would expect them to be allies and even friends, but Gloucester would therefore have known that Hasting's loyalty to Edward IV would never have allowed him to support his claim to the throne. Whatever your view of Richard of Gloucester, the removal of Hastings was a ruthless act that he may have had cause to regret.

From their place of sanctuary, the bad news kept on coming as the women learned of the deaths of the queen's brother and son, Anthony Woodville and Richard Grey, in Pontefract. Then came accusations that Edward IV's marriage to Elizabeth was invalid as before he married her in 1464, he was already pre-contracted to an Eleanor Butler. If this were true, then the York children would be bastards and unable to inherit the throne. This was followed by even more salacious rumours that Edward himself was a bastard son, a result of his mother's affair, a hugely controversial claim considering Cecily Neville, mother to Edward and Richard, was still alive. Edward's planned coronation day, 22 June, came and went and finally, on 6 July 1483 a coronation took place. But it was not that of the young prince. Instead, Richard, Duke of Gloucester, was crowned King Richard III at Westminster Abbey in a joint coronation with his wife, Anne Neville, just a stone's throw away from where the queen and her daughters were confined. By then, rumours must have reached Elizabeth and her daughters of the 'disappearance' of the two princes, who had been seen less and less until finally not at all and were presumed dead. For all of them, this was the worst possible conclusion.

For the women in sanctuary, this time there was no hope of Edward coming back to save them; they were on their own. Having lost her father and brother many years before on the orders of members of her husband's family, the queen had now lost another brother and her son. She must have been in the depths of despair, and also desperate for news of her two youngest sons. According to the Croyland Chronicle, plans were being made for the princesses to escape from sanctuary and flee overseas: 'There was also a report that it had been recommended by those men who had taken refuge in the sanctuaries, that some of the king's daughters should leave Westminster, and go in disguise to the parts beyond the sea; in order that, if any fatal mishap should befall the said male children of the late king in the Tower, the kingdom might still, in consequence of the safety of his daughters, someday fall again into the hands of the rightful heirs'.

If this were true, Elizabeth and her sisters may have been embroiled in escape plots and plans which would have perhaps been both exhilarating and terrifying in equal measure! Once news of these plans reached Gloucester's ears, he immediately turned the tower into a fortress, hiring a man named John Nesfield to ensure that no one could enter or leave the sanctuary precincts without his permission.

Having successfully dispatched Hastings and taken the throne, Richard III was now intent on finding Dorset and rounding up all the remaining Woodvilles. But Dorset, realising that sanctuary may not be enough to protect him, had already made his escape from the abbey confines. Completely unaware of his whereabouts, the king targeted Jane Shore; he at least was under the impression that she and Dorset were or had been lovers. Suspecting Jane had been harbouring him, but unable to locate Dorset with her, she received the full extent of his anger.

Jane was arrested and made to do public penance. Deemed a harlot, she was forced to walk barefoot through the streets dressed only in her kirtle and carrying a candle before being thrown into prison. Allegedly, although this punishment was designed to humiliate her, as she paraded through the streets, the people of London took pity on her and were won over by her beauty and humility.

During the next few months, Dorset remained undetected. Now he was king, Gloucester decided it was time to show himself off to the people and set off on progress to the north, an area where his popularity was already guaranteed, having acted as his brother's caretaker in the north for much of his reign. During his absence, rumours began to spread that Elizabeth's boys, the princes in the tower, had died 'a violent death'. But with a lack of evidence, no one could report how. Much has been debated about how much information Elizabeth Woodville knew about the whereabouts of her sons during their time in captivity. Conspiracies abound then and now as to who killed them, if indeed they were killed, and why. But there has never been any conclusive proof of their deaths, or indeed the perpetrators of their disappearance. If they were not killed, another possibility is that they were spirited away, either with the knowledge of their mother, or by someone following Gloucester's instructions, who needed them out of the way or they would forever be targets for insurrection.

Whatever Elizabeth knew or didn't know, what is certain is that at some point, a plot began to be formed through messages that were smuggled into the sanctuary precincts, primarily from Margaret Beaufort. Margaret Beaufort was mother to the last Lancastrian claimant to the throne, Henry Tudor, who had spent a large majority of his life in exile in France. The plan, formulated between the two women, would see an alliance between the Houses of York and Lancaster, uniting them by the marriage of Henry with Princess Elizabeth. The messages were conveyed by Margaret's physician, Lewis Caerleon. Elizabeth Woodville, who we can only assume at this stage either knew both her sons were dead or had no idea of what had become of them, had nothing to lose but to throw in her lot with Margaret and attempt to remove her brother-in-law from the throne.

Meanwhile, on 24 September, whilst the king was still on progress, the Duke of Buckingham, who had been hugely supportive of Richard since Edward's death, defected. What caused him to suddenly distance himself from the king is unknown, but he left Gloucester during his progress and returned to his home in Brecon. Whilst there, it is thought that he was persuaded by John Morton, Bishop of Ely, to turn coat. John Morton had been an important part of Edward IV's court and was an executor of his will. He had been held in custody at the duke's home in Brecon since the infamous council meeting that led to Hastings' death. John Morton was also a close friend of Margaret Beaufort and it is thought that it was through her that they began to communicate with Queen Elizabeth.

From his home in Brecon, Buckingham also wrote to the exiled Henry Tudor asking him to bring an army to assist in overthrowing the king. He then began to do the same himself, assembling men and arms at Brecon castle. By Saturday 18 October, he was ready to move, aiming to meet up with Dorset, who had made his way to Exeter and raised the standard of rebellion there. On 23 October, King Richard issued a proclamation offering a reward of 1000 marks in money or 100 marks a year in land for taking Thomas 'late marquis of Dorset' who 'not having the fear of God, nor the salvation of his own soul, before his eyes, had damnably debauched and defiled many maids, widows, and wives, and lived in actual adultery with the wife of Shore'.[12] As Buckingham and his men began their journey, nature was to prove a valiant enemy, and in a flood of torrential rain Buckingham reached the River Severn to discover the banks had burst and had to turn back. Many of his men, who had never been that keen to fight in the first place, turned around and returned to their homes.

Having to quickly revise his plans, the duke decided to make his way to Weobley in Herefordshire, to the home of Lord Ferrers. From Weobley, Buckingham continued to attempt to raise an army, but the men of Herefordshire would not rise, hearing reports that the king and his army were on their way. By this time, Buckingham was a wanted man with a reward on his head. His castle in Wales had been raided and seized by members of the Vaughan family, loyal to the king, who looted the castle and took his daughters into their custody. Realising he was in trouble he disguised his eldest son, who had travelled with him, as a girl and had him smuggled away by loyal retainers. Buckingham and his wife Katherine then went into hiding in Shropshire in the house of a servant, Ralph Bannister. But Bannister sold them out and on 1 November, the duke was captured and taken to the king at Salisbury, where the following day he was beheaded in the marketplace, without trial. Katherine and her younger son were taken to London into custody.

Elizabeth's brothers, Lionel and Richard Woodville, had also aligned themselves with the rebels alongside Thomas St Leger, Anne of York's second husband, who took up arms against his brother-in-law, the king. Unaware of Buckingham's capture and subsequent death, rebels at Bodmin declared Henry Tudor king. Henry Tudor had set sail from France as requested, but as he neared the English coast, he sensed luck was not on his side and his small fleet turned and sailed back to Brittany. Dorset, hearing the news of Buckingham's fate and Henry Tudor's retreat, realised he had little choice but to flee the country himself and he crossed the channel to join Henry and his men. The rebellion may have failed in the short term, but at dawn on Christmas Day 1483 in Rennes Cathedral, in the presence of 500 supporters, Henry Tudor made a public promise to marry Princess Elizabeth as soon as he was king. He then began to plan his invasion.

What did the young Princess Elizabeth feel about this? As with her earlier betrothal with the Dauphin of France, Elizabeth did not know her intended spouse so could have had no personal feelings for him. We cannot know how much Elizabeth was involved in these plans arranged by her mother and whether she had any say at all, but arguably the anger she would have felt at the treatment of her family and the disappearance of her younger brothers would have given her a determination to see this plan through and reclaim what rightfully belonged to her and her family. As the eldest York child, she most likely would have considered it her duty to do what she could to help her family in any way she could.

As 1483 turned into 1484 and the women remained in sanctuary, the queen must have been assessing the future of herself and her girls. Although she had agreed to the plans involving Henry Tudor, she had no power to bring them to fruition and there was always the possibility that they would fail. She and her girls could not remain in the Westminster sanctuary indefinitely so she had to give some thought to their next move. She may have felt she was exhausting the hospitality of the abbot and his monks at Westminster, and although the king had not breached sanctuary, he could make life difficult for her. She knew it was time to leave, a decision that she has been heavily criticised for over the centuries, for making a deal with the supposed murderer of her sons. But in reality, she had little choice, and of course, we do not know at that point what information she had and knew about her sons. Had they been spirited away she may have known they were safe. Alternatively, if she knew for sure they were dead, she could do nothing else for them. But she could and needed to look after her daughters and before she left the confines of Westminster, she took steps to ensure her girls were going to be safe. She did this by exacting a solemn oath from the king, guaranteeing the safety of her daughters. The terms of her surrender were tough, she had to acknowledge that she and the princesses now had no royal status, they were merely gentlewomen. She also had to allow herself to be placed under house arrest, with the money for her upkeep being paid directly to John Nesfield, who would house her at one of his properties, most likely at Hertford Castle or Heytesbury manor. In return, Richard agreed to commit to paper the following pledge:

> I, Richard, by the Grace of God, King of England and of France, and Lord of Ireland, in the presence of you my Lords spiritual and temporal, and you Mayor and Aldermen of my City of London, promise and swear verbo regio upon these holy Evangels of God by me personally touched, that if the daughters of dame Elizabeth Gray late calling her self Quene of England, that is to wit Elizabeth, Cecill, Anne, Kateryn, and Briggitte, will come unto me out of the Sanctuary of Westminster and be guided, ruled, and demeaned after me, than I shall see that they shall be in surety of their lives, and also not suffer any manner hurt by any manner person or persons to them or any of them or their bodies and persons, to be done by way of ravishment or defouling contrary their wills, nor them or any of them imprison within the Tower of London or other prison ; but that I shall put them in honest places of good name and fame, and them honestly and courteously shall see to be found and entreated, and to have all things requisite and necessary for their exhibition and findings as my kinswomen, and that I shall marry such of them as now be marriageable to gentlemen born, and every of them give in marriage lands and tenements to the yearly value of 200 marks for the term of their lives; and in likewise to the other daughters when they come to lawful age of marriage if they live. And such gentlemen as shall

96

happen to marry with them, shall straitly charge, from time
to time, lovingly to love and entreat them as their wives and
my kinswomen, as they will avoid and eschew my pleasure[13]

As they emerged back into a vastly different world from that which
they had left, Elizabeth needed to dig deep into her reserves to remain
strong for her family and dignified in defeat. She was immediately
placed into Nesfield's care and would remain under his watchful eye
for the foreseeable future. Her daughters most likely remained with
her, particularly the younger ones, but certainly Princess Elizabeth and
Cecily would have spent some time at court possibly in attendance on
the new queen Anne, their aunt. They were certainly at court for the
Christmas of 1484 where one of the most puzzling and intriguing stories
concerning the young Princess Elizabeth apparently took place. For
it was around this time that rumours began to circulate that the king
was enamoured with his niece. Even more bizarrely, there is a train of
thought that perhaps the attraction was mutual.

One source of this story was the writer of the Croyland Chronicle
who tells us that during the feast of Christmas, 'far too much attention
was given to dancing and gaiety, and vain changes of apparal presented
to Queen Anne and the lady Elizabeth, the eldest daughter of the late
king, being of similar colour and shape; a thing that caused the people
to murmur and the nobles and prelates greatly to wonder thereat'.
According to the writer of the Chronicle, even more sinister rumours
existed that the king was anticipating either divorce or an early death of
the queen, so he could contract a marriage with Elizabeth. Vergil tells
us that the king, hearing word of the conspiracies against him, vowed to
marry his niece to thwart Henry Tudor's plans.

Earlier in 1484, the king and queen had lost their only child and the
pair had been heartbroken. From the time of his death, Queen Anne's
health had suffered and during the Christmas celebrations, she was still
in mourning. During the festivities, the king received news from his
spies abroad that Henry Tudor and other York supporters would surely
invade England the following summer. The king was aware that Henry
intended to marry Elizabeth if his invasion was successful, and some
historians surmise that it was for this very reason that Richard may have
considered marrying Elizabeth himself. But as he was already married,
this was problematic.

Throughout early 1485, the health of the queen continued to deteriorate and on 16 March, during an eclipse of the sun, Queen Anne died. Because of the earlier rumours concerning Richard's plans towards his niece, the queen's death led some to suspect she had been poisoned. But were these just rumours or was there any truth in this? Vergil, certainly believed that an attraction did exist, but only one way: 'The King, thus lowysd from the bond of matrimony, began to cast an eye upon Elyzabeth his nece, and to desire hir in maryage; but because both the yowng lady hirself, and all others, did abhorre the wickednes so detestable, he determyned therefor to do everything by leisure'.[14]

To our modern sensitivities, a marriage between an uncle and his niece would be unspeakable. Even in the fifteenth century, when it was not considered out of the ordinary to marry someone you were distantly related to, the possibility of a marriage between the king and his niece was considered objectionable. It certainly would have required a special dispensation from the Pope, but this was not unusual – Richard had had to write for a dispensation when he married Anne Neville because of their close affinity. But it certainly was not beyond the realms of possibility if both parties had been in agreement.

But was it even considered or was it simply rumour? The majority of Richard's council felt the need to discuss it and were horrified at the idea, including his closest friends and advisors, Sir Richard Ratclyffe and William Catesby, although some suspected that they mostly feared Elizabeth taking the throne because she may then have chosen to avenge her brothers, as well as punish them for the murders of her uncle Anthony and elder brother Richard Grey. But the council made it clear to the king in no uncertain terms that the public would never accept such an act, even presenting to him more than twelve Doctors of Divinity, who asserted that the Pope could grant no dispensation in the case of such a degree of consanguinity.

Whether it was fact or rumour, the king was eventually forced to make a public statement in front of the mayor and citizens of London denying that he had ever considered taking Princess Elizabeth as his wife. But with so much effort put into the discussion of the subject, does that perhaps signal that it did indeed cross Richard's mind? One possible scenario is that Richard had considered it as a political move to thwart Henry Tudor's plans to marry Elizabeth. After the way Elizabeth and her siblings had been treated by the king, it would seem to be a safe assumption that Vergil was correct to write that Elizabeth must have found the idea totally abhorrent. But then there is the infamous George Buck letter which tells a completely different story.

George Buck was a historian in the late sixteenth and seventeenth centuries who wrote *The History of King Richard the Third*. The work was completed by 1619 but did not get published before his death. His draft manuscripts were then used by his nephew, also named George Buck, who published them in 1646 under his own name. The younger George Buck was not well considered in the literary world, taking credit for work that belonged to his uncle and facing accusations that he was careless in his transcription of his uncle's original text and that he had invented sources.

In 1979, the editor, Arthur Kincaid, finally published an authentic version of Buck's original history, having meticulously gone through all Buck's original notes and sources. Central to this story is a letter that George Buck (the elder) had allegedly seen in a household cabinet belonging to the Earl of Arundel. The letter has never been seen again, leading some to doubt it ever existed. But if authentic, this extraordinary letter, written in the hand of Princess Elizabeth to the Duke of Norfolk (an ancestor of the Earl of Arundel) is an astounding piece of evidence in the story of Princess Elizabeth and Richard III. In the letter, written in February 1485, Elizabeth seems to ask Norfolk to be a mediator in 'the cause of her marriage to the King', who was 'her only joy and maker in this world', that she was his 'in heart and thought' and that she 'feared the Queen would never die'. Apart from the doubt surrounding its authenticity, this letter has caused much controversy, mainly because the contents have been passed down to us incomplete. Buck, the Younger, wrote his own interpretation of the letter from his uncle's notes and Arthur Kincaid, using the original manuscript has since put together a very credible interpretation of how the full letter likely read.

For those who doubt either the existence of the letter, or the interpretation of the letter, arguments are robust against the idea that Elizabeth would have ever contemplated marriage with her uncle. The most contentious part of the letter of course is that she asks Norfolk to 'be a mediator in the cause of her marriage to the king'. This does appear incriminating, however on 22 March 1485, shortly after Queen Anne died, Richard had reportedly sent a gentleman named Edward Brampton to Portugal, supposedly to negotiate two marriages – one for himself with Joana of Portugal, daughter of King Alfonso, and the other for the Princess Elizabeth to a nephew of Alphonso, the sixteen-year-old Manuel, Duke of Beja.[15] Those arguing that the letter is not referring to a marriage between Richard and Elizabeth quite rightly point out that if a simple comma is inserted after the word marriage, the meaning of the sentence is changed. Elizabeth asks Norfolk to be a mediator 'in the cause of her marriage, to the King' – in other words, she is requesting Norfolk to mediate on her behalf to the king in the cause of her marriage – possibly to Alphonso, and not to the king himself.

The phrase 'she fears the queen would never die' also does not paint Elizabeth in a good light, if we assume she is hoping for the queen's death so she can then marry the king. But then, of course, this can also be interpreted differently – Elizabeth may have witnessed her aunt suffering a slow and even painful death and be simply wishing to end her aunt's misery? And was the king her only 'joy and maker in this world' and was she his 'in heart and thought'? Certainly, he was her only hope at that current moment in time of securing her a good marriage and perhaps she even had a fondness for him that she had harboured since childhood? Medieval language was also much more descriptive and 'flowery' than modern language, so perhaps this is not as much of a declaration of love as it first appears to be.

The truth, of course, will never be known, and this letter has been much debated over the centuries. The Richard III Society has some interesting articles by Alison Hanham and Arthur Kincaid debating the letter. But for all the evidence that can be given to disprove any feelings between uncle and niece, there is always the small and intriguing possibility that Elizabeth, a young girl of just eighteen, who had recently lost her father and her position in life, did come to see her uncle in a different light. He was only thirty-two years old at the time and if, as some suggest, he made her feel special and told her he wanted to marry her, she may even have fallen for him for a short while. Whatever the truth of the matter, we can only now ever surmise.

What we do know though is that Richard's public denial at the time simply fuelled rumours even more. And if there were plans for them to marry, it became virtually impossible once the rumours of poison began. What Elizabeth Woodville thought of the idea of her eldest daughter marrying the king is also not recorded. Her opinion on that also depends on her opinion of the king and what she knew or believed to be true about his involvement in her sons' disappearance. There are so many spokes in this wheel, that it is impossible to figure out what each party thought and felt at the time. But what is fact is that the king was forced to make a public denial, after which Princess Elizabeth was sent from court to reside at Sheriff Hutton, one of the king's homes in the north. He clearly needed to dispel the rumours, particularly that he had been involved somehow in his wife's death. Sheriff Hutton was also far enough away from London to keep Elizabeth out of the way of any who might want to use her to challenge his rule. Clarence's children, the young Earl of Warwick and his sister, Margaret, were also housed there. It is likely that Princess Elizabeth remained there throughout the summer and she was certainly there on 7 August 1485 when Henry Tudor eventually landed back on England's shores, in Milford Haven on the coast of Wales.

Tudor had set sail from France, determined this time to complete his mission. Unable to raise enough money for the ships and men he required, he borrowed heavily from the Captain of the Bastille, Philippe Luillier, pledging all his personal belongings in return. He was also required to leave behind two men as a pledge that he would keep his word and repay his debts. The two men left behind on French shores were Sir John Bourchier and the Marquis of Dorset. Henry Tudor also had to agree to pay for their upkeep at the Bastille during their time there and both men, as Knights of the Garter, had also provided their own letters of assurances.

The king, who was expecting him, had also gathered together an army. Marching towards each other, both men knew what was at stake. The two parties eventually met at Bosworth field and after a fierce battle, Richard, who fought valiantly was defeated. Ever a good soldier, even Richard's detractors agree that he fought bravely, but it wasn't enough. Vergil tells us that he had realised he was in danger and could have saved himself by fleeing the field, but he was determined that this battle be the final word, that 'that very day he wold make end ether of warre or lyfe'.[16] If he had defeated Henry Tudor, he could, in time, have brought peace to the realm; but the battle had to end with a death, and it was Richard who had fought so valiantly many times before alongside his brother Edward who met his fate that day.

The dead king's body was thrown naked upon a horse and taken to buried at the Grey Friars in Leicester, a Franciscan priory, where he would remain until 2012 where he was eventually discovered as part of the excavations that have since made him famous once more as 'the king in the car park'.

After his victory, Henry Tudor knelt and gave thanks to Almighty God, before his father-in-law, Sir Thomas Stanley, took Richard's crown and placed it upon his head. He and his men also proceeded to Leicester, where they stayed for two days, making plans for his journey to England's capital city, where he would be officially recognised as England's new king.

As news of the king's death spread and it reached the ears of both our Elizabeth's, mother and daughter, it may have been received with differing reactions. Elizabeth Woodville may have felt relief, and finally avenged for the deaths of her family members. For her daughter, if she had harboured feelings for her uncle, his death may have been bittersweet. But putting her personal emotions aside, she now had her duty to do; as planned so many months before by her mother and soon to be mother-in-law, Princess Elizabeth was now finally about to fulfil her destiny and become queen – not of France as she had once thought but of England.

Before he departed from Leicester, Henry dispatched Sir Robert Willoughby north to Sheriff Hutton to collect Princess Elizabeth and escort her to London. Clarence's children were also to make the same journey, but with differing destinations – Margaret Plantagenet would remain with her cousins, the York princesses, but as a male Yorkist heir, the young Edward Plantagenet, the little Earl of Warwick, was conveyed to the Tower of London, out of the way of any disaffected Yorkists who may have caused trouble.

Elizabeth Woodville was also released from her house arrest and made her way to London, where she would be reunited with her daughter. The men may have fought the battle, but the plan put together by women in their darkest of days, was finally about to come to fruition. The Tudor era had begun.

Chapter 6

And then there were two Queens

With Henry on his way to the capital, Elizabeth Woodville and her daughters were reunited at Coldharbour Place in London, the home of Henry's mother, Margaret Beaufort. The formidable Margaret Beaufort, whose own life story was one of stoicism and perseverance, had triumphed and her only son from whom she had been separated for much of his life, was now England's new king. She very much intended to play an active role in supporting her son going forward and it is highly likely that in these early days of Henry's rule at Coldharbour, that this group of strong women danced around each other, each finding her own place in this new world they were living in. It is often inferred that Margaret's intimidating personality overshadowed her daughter-in-law, Elizabeth, throughout the rest of her life, although there is no direct evidence to give this credence. But over the next few years, Elizabeth's sister, Princess Cecily and Margaret Beaufort would form a close friendship, which perhaps began during this time spent at Coldharbour, and perhaps illustrates that the picture we have today of a cold-hearted and domineering Margaret is not the whole truth.

As Henry approached his capital, the writer, Francis Bacon, who penned a history of Henry's reign in the seventeenth century, tells us that he was met with applause and acclamations in all the towns and villages that he travelled through. He finally made his entry into London on a Saturday and was received by the mayor and livery company representatives at Shoreditch, who accompanied him into the city. His first port of call was St Paul's, where the Te Deum was sung and he gave thanks no doubt for his victory, before heading to his lodgings at the Bishop of London's Palace.[1]

With his arrival in London, plans soon began in earnest for his formal coronation. Assembling his council, he renewed his vow to marry Princess Elizabeth of York, a formal recognition which may have gone some way to reassuring Elizabeth as according to Bacon, rumours were circulating that he had had thoughts of marrying Anne of Brittany, rumours which according to Bacon had reached Elizabeth's ears and 'did much afflict her'.[2] She had already experienced rejection from her last betrothal, and she would have been well aware of how important this marriage was. The union was so much more than a personal matter, and if it fell through now the reverberations would be felt by many.

Many historians have reflected on how much Henry Tudor needed Elizabeth. After all the troubles of the last thirty years, the people of England wanted some peace and stability. Edward IV had been a popular ruler and although the people were prepared to accept this new young king, it almost certainly was on the condition that he ruled alongside the popular Elizabeth. As for Elizabeth Woodville, she would surely have been pushing hard from behind the scenes to see her daughter take her rightful place upon the throne. Margaret Beaufort was nothing if not an honourable woman and she too, no doubt, would have persuaded Henry that his choice of bride had to be Elizabeth. By his side, she gave him the legitimacy he perhaps lacked on his own.

But before he could marry Princess Elizabeth, he had to make her legitimate again. When Richard had taken the throne in 1483, he had drawn up a document entitled *Titulus Regius* (Royal Title), establishing his right to the Crown of England. This had been legally enshrined as an act of parliament in January/February 1484 and had consequently rendered the York children bastards in the eyes of the law.

In the *Titulus Regius*, we once again see accusations of witchcraft bought against Elizabeth and her mother, a charge that had been included in the parliamentary act to emphasise the 'wickedness' of the king's marriage to the sorceress Elizabeth Grey.

> And here also we considre howe that the said pretensed marriage, bitwixt the above named King Edward and Elizabeth Grey, was made of grete presumption, without the knowying or assent of the lords of this lond, and alsoe by sorcerie and wichecrafte, committed by the said Elizabeth and her moder, Jaquett Duchess of Bedford, as the common opinion of the people and the publique voice and fame is through all this land; and hereafter, if and as the case shall require, shall bee proved suffyciently in tyme and place convenient. And here also we considre how that the said

pretenced marriage was made privatly and secretly, without edition of banns, in a private chamber, a profane place, and not openly in the face of church, aftre the lawe of Godds churche, but contrarie thereunto, and the laudable custome of the Churche of England[3]

The same document also raised the issue of the alleged pre-contract between Edward IV and Dame Eleanor Butler, the daughter of the Earl of Shrewsbury, the accusation which neither party were alive to defend, made bastards of Edward's children and formed the basis of Richard's argument for his claim to the throne:

And howe also, that at the tyme of contract of the same pretensed marriage, and bifore and longe tyme after, the said King Edward was and stoode marryed and trouth plyght to oone Dame Elianor Butteler, doughter of the old Earl of Shrewesbury, with whom the saide King Edward had made a precontracte of matrimonie, longe tyme bifore he made the said pretensed mariage with the said Elizabeth Grey in manner and fourme aforesaide. Which premises being true, as in veray trouth they been true, it appeareth and followeth evidently, that the said King Edward duryng his lyfe and the said Elizabeth lived togather sinfully and dampnably in adultery, against the lawe of God and his church; and therefore noe marvaile that the souverain lord and head of this londe, being of such ungodly disposicion, and provokyng the ire and indignation of oure Lorde God, such haynous mischiefs and inconvenients as is above remembered, were used and committed in the reame amongst the subjects. Also it appeareth evidently and followeth that all th issue and children of the said king beene bastards, and unable to inherite or to clayme anything by inheritance, by the lawe and custome of England[4]

One of Henry's first official acts had to be to repeal this act and this he did, ordering that all copies be destroyed, although a copy survived in the parliament roll, allowing us sight of the act today. In his bill annulling the act, Henry ordered that: 'for its false and seditious contrivance and untruth, [the bill] be void, annulled, repealed, cancelled and of no effect or force. And that it be ordained by the said authority that the said bill be cancelled and destroyed, and that the said act, record and enrolment be taken and removed from the roll and records of the said parliament of the said late king and burnt and entirely destroyed'.[5]

To re-instate Elizabeth as her father's rightful heir was a precarious move for Henry to make, but a necessary one. As far as has ever been known, when Henry took the throne the fate of Elizabeth's brothers was still a mystery and neither Henry himself nor Elizabeth had any idea of their fate or whereabouts. The assumption was that they must be dead, but Henry was still taking a chance because if one or both of them had survived, the very act of repealing *Titulus Regius* would mean that he had reinstated them also. And they had a far stronger right to the throne than Henry ever did. Henry never made an announcement on their whereabouts, nor did he ever directly accuse Richard of murdering them. As part of official proceedings, Henry also cleverly dated his reign to the day before Bosworth, thus making traitors out of anyone who fought for King Richard.

With the act repealed, Elizabeth Woodville could also now take up her rightful place as dowager queen and she was reportedly treated honourably by the new king. She was finally awarded possession of some of her dower palaces, which had been denied her by Richard III and was awarded a pension from Henry's annual revenues that would enable her to live a comfortable lifestyle, suitable for the mother of a queen.[6] For Elizabeth, now in her mid-forties, this would not eradicate the trauma and sadness of the past few years but would go some way to securing a comfortable future for herself.

As Henry's coronation neared, the first occurrence of what would become known to history as the sweating sickness appeared in London. It was first recorded in the city towards the end of September and victims were famously said to have been 'well at breakfast and dead by supper'. This first outbreak purportedly carried away two mayors in quick succession according to the Chronicle of London – Thomas Hill the existing mayor who died first, then Sir William Stoker, who died within five days of his appointment of the same disease, the position of mayor then being awarded to Sir John Warde until a new mayor could be elected. But the epidemic disappeared as quickly and mysteriously as it had arrived and had all but disappeared by the time of the king's coronation at the end of October, although it would resurface again periodically over the next few decades.

Henry's coronation, which took place on 30 October, was therefore unaffected by the disease and it was upon that auspicious day that Henry Tudor became the first Tudor king of England, and the father of the dynasty. Princess Elizabeth was not present at his coronation but this was not in itself unusual – her father was not present at the coronation of her mother so as not to steal the limelight. It may also have been that Henry was keen to demonstrate that he was now England's new ruler in his own right, not because of his intended union with a Princess of York.

Elizabeth may not have been at Henry's coronation, but by then they would certainly have met. How must she have felt when she came face to face with her intended husband, a union that had been planned for over two years ago? No record of their first meeting exists, but if later reports of their marriage are to be believed, the pair did find they had a liking for each other, maybe even an initial attraction. Finally, on 10 December of that year, plans began for their wedding and the celebratory tournament which would follow and Elizabeth was formerly named Duchess of York.[7] With Christmas approaching, Henry dissolved his first parliament and made good his vow to repay the Captain of the Bastille, thus redeeming Dorset and Sir John Bourchier who were now free to leave Paris and return to England. Dorset arrived back in England in time to celebrate the Christmas period, much to the relief no doubt of his mother and family.

As the new year dawned, the marriage of Henry Tudor and Elizabeth of York finally took place, on 18 January 1486. The bridegroom was twenty-nine, his bride a mere twenty years old. A proposition that had been put into action in Elizabeth Woodville's darkest days in sanctuary finally saw her daughter marry the king and become queen. Perhaps for her, this would go some way to fixing the wrongs that had occurred that should have seen her eldest son Edward on the throne. For Princess Elizabeth, she must have felt some pride that she could bring her family back into good fortune. She would have been well aware that it should have been her brother on the throne, but at least she was now standing alongside England's king and her family was once again back in the royal court where they belonged.

The marriage ceremony took place in Westminster Abbey and Princess Elizabeth wore a wedding dress of silk damask and crimson satin with a kirtle of white cloth of gold damask and a mantle furred with ermine to protect her from the winter weather. Her loose blonde hair was threaded with jewels. The king was attired in cloth of gold.[8] All across the land, the people celebrated to see the popular York princess take her rightful place beside England's new king. Bernard Andre, a contemporary of Henry Tudor who wrote his biography, witnessed the event and recorded that feasts, dances and tournaments were held throughout the land and great gladness filled all the kingdom. When people heard that Henry and Elizabeth were joined in happy marriage, they built fires for joy far and wide, finally hoping that this union would bring peace and prosperity to England.[9]

The union of Henry Tudor and Princess Elizabeth really was seen as a great joining of royal houses and an end to all the enmity between Lancaster and York that had blighted England's peace for so many years. Shakespeare in his 'Richard III' wrote 'we will unite the white rose and the red. Smile Heaven upon this fair conjunction, that long hath frowned upon their enmity'. The frontispiece to the historian Edward Hall's printed edition of *The Union of the Two Noble and Illustre Families of Lancaster and York* in 1550 also reflects this sentiment and features two rose trellises surrounding the title with Henry VII and Elizabeth of York kneeling hand in hand at the top of each.

But despite the agreement to make her queen, Princess Elizabeth's coronation would not take place for nearly another two years, partly perhaps because sometime shortly after her wedding, Elizabeth may have known or suspected that she was pregnant. This may illustrate that there was indeed an attraction between the couple right from the start. According to Bacon, Henry would prove to be a good husband to Elizabeth and an affection was borne, although Bacon reflects that as much as he may have grown to love his wife during their marriage, there was always a part of him that remained wary of her and her Yorkist roots: 'And it is true, that all his lifetime, while the lady Elizabeth lived with him, for she died before him, he shewed himself no very indulgent husband towards her, though she was beautiful, gentle, and fruitful. But his aversion towards the house of York was so predominant in him, as it found place not only in his wars and councils, but in his chamber and bed'.[10]

But even though he was wary of her, it seems that Elizabeth with her kind and loving nature did win him over. As well as being described as beautiful and gentle by Bacon, Andre, who was predominantly Henry's biographer, also credits her with an array of good qualities. 'She had a marvellous piety and fear of God, a remarkable respect towards her parents, an almost incredible love towards her brothers and sisters and a noble and singular affection toward the poor and ministers of Christ which had been instilled in her from childhood'.[11] It seems it was not just because of her descent from Edward that she was loved by the people, but that she possessed many qualities herself that made them love her.

After their January wedding, the king, like his predecessor Richard III, set off on progress to the north. But unlike Richard, he was not as sure of a good reception. Aware that the people in the north in particular had held a real affection for Richard III, the progress was an opportunity for Henry to present himself as their new king and to try and unite the kingdom. So, in the summer of 1486, he departed from London, leaving a pregnant Elizabeth behind at the Palace of Placentia in Greenwich. Elizabeth Woodville remained with her daughter in the residence that had once belonged to Humphrey, Duke of Gloucester. The palace would later become one of Henry's favourite residences and he would rename it Greenwich Palace. Henry returned to London some three months later, joining Elizabeth at Sheen.

Whilst the king was away, Elizabeth would have been preparing for the exciting arrival of her first child. Towards the end of August, with her husband back by her side, the couple moved to Winchester where it was planned Elizabeth would give birth. But her destination was not Winchester Castle, which had in recent years been left to ruin and was therefore uncomfortable and draughty, but the prior's house, a three-storey stone building and one of the richest monastic houses in the land, surrounded by beautiful gardens. To support her during her first pregnancy and birth, Elizabeth was accompanied by her mother, her sisters and Lady Margaret Beaufort, who had been busy drawing up a set of ordinances governing a set procedure for a royal birth.

Detailing practices that would have been followed by women for centuries, but carefully compiled by Margaret into a comprehensive set of instructions to accompany a royal birth, many of the things that Elizabeth did to prepare for the arrival of her child would have been familiar to her mother during her many confinements. Within the priory, Elizabeth would have retired to a set of rooms, with only her women for company. The staff who would serve her during this time would be all women, who would take on male roles such as that of a butler, bringing provisions to the door of the chamber for those inside. Herbal potions and religious objects would all be present, as they were when her mother gave birth to her some twenty years previously.

Just over eight months after their wedding nuptials, on 21 September 1486, Elizabeth gave birth to a baby boy. The new prince, whom they named Arthur, may have surprised his parents, arriving a few weeks prematurely at just eight months gestation or Elizabeth may have been in the early stage of pregnancy on her wedding day, perhaps another indication of how well Henry and Elizabeth liked each other from their first meeting.

As soon as the baby boy emerged into the world and the umbilical cord was cut, the young prince would have been washed in a mixture of wine, herbs, milk, sweet butter or barley water and then swaddled in linen, to help his limbs form correctly. Elizabeth would also be washed with a linen cloth and herbal ointments applied to her skin. No matter how tired she was, she would not be able to sleep until two hours later as tradition dictated.[12] Her chamber would remain in darkness for three days after the birth. But shortly after Arthur's birth, Elizabeth fell into a fever. All the gathered women could do was to make her comfortable and wait to see if she survived. Thankfully on this occasion, she pulled through.

The new young prince was christened on the following Sunday, a cold and wet day, the event reportedly being delayed because one of the godfathers, the Earl of Oxford, needed to return from Suffolk for the occasion, a journey which may have been slowed down due to the inclement weather conditions.[13] The location of the christening was the cathedral church of Winchester. Both the young prince's chosen Christian name and the choice of location for his birth and christening were designed to illustrate the power of the new Tudor regime. Winchester was the home of the legendary King Arthur and by association, it invoked a sense of awe and majesty that this new dynasty of Tudor kings would bring to the country. The church was decked out in all its finery, with the main body of the church awash with rich arras cloth that had been hung for the occasion.

The day began with a procession headed up by yeomen carrying unlit torches. Behind them came the men and women of the court. As would be expected, the christening was a real family affair but as was tradition, it was not attended by the king or queen. Elizabeth's sister, Princess Anne of York was accompanied to the cathedral by Sir Richard Guildford on her right and Sir John Turbeville on her left, both bearing their staves of office. Pinned to her right breast and draped over her arm on 'a kerchief of fine ermines' was a rich chrisom to be placed on the anointed infants head. A chrisom was a square of white linen placed by the minister on the forehead of the child after the anointing oil. It was often allowed to remain there until the infant was a month old. Another of the queen's sisters, Lady Cecily of York, was given the honour of carrying baby Arthur.[14] The baby prince, completely oblivious to the importance of the occasion, was wrapped in a mantle of crimson cloth of gold, furred with ermine, with a train, which was supported by Cecily Dorset. Dorset also accompanied the ladies along with the Earl of Lincoln. The Earl, nephew of Edward IV and therefore someone with a strong Yorkist claim to the throne should he have chosen to follow that up, was seemingly at this stage welcome at the Tudor court.

The christening party proceeded through the cloisters of the abbey through a little door into the southern part of the church. Leland tells us that the weather was too cold and foul for the ceremony to take part in the west end. Waiting at the font to welcome her grandson was Elizabeth Woodville. According to Leland, the gathered guests were informed at this point that the Earl of Oxford was a mere mile away, hastening to the church as fast as he could. Several hours later, upon the orders of the king and probably much to the relief of all present, The Bishop of Worcester performed the christening without the Earl's presence as he had still not arrived. The Earl of Derby and Lord Maltravers, the husband of Margaret Woodville, were godfathers at the font, and Elizabeth Woodville stood as godmother. Shortly after the prince was christened, and the Officers of Arms had put on their coats and lit the torches, the Earl of Oxford finally made his appearance, just in time to witness the young prince being confirmed by the Bishop of Exeter.

The prince was then returned in procession to his parents, once again carried by his aunt, the Lady Cecily. As they entered the royal nursery, they were met by the king's trumpeters and minstrels playing their instruments. Arthur was then returned to his parents for their blessing and as was the custom, his mother was the first one to call him by his name. For the honoured guests, the celebrations continued for the rest of the day with Leland reporting that in the churchyard there were 'Pipes of Wyne, that every Man myght drynke ynows'.

After the christening festivities, the king, queen and court moved to Greenwich where they celebrated the solemn feast of All Hallows, the precursor to our modern-day festival of Halloween. This was an important time in the medieval year when it was believed that during All Hallows Eve, the curtain between the physical and supernatural worlds was at its thinnest. The court then remained at Greenwich for the celebrations of Christmas and New Year.

Henry's reign had begun well; the new king and queen had won over the people and had a royal heir in the cradle. For Elizabeth Woodville too, she was able to look on with pride at how well her daughter had performed and was representing the House of York. But there was still a final act that had been agreed upon and that hadn't yet taken place – that of Elizabeth's formal coronation. As the months passed, Bacon tells us that murmurs of discord slowly began to spread at the delay in organising her coronation and this 'did alienate the hearts of the subjects from him [the king] daily more and more, especially when they saw, that after his marriage, and after a son born, the king did nevertheless not so much as proceed to the coronation of the queen, not vouchsafing her the honour of a matrimonial crown'.[15]

The delay in formerly crowning Elizabeth also began to fuel rumours that that at least one of the children of Edward IV may still be living. These rumour sparks turned to a small flame, when in early 1487, the first threat to the Tudors came in the shape of a pretender, eventually revealed to be a young man by the name of Lambert Simnel.

Simnel came to the palace's attention in the spring of 1487 when it reached the king's ears that a young man had surfaced proclaiming his right to the English throne. This young man and his supporters had made their way to Ireland to begin their campaign where they were most assured of gaining support.

Unlike Scotland, Ireland was under English control and subject to the rules of the kings of England, although in practice much of Ireland lived under its own rule. But with the wide expanse of Irish Sea between the two countries, it was a notoriously difficult region to oversee and factions had formed in Ireland over the centuries that often took the law into their own hands. In the early 1300s, three earldoms had been created in Ireland, that of Kildare, Desmond and Ormond. The powerful families of these earls were often at loggerheads and although English kings had sent representatives to the country over the years to maintain law and order, often the land of Ireland was a law unto itself.

In 1449, Richard, Duke of York had been made Viceroy of Ireland and had held the post for ten years. Rather than attempt to rule Ireland with a strong hand, he chose the path of reconciliation and had consequently received the support of many of the Irish clans, almost creating a Yorkist party across the sea. When he returned from Ireland, he left the reins of government to the Earl of Kildare.

After the death of the Duke of York, subsequent viceroys had included George, Duke of Clarence, two of Edward IV's young sons and Prince Edward, the son of Richard III and Anne Neville. Unlike the Duke of York, none of these ever visited Ireland and the country remained under the local rule of the House of Kildare. When Henry Tudor took the throne, he appointed Jasper Tudor as Lord Lieutenant of Ireland and the Earl of Kildare became his deputy. But Ireland still held a strong affiliation towards the House of York and it was the Earl of Kildare who received Lambert Simnel and his party when they landed on Irish shores. Bacon clearly thought that Henry had not yet done enough to remove the Yorkist affection from Irish shores, writing that Henry: 'had not removed 5 officers and counsellors, and put in their places, or at least intermingled, persons of whom he stood assured, as he should have done, since he knew the strong bent of that country towards the house of York; and that it was a ticklish and unsettled state, more easy to receive distempers and mutations than England was. But trusting to the reputation of his victories and successes in England, he thought he should have time enough to extend his cares afterwards to that second kingdom'.[16]

Managing to convince the Earl of Kildare and others of his claim, Simnel had himself crowned Edward, King of England, on 27 May 1487 in Christ Church, Dublin. But he was not claiming to be one of the missing York princes, his supporters claimed that the man they had crowned king was Edward, Earl of Warwick, Clarence's son, whom they argued had a stronger right to the throne than Henry Tudor. Even though he had been barred from the accession due to the attainder and execution of his father, the young earl probably did have a strong claim. But in 1487, Warwick was just eleven or twelve years old. Rumoured to be a weak lad, perhaps even with some form of mental disability, he was no candidate for a strong King of England. He was also nowhere near Dublin, but still locked up in the Tower of London.

Henry soon learned of the involvement of the Earl of Lincoln in this plot as well as Margaret of Burgundy, Lincoln's aunt, who had agreed to send troops in support. Lincoln and Francis Lovell, an old associate of Richard III, had also arrived in Dublin just before the coronation accompanied by two thousand of Margaret's troops. They then set sail for England with their 'new king', arriving ten days later in Lancashire where they made land and began their march south. As a precaution against the arrival of further of Margaret's men, Henry made the decision to fortify the whole east coast. He set off to Bury St Edmunds, leaving Elizabeth and Prince Arthur in the safety of Kenilworth Castle, to personally see this was done. Once again, Elizabeth was faced with the prospect of close family members taking up arms, not against her personally, but against her husband who even at this stage, she may well have had real affection for.

In a bizarre set of circumstances, her half-brother, Dorset, was also headed towards the east coast around this time. His reasons for travelling there are unclear but when questioned he claimed he was visiting the Shrine of St Edmund. Residing in the Abbey Church of Bury St Edmunds, the shrine was a place of pilgrimage during the Middle Ages and it was here that Dorset alleged he was heading.

Henry, who had been suspicious of Dorset's loyalty since the Marquis had tried to flee his camp when they were in exile together in France, had him apprehended by the Earl of Oxford and taken to the tower. According to Francis Bacon, 'He sent the Earl of Oxford to meet [Dorset] to accompany him back to London and forthwith to carry him to the Tower; with a fair message nevertheless that he should bear that disgrace with patience, for that the king meant not his hurt, but only to preserve him from doing hurt either to the king's service or to himself'.[17] What Dorset's real motives were for this trip to the east coast we will never know. Was it just an inconvenient coincidence that the rebels disturbed his pilgrimage or was he actually involved in the plot to remove Henry? It would seem unlikely that he was unaware that the young Earl of Warwick, who had once been his ward, was actually being held in London, or that he would make a move against his half-sister, for to remove Henry from the throne would also remove Elizabeth and Arthur.

To prevent the rebellion from spreading, Henry had the real Earl of Warwick bought from the tower and paraded through the streets of London. Lincoln, Lovell and their army finally met up with the king's men on 16 June on the battlefield at Stoke. Henry emerged victorious. The Earl of Lincoln was killed in the fighting and Lord Lovell fled when it became clear they were defeated. Where he fled to is a mystery, although legend tells that he eventually ended up in his house at Minster Lovell, where he was hidden by a servant in a secret underground chamber. It is said that in the early eighteenth century, during building work at the hall, an underground room was discovered. In this room, a skeleton was found, sitting upright at a table, surrounded by books, paper and pens. According to the tale, the loyal servant died before Lovell, and with no one else knowing he was there, Lovell was unable to escape the room from the inside and starved to death.

Whatever Dorset's motives were for his east coast trip, other close family members did turn out to fight for the king including one of Elizabeth Woodville's brothers, Edward Woodville. The impostor 'Warwick' was captured and Simnel's real identity was revealed. Once it was established who he actually was, it came to light that he was a baker's son, and a pupil of a priest called Richard Simon, who lived in Oxford. It is said that Henry took pity on the young lad and he was taken to London and given a job in the royal kitchens.

But Dorset was not the only one who fell under Henry's suspicion at this time, it seemed he may also have suspected Elizabeth Woodville herself as having some involvement in the plot. She had so far been treated graciously by her son-in-law, so would she really have schemed against him and her daughter, after working so hard to put them on the throne in the first place?

In 1486, just after Henry had become king, Elizabeth Woodville had taken out a forty-year lease on Cheneygates, the Abbot's House at Westminster where she had taken sanctuary a few years before, which suggests she planned to make it her home for some considerable time. There were also suggestions early on that Henry had wanted her to marry James III as part of a three-year peace deal.[18] What her thoughts were with regards to the Scottish plan went unrecorded but it is doubtful that she would have relished the idea of a new life in Scotland away from her family. But around the time that the Simnel plot was playing out, Elizabeth Woodville suddenly retired to the Abbey of Bermondsey, a Benedictine monastery in Southwark. Her reasons for moving there are unclear, but it is possible she was banished there by the king, who either suspected or knew that she supported the Simnel plot to overthrow him.

It seems unlikely that she would have plotted against Henry to remove him from the throne, as this would directly affect her daughter and grandson too. It seems even more unlikely that she would do all this for a son of Clarence. But the fact is, she suddenly retired from public life at the same time that the Simnel affair was taking place and it would be remiss to not even consider that the two things could be connected. Bacon certainly believed that she did play a part in the Simnel plot because she was unhappy with the king and his delay in crowning her daughter and because she believed that the king's treatment of Princess Elizabeth was causing her daughter to feel discontented and depressed. He writes: 'one of the King's first acts was to cloister the queen dowager in the nunnery of Bermondsey, and to take away all her lands and estate'.[19] But rather than directly accuse her of involvement in the plot, Bacon alleges that the king told Elizabeth that he was displeased with the fact that she had delivered her daughters out of sanctuary into the hands of Richard, thereby putting their agreement in danger. When Richard became aware of Henry's plan to marry Princess Elizabeth, he could have jeopardised it by marrying her daughters off, or even by marrying Princess Elizabeth himself and by coming out of sanctuary and releasing her girls into his care, Henry believed that Elizabeth had gone against her word. Hall, in his chronicle, seems to agree with this theory:

> It was determyned that the lady Elizabeth wyfe … shoulde loase and forfeyte all her Landes and possessyons, because she had voluntarely sutunytted her selfe and her daughters wholy to the handes of kyng Richarde, contrarye to the promes made to the lordes and nobles of thys realme in the begynnyng of the conspiracy ymagyned agaynst kyng Richard[20]

If this had indeed been the case, Henry would surely have punished Elizabeth right at the very beginning of his reign, rather than after all these months and thus far he had treated her fairly and honourably. Whether it was her own choice or not to relocate to the abbey, what was certain is that she was deprived of all her possessions and allocated a small pension of 400 marks to be paid in instalments, considerably less even than she received from Richard III.

Arriving at the abbey, she registered as a border and was lodged in an old range of apartments within the precincts. Although her life within the abbey walls would be one of relative seclusion, the abbey itself was a beautiful building, just across the Thames from the tower, with gardens, orchards and even a vineyard in which she could spend her time. But it still took her away from the court, which was no doubt Henry's intention.

Elizabeth Woodville's involvement along with her son Dorset's is all conjecture and it seems unlikely that they would risk Elizabeth's position for a young lad not even of their blood. What was actually going on can once again only be speculated on, but if indeed her mother and half-brother had been involved in a plot to remove Henry from the throne, it may have been hugely upsetting to Elizabeth when she learned of their disloyalty towards her.

The Marquis of Dorset remained in the Tower for several months after the Simnel affair and with Elizabeth Woodville also safely ensconced in Bermondsey Abbey, sadly neither of them was there to witness Princess Elizabeth's moment of triumph when it came; her coronation, which finally made her England's official queen, took place in November of that year.

As with her mother's coronation some twenty years before, Elizabeth's coronation festivities also took place over several days. On Friday 23 November 1487, Elizabeth, wearing her royal robes, left Greenwich by water, escorted by the Lord Mayor, sheriffs and aldermen of London, in a grand procession of barges down the great River Thames. Her sisters were all by her side to celebrate with her and support her. The populace watching from the banks were treated to a magnificent and colourful display, as the barge belonging to the students of Lincoln's Inn contained a large red dragon, representing the king's Welsh roots and the House of Tudor, which breathed flames of fire into the river along the journey. Reportedly this barge kept pace with Elizabeth's and as well as the awe-inspiring dragon, the boat was filled with the most handsome rowers and played a sweet melody all along the route.[21]

Elizabeth and Henry spent that night at Greenwich, where Henry created eleven new Knights of the Bath. Then the next day, 24 November, her sisters helped her dress for her state entry into London and there was a grand procession through the streets of the city. Elizabeth's train was carried by Cecily of York, who rode in a carriage behind the queen alongside Katherine Woodville, the new Duchess of Bedford. Katherine, the youngest Woodville daughter, who was carried on the shoulders of a squire at her sister's coronation, was now a grown-up woman of twenty-nine years old. After the death of her first husband, the Duke of

Buckingham, she had remained in London and had recently become the wife of Jasper Tudor, the king's uncle, acquiring the title of Duchess of Bedford. That she also played a prominent role in the coronation of her niece illustrates how close the Woodville family remained to each other over the years. The wedding party spent the night at Westminster, and the following morning, 25 November, Elizabeth proceeded to Westminster Abbey accompanied by her ladies.

Elizabeth's sister Cecily once again played a supportive role, bearing her train whilst the Dukes of Suffolk and Bedford carried the sword and sceptre. The procession itself was hugely eventful with reports that amidst such huge crowds that had formed to try and cut a piece of the woollen floor covering that the queen walked on (as was the custom), a number of people were killed: 'ther was so Hoge a people inordyantly presing to cut the Ray Cloth … in the presence certeyne Persons were slayne, and the Order of the ladies folowing the Quene was broken and distrobled'.[22] As they entered the abbey, the king was already present, watching the proceedings from a latticed box, positioned between the altar and the pulpit so as to remain out of sight and not to detract attention from his wife on this special occasion.

The coronation ceremony was followed by a state banquet in Westminster Hall, where once again the king and his mother were unseen spectators. Then the festivities came to an end the next evening when a grand dinner and ball was held with much dancing from Elizabeth and her ladies. The royal party all returned to Greenwich the next day.

Agnes Strickland paints a vivid picture of Elizabeth on her coronation day, recounting her renowned beauty that she had inherited from her mother: 'She was not quite twenty-two; her figure was tall and handsome; her complexion fair and brilliant. She had, besides, soft blue eyes and delicate features, set off by a profusion of yellow hair. Her costume on this occasion was a gown of white silk, brocaded with gold, and a mantle of the same material, bordered with ermine and fastened across the breast with gold cords and tassels. A close-fitting cap, formed of rich gems in a golden network, encircled her head, and her hair fell loosely around her shoulders'.[23] It must have been a real blow to Elizabeth Woodville to not have been denied the chance to see her daughter, resplendent in her finery, take her place upon the throne of England. Although Dorset was released not long after Elizabeth's coronation, Elizabeth Woodville would receive no second chance and would spend the rest of her days in quiet seclusion. An apt punishment for an act of treachery against her daughter and son-in-law or a terrible injustice, we will never now know.

Life at court after the coronation continued much as it had done before. Her sister Cecily had been appointed as her chief lady-in-waiting and her other sisters also remained at court with her until they were found husbands, with the exception of the youngest York daughter, Bridget, who at the age of ten, was sent into the care of the nuns at Dartford Priory. Here she would be schooled and cared for and when old enough, she would take the veil and enter the monastic life herself.

After the death of their father and Uncle Richard, Elizabeth and her sisters were co-heiresses to the lands of Mortimer, Earls of March and Clare, which belonged to the House of York. On his ascension to the throne, however, Henry VII incorporated them into Crown lands, leaving all the York girls without dowries. As the eldest, Elizabeth took responsibility for her sisters, supporting them from her own privy purse. She gave them each £50 per year, supplemented by arbitrary gifts of cash whenever she could. It was down to the king to find them marriages, and when they married, Elizabeth paid their husbands £120 for their maintenance.

Shortly after Elizabeth's coronation, her sister Cecily was found a husband and they married in December 1487. Her spouse was a favoured uncle of Henry's, John, Viscount Welles. The groom was thirty-seven at the time of their wedding, Cecily still only eighteen. Both the king and queen were guests at the wedding but there is no record of whether Elizabeth Woodville had been forgiven enough to attend the wedding of her third eldest daughter. John Welles was Margaret Beaufort's half-brother and had been an ardent York supporter, in high favour with Edward IV. He was one of the men who watched over his body after his death. Disillusioned with the actions of Richard III, he had sailed to France to join Henry Tudor in Brittany during Richard's reign and remained in exile with Henry, returning with him in 1485. Knighted by Henry Tudor near Milford Haven on 7 August 1485, he fought alongside him at Bosworth and was created Viscount Welles. Cecily reportedly had a close relationship with Lady Margaret whom she would often visit at her home at Collyweston, and it may well have been Margaret's suggestion for Cecily to marry her half-brother.

The Christmas of 1487 was 'kept full honourably' at Greenwich, with Cecily and her new husband included as part of the festivities. The king presided over feasts in the great hall and it seems that for the festive season, Elizabeth Woodville was granted leave to return to court. The queen dined with her mother and Lady Margaret and Cecily 'the noble princess, sister to the queen, our sovereign lady'. The royal party stayed at Greenwich for a week after Christmas and on New Years' Day gifts were distributed to the members of the household of the king and queen as was custom.

The new year bought with it preparations for Prince Arthur's future, when in March 1488 Henry and Elizabeth began negotiations for the betrothal of the two-year-old prince to Katherine of Aragon, one of the daughters of Ferdinand of Aragon and Isabella of Castile. With Arthur destined to be the next Tudor king, he needed a suitable bride and none could be better than a daughter of the two great Spanish leaders. At this point, the royal nursery only contained one child, with Elizabeth seemingly not quite as fertile as her mother had been. Their second child, a daughter, would not arrive for another eighteen months.

Then in April 1488, the first garter ceremony of Henry's reign took place. Queen Elizabeth and the king's mother, Lady Margaret Beaufort, rode together in procession through the grounds of Windsor Castle in a chariot covered in cloth of gold. Elizabeth's sister, Anne of York, who had taken Cecily's place as Elizabeth's main lady-in-waiting after her marriage, rode behind them, wearing a crimson velvet robe of the Order and accompanied by nineteen other ladies similarly dressed, on white palfreys with cloth of gold saddles. The royal party attended Mass at the castle followed by a great feast in St George's Hall.[24] During the ceremony, Margaret Beaufort was invested as a Lady of the Garter as the queen and Elizabeth Woodville had been during Edward's reign. The tradition was then brought to an end for the next 400 years. Future kings and queens did not have quite the same passion for this chivalric order as King Edward IV had had, and it was not until 1901 that ladies would once again be invited to join, when King Edward VII invested his wife Queen Alexandra.

By 1489, Elizabeth Woodville may have proved her loyalty enough to allow herself back into the royal fold, as she was present at court in November of that year to support her daughter in her second period of confinement ahead of the birth of her second child. This time, Elizabeth would give birth in the Palace of Westminster, and she took to her chamber on All Hallows Eve, accompanied by the king's mother and others of her ladies. In a formal procession, she was led to her rooms by the Earl of Oxford and the Earl of Derby, where the Bishop of Exeter said Mass. After the Agnus Dei was sung, the queen lingered a while to take refreshments in her antechamber, standing under her cloth of estate. After taking their fill, the queen's chamberlain desired all her people to 'pray that God would send her a good hour', before she entered her inner chamber, where she would remain until after the birth. The room was hung floor to ceiling with blue cloth of arras, enriched with gold fleur-de-lis. No tapestries with human figures were allowed within the chamber.[25]

Within her room at Westminster was a rich bed and pallet. The pallet had a fine canopy of velvet of many colours, striped with gold and garnished with red roses. The familiar altar furnished with relics was also there. Her only surviving accounts from the year 1502/3 show payment to a monk for the use of 'The Girdle of Our Lady', which belonged to Westminster Abbey and it may have been an object that she used for all her births. On this occasion, the wholly female gathering was broken by the arrival of the Prince of Luxembourg, a near relative through her mother's side of the family, who most earnestly desired to see the queen and for whom the rules were temporarily relaxed so she could grant him an audience. He was shown into the queen's bedchamber by Elizabeth Woodville.

A few weeks after her confinement began, Elizabeth was delivered of a baby girl, named Margaret in honour of the king's mother, who presented the infant with a silver box full of gold pieces. The Princess Margaret was born on 29 November, and the same day, her elder brother, Arthur, was brought to Westminster and made a Knight of the Bath. The newborn Margaret was baptised the following day, 30 November, at St Stephens Chapel, Westminster where Elizabeth's sister, Anne, once again took on the role of bearing the chrisom during the ceremony. Then due to an outbreak of measles at the palace, the queen was churched a month later in private on 27 December, before removing to Greenwich on 29 December.

Then eighteen months after the birth of Margaret, the king and queen's third and perhaps most famous (some would say infamous) of their offspring was born at Greenwich Palace, on St Peters Eve, 28 June 1491. Christened Henry after his father, he of course would go on to become the great Henry VIII, although at the time of his birth he was the second male child and therefore considered only as the spare, rather than the heir.

All was going well for the new king and queen, they had three children in the royal nursery at Eltham and after six years on the throne, Henry could have been forgiven for thinking that any threats to his kingship were long past. But two months after the birth of Prince Henry, in August 1491, a young man of considerable refinement sailed into the Irish town of Cork, who would become perhaps the greatest threat that the court of Henry and Elizabeth would face. For according to this sixteen-year-old youth, he was none other than Richard of York, the younger of the missing York princes. When news of his appearance reached the English court, it caused a certain amount of worry to the king and his advisors. But to Queen Elizabeth and her sisters, as well as for their mother, Elizabeth Woodville, it must have stirred up a real flurry of emotions, particularly if they truly were ignorant of what fate had befallen the princes. Could the young Prince Richard have escaped his uncle's clutches or been smuggled away to safety? To ascertain what sort of a threat the boy presented, Henry sent his advisors to uncover his real identity. His presence in Ireland was at the moment just a distant threat but could it become something more? Could it even topple this fledgling Tudor dynasty?

The Christmas of 1491 must have passed with the usual celebrations, but perhaps with a shadow of worry and fear lurking in the background for the king and his family. As 1492 dawned afresh, Elizabeth Woodville had been in retirement for five years. Perhaps she had used the past few years as a period of reflection, and the news from Ireland may have sparked a sudden flame of hope within her that she might see one of her boys again.

By now, Elizabeth was indeed the great survivor of her family. Her parents had of course died many years before and by 1492, all but one of her siblings had also died. Out of her remaining brothers who had survived Richard III's reign, Edward Woodville had died in July 1488 and her last living brother, Richard, who had become the third Earl Rivers after Anthony, had died on 6 March 1491. Upon his death, he had bequeathed the family home of Grafton to Elizabeth's son, Thomas Grey, Marquis of Dorset. As for her female siblings, they had all slowly passed away over the years, with only the youngest, Katherine Woodville, surviving until 1497.[26] On 10 April 1492, Elizabeth herself made her will; perhaps she too was ill. From the quiet solitude of the priory, she may have been well aware that time was no longer her friend.

Above left: Elizabeth Woodville, the eldest of the Woodville girls born to Richard Woodville and his wife Jacquetta between c.1437 and c.1440. She would later marry King Edward IV and become the first English-born queen since the twelfth century. (Unidentified painter, via Wikimedia Commons. Public domain image)

Above right: Edward Earl of March, who became King Edward IV of England in 1461 aged just eighteen, after a resounding victory for the House of York at the Battle of Towton that removed King Henry VI from the throne. Edward married Elizabeth Woodville in 1464; she was the first and only woman he married, although after his death allegations would be made that in his younger years he had been pre-contracted to another woman, Eleanor Talbot. (Unknown author, Anglo-Flemish School, via Wikimedia Commons. Public domain image)

An artist's impression of Grafton Manor, Elizabeth Woodville's childhood home in the Northamptonshire village of Grafton Regis. (A watercolour by Thomas Trotter, painted in 1789)

Above left: The Queen's Oak at Pottersbury, near Grafton, just off the A5, so-named because it is believed to be the tree that Elizabeth stood next to with her two sons, waiting for King Edward to pass so she could enlist his help with her sons inheritance. The oak tree burned down in 1994 and died in 1997, with only a blackened stump now remaining. (Photograph courtesy of Jean Glanville)

Above right: The site of the Woodville hermitage was extensively excavated in 1964-5 and floor tiles were discovered in the chapel, decorated with the arms of Woodville and the House of York. This discovery lends even more evidence to the suggestion that the chapel was indeed the scene of Edward and Elizabeth's marriage on May Day, 1464. The photo is of a village resident called Joe Sargeant when the tiles at the Hermitage were discovered. (Photograph courtesy of John Kliene)

An artists impression of the Hermitage at Grafton, the suggested location of Elizabeth Woodville's secret wedding to Kind Edward. Once a small, religious community it is believed to have gone into decline in the fourteenth century and eventually become the Woodville family's private chapel. (Painting courtesy of John Kliene)

Above and right: The beautiful church of St Mary the Virgin in Grafton and the sign on display in the church porch. Although the church is situated close to the manor house, perhaps it was too visible a location for Elizabeth Woodville's clandestine May Day wedding. (Images author's own)

Grafton manor as it is today. The old manor that Elizabeth would have known was deliberately burnt down by the Parliamentarians on Christmas Day 1643 during the English Civil War. The new manor house was rebuilt over the ruins of the old manor by 1661 and was modernised in 1833. It is now a head injury rehabilitation hospital. (The back of Grafton Manor from the air; courtesy of Jonathan Feakin, 2015)

A 1923 painting by Ernest Board depicting Edward IV and Elizabeth Woodville at Reading Abbey on Michaelmas Day, (29th September) 1464. (Image courtesy of Reading Museum)

Above left: Elizabeth of York. Born in 1466, she was the eldest child born to Edward IV and Elizabeth Woodville. As a female, she was never destined to be queen of England, but after the disappearance of her brothers, infamously now known as the Princes in the Tower, Elizabeth married Henry Tudor and they took their place in history as the first Tudor King and Queen of England. (Late 16th century oil painting via Wikimedia Commons. Public domain image)

Above right: Stained glass windows at Cardiff Castle depicting Elizabeth of York and Henry Tudor, who married in 1486. Their union brought together the Houses of Lancaster and York, bringing an end to the period we now refer to as 'The Wars of the Roses'. (Image by Kramerw from Pixabay)

The Royal Castle of Blois in the Loire Valley, France. As one of the main residences of the French Queen Claude, Elizabeth Grey would have most likely visited and stayed here during her time in France. (Adobe Stock Images; photo by Leonid Andronov)

Katherine of Aragon pleads her case against divorce from Henry VIII at the Blackfriars Court. Elizabeth Grey was one of many women who supported the queen. (Painting by Henry Nelson O'Neil, via Wikimedia Commons. Public domain image)

The Woodville manor at Grafton was the location of the last meeting of Henry VIII and Cardinal Wolsey after Wolsey met with Cardinal Campeggio, the Pope's envoy. Wolsey had to break the news to Henry that the Pope would not grant Henry a divorce from Katherine of Aragon. Anne Boleyn, also depicted in the painting, was with Henry at Grafton. Shortly after this Henry left the Church of Rome and the Church of England was formed. This painting is on the wall of Grafton Village Hall. (Painting by Brian Tite)

Gerald Fitzgerald, 9th Earl of Kildare, became Elizabeth Grey's husband sometime around 1520. The pair were reportedly much in love and when Gerald was dying in the tower, Elizabeth remained with him until the end. (Unknown author, via Wikimedia Commons. Public Domain Image)

The meeting known as the 'Field of the Cloth of Gold', between Henry VIII and Francis I, took place in a field near Guisnes between 7th and 24 June 1520. It was so named because of the luxuriousness of the materials used for the tents and pavilions. Elizabeth Grey attended in the English party and it may have been here that she first met her husband, Gerald Fitzgerald, Earl of Kildare. (Royal Collections Trust, public domain image)

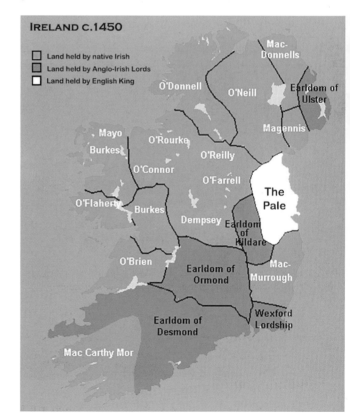

Map showing the division of Ireland, c.1450. The area under the control of the English king was known as The Pale. (via Wikimedia Commons. Public Domain Image)

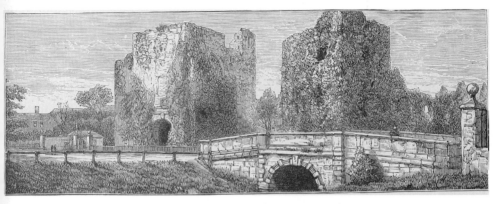

A drawing of the remains of Maynooth Castle in 1885, the place that Elizabeth Grey called home during her time in Ireland. It had been the stronghold of the Earls of Kildare since the early thirteenth century. (Internet Archive Book Images on Flickr. (Image from p. 671 of "Picturesque Ireland" by John Savage, 1885). Public domain)

We have no contemporary image of Elizabeth Grey, but her daughter, Elizabeth Fitzgerald, Countess of Lincoln, was considered to be an attractive woman. Perhaps in her image, we can see traces of what Elizabeth Grey may have looked like? (Attributed to Steven van der Meulen, via Wikimedia Commons. Public domain image)

Chapter 7

An End and a Beginning

Elizabeth Woodville, England's dowager queen, took her last breaths on Friday 8 June 1492 at Bermondsey. She was around fifty-three years old.

Her funeral which took place quickly after her death, was a simple and modest affair for a woman who had been queen but was as she had requested. She desired in her will to be buried at Windsor with her husband, Edward, 'without pompes entring or costlie expensis donne thereabought'. Her journey down river from Bermondsey to Windsor took place two days after her death, on Sunday 10 June. The late queen's body was accompanied by just five attendants including a gentleman named Edward Haute who was her second cousin and a young woman named Grace, an illegitimate daughter of Edward IV's. Her presence perhaps gives us an indication of Elizabeth's character. Grace's mother is unknown, and it is assumed that the young girl may have been brought up by the king and queen. That she was one of the women to accompany Elizabeth's body that Sunday, is perhaps an indication of the close relationship that they had, and that although Elizabeth may not understandably have been completely accepting of Edward's womanising ways, she was prepared to give this young girl a home and her care.

Upon arrival at Windsor, Elizabeth's body was taken through the Little Park to St George's Chapel. The funeral cortege arrived at 11 pm and was met by a single priest, accompanied by a clerk; she was buried immediately in the tomb alongside Edward. Presumably, the news of her death took time to filter to those close to her, but by the Tuesday mourners were arriving and during the next few days memorial services were held. Her female relatives were the first to arrive on Tuesday, in the form of her daughters Bridget, Katherine and Anne of York, alongside Cecily Dorset and one of her daughters, presumably Eleanor the eldest, Elizabeth's granddaughter.

On the Tewsday theder came by water iii of kynges Edwardes doughters and heirs, that is to say the lady Anne,

123

> the lady Katherine, the lady Bregett, accompeygned by the
> lady marquys of Dorsset, the Duc of Buckyngham daughter
> of nyce of the fore said Queen, also the daughter of the
> marquys of Dorsett...[1]

Her other two surviving daughters, Cecily of York, and of course Queen Elizabeth, were unable to attend, Cecily for unknown reasons and the queen because she was in confinement for her latest pregnancy. This must have been a cause of real sadness to Queen Elizabeth, unable to honour her mother at this final hour. When she gave birth on 2 July, she named her newborn daughter Elizabeth, in what can only have been a tribute to her recently departed mother who she had been so close to throughout her life.

Elizabeth Woodville's firstborn, Thomas Grey, Marquis of Dorset arrived on the Wednesday after the women and further services were held. Then on Thursday 14 June one of the canons sang the Mass of Our Lady and Dorset offered a gold piece, and a second gold piece, at the following Mass of the Trinity. The ladies did not attend these Masses.

Elizabeth Woodville has always been a contentious figure and she and her family still have a bad reputation to contend with even today. She climbed high with her marriage and that elevation put her in a position where some would attempt to knock her down. But whatever her faults, there is no doubt that her children loved her dearly and they all would have felt her loss keenly. From fairly normal beginnings, she undeniably went on to lead an eventful life, perhaps no better summed up than in this description by Francis Bacon:

> This lady was amongst the examples of great variety of
> fortune. She had first from a distressed suitor, and desolate
> widow, been taken to the marriage bed of a bachelor king,
> the goodliest personage of his time, and even in his reign
> she had endured a strange eclipse by the King's flight, and
> temporary depriving from the crown. She was also very
> happy, in that she had by him fair issue; and continued his
> nuptial love, helping herself by some obsequious bearing
> and dissembling of his pleasures, to the very end. She was
> much affectionate to her own kindred, even unto faction;
> which did stir great envy in the lords of the King's side, who

counted her blood a disparagement to be mingled with the King's. With which lords of the King's blood joined also the King's favourite, the lord Hastings; who, notwithstanding the King's great affection to him, was thought at times, through her malice and spleen, not to be out of danger of falling. After her husband's death she was matter of tragedy, having lived to see her brother beheaded, and her two sons deposed from the crown, bastarded in their blood, and cruelly murdered. All this while nevertheless she enjoyed her liberty, state, and fortunes: but afterwards again, upon the rise of the wheel, when she had a King to her son-in-law, and was made grandmother to a grandchild of the best sex; yet was she, upon dark and unknown reasons, and no less strange pretences, precipitated and banished the world into a nunnery; where it was almost thought dangerous to visit her, or see her; and where not long after she ended her life: but was by the king's commandment buried with the King her husband at Windsor . She was foundress of Queen's college in Cambridge.[2]

It has never been established whether Elizabeth Woodville eventually discovered the fate of her sons, with many differing theories being proffered, including that she had, in fact, managed to smuggle one or both of them away to safety. But she may simply have died not having any idea of what had become of them. But in her living children and her ever-expanding number of grandchildren, her legacy would continue.

One of those grandchildren, Elizabeth Grey, is the third protagonist in our story. The eleventh child of Thomas Grey and his wife Cecily, she too was more than likely named after Elizabeth Woodville. Together, Cecily and Thomas had at least thirteen children, making Elizabeth Grey one of their youngest. Like many other families at that time, the birth dates and birth order of the children of Cecily and Thomas Dorset are very intertwined and almost impossible to establish accurately from this distance of time. Melita Thomas in her book *The House of Grey* has made perfectly good arguments for the birth date and order of the Dorset children and following that order places Elizabeth Grey's birth sometime in 1492. Given her name, it would seem likely that like her cousin, the newborn Princess Elizabeth, she too was born slightly after

Elizabeth Woodville's death and named in her honour. As cousins, the two Elizabeth's, same age and name, could have grown up together as playmates, but sadly Princess Elizabeth did not make it beyond the age of three; much to the sadness of the king and queen, Princess Elizabeth died on 14 September 1495. Her tiny coffin was brought from Eltham Palace and buried in St Edward the Confessor's shrine in Westminster Abbey and her small tomb with a black marble slab can still be seen in the abbey today. The inscription on the verge had disappeared by the 1700s but it read:

> Elizabeth, second child [daughter] of Henry the Seventh King of England, France and Ireland and of the most serene lady Queen Elizabeth his consort, who was born on the second day of the month of July in the year of Our Lord 1492 and died on the 14th day of the month of September in the year of Our Lord 1495, upon whose soul may God have mercy. Amen.

The tomb also had a gilt effigy which has now gone and a plate at the feet of her likeness read:

> Hereafter Death has a royal offspring in this tomb viz. the young and noble Elizabeth daughter of that illustrious prince, Henry the Seventh, who swayed the sceptre of two kingdoms, Attrapos, the most severe messenger of Death, snatched her away but may she have eternal life in Heaven[3]

1492 was proving to be a year of mixed emotions for the royal family. The death of her mother was obviously a real blow to the queen, although her sadness would have been mixed with joy a few weeks later at the safe arrival of her baby daughter. But that same year the royal court would have received the worrying news that the young man identifying as Richard of York had left Ireland and had arrived at the court of Margaret of Burgundy. And even more worryingly for King Henry, Margaret had claimed to 'recognise' him and had declared him to be her true nephew, throwing her full support behind him and his claim to the English throne. The news that she had appointed a guard of thirty halberdiers to guard his person and bestowed upon him the title of 'The White Rose of

England' spread across the continent and back across the sea to England, where Queen Elizabeth must have received it with a mixture of wonder and fear.[4]

Henry had not been idle since the young man's appearance in Ireland, he had sent his spymasters far and wide to out to find out the young man's 'true' identity. The officials had seemingly managed to identify him as a young man called Perkin Warbeck, the son of a peasant couple from Tournai (in modern-day Belgium), but even with his supposed identity revealed, he was still very much a magnet for any disaffected Yorkists and therefore a worry to this still very fledgling Tudor court.

Across the channel in Ireland where the pretender had first declared himself, the Earl of Kildare was suddenly dismissed from his post as Deputy of Ireland. After the Simnel affair, the Earl had been careful not to appear to support this new claimant to the English throne, but Henry was clearly still aware of the support for the House of York in Ireland and wanted to ensure Ireland's loyalty. In his place, Henry installed someone whose loyalty he could depend upon, the Archbishop of Dublin, Walter Fitzsymons.[5]

Things were now becoming very real for Henry and Elizabeth. Just the existence of this new 'white rose of England' was a real challenge to Henry's kingship and it must have crossed his mind that if this was actually Richard of York, his claim to the throne was much stronger than his own. For Elizabeth, she must also have been in emotional turmoil – was this really her brother and if it were, she knew his very existence and survival would have both delighted her and been a very real threat to her family and position.

As well as being made welcome at the Burgundian court, the young man had also been accepted at the French court and given a warm welcome and by 1493, Maximillian, the Holy Roman Emperor, had also recognised the young man as King Richard IV. That same year it was reported that the pretender was in correspondence with the Earl of Kildare.[6] Although he had been removed from his post, his influence in Ireland was enormous; his removal from government the previous year had caused revolts and burning at the English borders. But who actually was this man, and why had so many royal courts already thrown their support behind him?

The answer to that, of course, has never been proved and there are strong and convincing arguments both to him being Perkin Warbeck and also that perhaps he was one of the lost princes who had indeed survived the reign of his uncle, Richard III. An existing letter from the young man himself that he wrote in 1493 to Queen Isabella of Spain attempts to explain his back story in his own words.

In the letter, he writes that his elder brother, Edward, Prince of Wales, had been assassinated. He, Richard, had been delivered to a gentleman who had meant to kill him but took pity on him, sparing his life on the condition that he did not divulge his name, birth or lineage for many years. He had been taken abroad under the care of two gentlemen and had spent nearly eight years of his life moving around Europe in hiding, spending some time in Portugal before arriving in Ireland and being 'recognised' and welcomed by the Earls of Ormond and Kildare.

He goes on to tell of his welcome from his aunt in Burgundy, as well as his support from Maximilian, and the Dukes of Austria and Saxony and the Kings of Denmark and Scotland. He also writes that 'many of the chief personages in England, whose indignation had been roused by the iniquitous conduct of the usurper, Henry Richmond, had done the same in secret'. The letter ends with the wish that Queen Isabella will also offer her support and entreat her husband to do the same and is signed: 'From the town of Andermund, 8th Sept. 1493. Richard Plantagenet, second son of the late King Edward and Duke of York'.[7]

Although the fates of both of the princes are still one of history's best-kept mysteries, it is generally accepted that the eldest son of York, Prince Edward, did in fact die, possibly through natural causes or perhaps through murder, either accidental (i.e. manslaughter), or through intention. But the fate of Prince Richard is less clear, and despite Henry's claims that the man now being accepted around the courts of Europe was only the son of a boatman, there is an element of doubt that this story is true. The story of the younger prince being smuggled away does have an air of truth to it, which is why the story of the lost princes have remained of interest even today.

To counter the claim of this so-called impostor, on 9 November 1494, Henry Tudor had his second son, Prince Henry, invested as Duke of York. The formal ceremony was followed by three days of festivities and tournaments held at Westminster. The king and queen watched the jousting from a purpose-built house covered in a blue cloth of arras with gold fleur-de-lis, hung inside with a cloth of gold. The winners of the tournament were awarded their prizes by Princess Margaret. On the surface, the king and queen were presenting a court that was business as usual, but behind the scenes, the stress and dismay at the amount of support this young man was receiving must have been hugely troubling.

Worried that the pretender would make his way back to Ireland and receive support there from the strong Yorkist faction, Henry decided to make an example of the Earl of Kildare. In 1494, he was arrested for high treason, although other than reports of his alleged support for the pretender, there was no evidence to prove he was aiding him in any way. The earl was brought to England and a gentleman named Sir Edward Poynings was made Governor of Ireland and dispatched by the king; he arrived in Dublin in September 1494.

Arriving in London, the earl was held in the Tower of London for the next two years. It was reported that just a short while later, on 22 November 1494, his countess, Alison, died of grief at his imprisonment.[8]

The detention of the earl may have been a shrewd move by Henry as the following year, 1495, the pretender did arrive back in Cork but found little support there. Setting sail again, he landed for the first time on English shores at Deal, on the Kent coast. The men of Kent remained loyal to their king, however, and chased him away. He subsequently made his way to Scotland where he was received with honours by James IV who allowed him to live at the Scottish court and treated him as he would a son of Edward IV.

Now that he was just a border away from England, he was even more of a threat. In a hugely embarrassing turn of events for Henry, even some of his own family appeared to be keeping their options open. Henry's uncle by marriage, Sir William Stanley, the brother of Margaret Beaufort's husband, Thomas, was at this time found guilty of supporting the pretender. He had allegedly been heard to say he would not fight against him if he was the son of Edward IV. This viewpoint was likely held by many others, something the pretender had adhered to in his letter to Isabella of Castille. Henry had no choice but to arrest William and execute him for treason.

As the end of 1495 approached and their daughter Elizabeth, born just three years before, lost her life, things were looking bleak. As they buried their youngest child, the queen may have been aware that she was in the early stages of another pregnancy. On 18 March 1496, another daughter, Princess Mary, was born at Sheen. Her birth must have been a beacon of light in a period of turmoil. Holding her newborn daughter in her arms, Elizabeth would have known that this new addition to their family was another reason that she and Henry must fight for their family and throne.

By 1496, the troublesome Earl of Kildare had now been a prisoner in England for just over two years. A hugely powerful figure, the charismatic earl was a man who garnered much respect and made an extremely dangerous enemy. When charged with sacrilegiously burning down the church of Cashel he allegedly confessed the fact that he had indeed burned it down, pleading as his defence that 'he thought the archbishop was in it'. This frankness coupled with a dry sense of humour, seemingly earned him favour with Henry. It was reported that the king had advised the earl to provide himself with good counsel, fearing that his case would require it. To which the earl replied: 'I will then choose the best counsel in England'. When asked by Henry who that should be, he replied: 'Marry, the king himself', at which the king purportedly burst out laughing.[9]

During his trial, the counsel against Kildare evidently concluded that 'not all Ireland could govern this man' which led the king to reply: 'then is he the fittest man to govern all Ireland'. Upon which, by letters patent dated 6 August 1496, he was restored all his titles and estates by the king, made Lord Lieutenant of Ireland again and allowed to return to his homeland. Henry had obviously decided that this fierce and likeable earl was better to have as an ally than a foe. The only condition was that he left his eldest son Gerald behind on English soil as his promise of his allegiance.

After his release, the earl remarried, taking as his second wife Elizabeth, the eldest daughter of Oliver St. John of Lydiard Tregoze.[10] His son, young Gerald Kildare, was just nine years old when his father returned to Ireland and he would remain at the English court until 1503. He would later, well into the future, become the husband of Elizabeth Grey, who was five years his junior, and it is tempting to wonder if their paths ever met during his years spent at the English court. We do not know how often Elizabeth Grey may have attended court during her younger years, perhaps as a playmate to her cousins or whether she and the future 9th Earl of Kildare ever met as children, but as he spent eight years within the sphere of her family it is certainly a possibility.

Meanwhile, the pretender was still in residence at the Scottish court. During his months there, the Scottish King James had arranged a suitable marriage for him with a respectable lady named Katherine Gordon, the daughter of the Earl of Huntly. Supported by the Scottish king, he had made a further failed attempt to enter England from the north in 1496 but had not succeeded and had retreated back into Scotland.

The royal family spent the summer of 1497 in the palace of Woodstock in Oxfordshire. The manor of Woodstock, set deep in the beautiful Oxfordshire countryside, had begun its life as a hunting lodge during the time of Henry I. Subsequent kings had enlarged and improved the lodge into a magnificent palace, and it was obviously a favourite residence for Elizabeth and Henry as they spent over £4,000 on works there, including major alterations to the grand hall, and the addition of a large gatehouse, which contained some fourteen rooms. Henry is also said to have built the front and the outer court, the tennis courts and a conduit which was built to carry water to the king's houses in a vaulted tunnel.[11] In later years the palace would sadly be left to ruins. It was heavily damaged during the Civil War and was eventually pulled down to make way for the building of Blenheim Palace. All that remains of the Palace of Woodstock today is a single stone commemorating its existence in the grounds of Blenheim.

Whilst at Woodstock, we get a glimpse of the royal family at leisure, from the reports of a visiting Italian ambassador, Andrea Trevisan. The king received word that the Italian had arrived in London and he invited him to Oxford for an audience. Trevisan arrived there on 3 September and Henry received him in a small hall, hung with a beautiful tapestry. The king, wearing a violet gown, lined with cloth of gold and a multi-jewelled collar, was standing and leaning against a tall gilt chair, covered with cloth of gold. On his head, he wore a cap inset with a large diamond and pearl. His son, the twelve-year-old Prince Arthur, was by his side and various other lords were also present. Later the ambassador dined in the hall with four unnamed lords, before being granted a private audience with the king.[12]

Before he left Woodstock, Trevisan was also taken to visit the queen who received him at the end of the hall, dressed in cloth of gold. She was with her son and Margaret Beaufort, the king's mother. The ambassador recorded that the queen, who by then was in her early thirties, was a 'handsome woman'.

As their summer at Woodstock was coming to an end, news was received that the pretender had set sail from Scotland once again and was this time making his way to the south coast. Here he found that the men of Cornwall were not as loyal to their king as their Kentish counterparts had been. Disillusioned with Henry VII and his exorbitant taxes, they allowed him to land and march northwards through their lands. Collecting supporters along the way, he had himself declared Richard IV at Bodmin.

The threat that had been reverberating in the background for so many years had now become a reality and Henry had no choice but to set off to meet his challenger with an army. As the king drew near, many Cornishmen began to desert – a charge of treason was too serious a penalty for them to risk for a man whom they were not even certain was who he said he was. With his supporters fading away and knowing his cause was lost, the pretender went into hiding in Beaulieu Abbey, where he was finally captured. In the end, it was all over without any major battle. The captured Warbeck, as Henry declared him to be, was taken to Taunton and it was here on 3 October 1497 that the Tudor king and the alleged York king came face to face for the very first time. Official records tell us he admitted his deception at this meeting when he was put face to face with men he should know. One of these men who came to face him was Dorset, his half-brother. Official records tell us he failed to recognise Dorset and that none of the men present were able to recognise him. Or perhaps would not admit that they recognised him, for some might argue that no good could have come of it if they had admitted to knowing him and he them? He was then escorted back to London as a prisoner.

Before returning to London himself, Elizabeth Grey and her family had the honour of entertaining the king at their home at Shute Manor in Devon. The Grey family manor was set high up on a hill, just four miles from the beautiful Devon coastline and surrounded by lush green countryside. Henry had arrived at Taunton on 4 October and having met and dispatched Warbeck back to London, he then proceeded to Exeter, where he oversaw the hanging of some of the Cornish rebels. He also graciously received the wife of the pretender, Lady Katherine Gordon whilst at Exeter, before she too was sent to London. Leaving Exeter on 3 November, the king passed the night at Ottery St Mary and then proceeded to Newenham Abbey at Axminster, where he remained for nearly a week until 10 November. For the young Elizabeth Grey and her siblings, a visit from the king would have been an exciting event.

Even though Elizabeth would have been just five years old, she may have remembered the king arriving with his large entourage, the clatter of horses' hooves as they approached and the general melee of entertaining a king, which would have bought a hive of activity to their quiet little manor house, near the banks of the River Coly. The king spent some time with her father in the surrounding deer parks and at leisure, shooting the butts with the marquis, in the beautiful grounds surrounding their home.

But soon enough it was time to return to London to deal with the man who had been a shadow to his kingship for the last few years. Back at court, Lady Katherine Gordon was given a position as one of Queen Elizabeth's ladies. She was not allowed to spend time in private with her husband and sadly we have no records of her reaction to his arrest. She presumably believed his identity at first, although as was the fate of many women, she may have had little choice in marrying him. But their relationship remains a mystery. Did she love him, whomever he was? Did she come to disbelieve him and feel she had been duped or did she remain loyal to him to the end, perhaps believing he was who he claimed to be or simply because she loved him whoever he was? At court, Henry kept the young man close; he was not exactly a prisoner but also not at liberty. Interestingly, we also have no report of Elizabeth or her siblings meeting with him. For the king to disprove his claim, a statement by his queen declaring the pretender was not her brother would have surely held much weight but none ever came. In fact, the silence is almost deafening. What was their first meeting like, did she ever doubt who he was, and just supposing he was her brother Richard, and she knew it, would she have kept his real identity to herself knowing that revealing it would endanger her position and that of her children? And would he have asked that of her in the end? Of course, she was not the only York sibling still alive, her sisters may also have met him and any one of them could have either proved or disproved his claim. But there was only silence.

As Christmas 1497 came around, Elizabeth and Henry may have been glad to see the end of the year. According to Hall, 1497 had also been a plague year 'wherof men dyed in many places very sore, but specially and moost of all in the citie of Lodon, where dyed in that yere thirty thousand.[13] But misfortune had not yet finished with them and as the Christmas celebrations were in full swing, disaster struck when the palace of Sheen caught fire. According to accounts, the fire reportedly broke out in the queen's chamber and burned for three hours. The whole of the royal family had to escape from the building, including the children. Thankfully no one was hurt but much of the palace was destroyed and the monetary loss to the king was extensive. Henry would later demolish the remains and begin a new palace on the site, which he would name Richmond Palace.

Henry and Elizabeth are generally thought to have had a happy marriage. Unlike her father who had been a notorious womaniser, there were no reports that Henry was ever unfaithful to Elizabeth. But their marriage may have faltered ever so slightly around this time if rumours are to be believed that during her time at court, Henry developed an attraction towards Katherine Gordon. Hall writes that Henry was 'wondering at her beautie and amiable countenance' and 'began then a lytle to phantasie her person', which may clearly have upset Elizabeth if she learned of this, although there is no proof he ever acted on any feelings if they were there or that anything inappropriate occurred between them. Perhaps having grown up and witnessing her father's infidelities, Elizabeth considered herself lucky that her husband was as faithful to her as he was.

During 1498, Perkin Warbeck or Richard of York, whoever he really was, would finally meet his end. After making a failed attempt at an escape, he ended up in the Tower of London, where he was housed near to the young Earl of Warwick, Clarence's son. The two were then alleged to have plotted together and they were both arrested and executed for treason in November 1498. Evidence strongly indicates that this final act of rebellion was almost definitely a set-up, which the poor young Warwick also found himself caught up in. In one fell swoop, the threat from any male Yorkists was over. Hall reports 'Edward erle of Warwieke whiche as the fame went, consented to breake pryson, and to departe out of the realme with Perkyn (which in prysoners is high treason)'. Both men were bought before the Earl of Oxford, in his position at High Constable, and after being found guilty, were beheaded on Tower Hill on 18 November.

Once more we have no record of how Elizabeth felt about their deaths. For her cousin, Warwick, she may have grieved enormously. He was a young and simple lad and his only crime was his parentage, which made him a magnet for those who still believed the House of York had a greater right to the throne. The death of the pretender, and its effect on Elizabeth, would depend on who she knew or believed he was. We cannot ever know the character of a person from such a distance of time, but her reputation as a kind and honourable woman is generally believed to be representative of who she was. It is possible she had to find a ruthless streak, the kind she had seen her father exhibit when he executed his own brother, that she too would have to call upon. She may have had little choice on the fate of both the pretender and the young Warwick, other than to plead their cases. If the young man was the son of a boatman from Tournai and that is what she knew to be true, then his death would have made little difference. Or did she watch her brother go to the scaffold after all these years? We will never really know.

What we do know is that the death of the pretender paved the way for the planned marriage of their eldest son to the Spanish princess to now go ahead. Plans had begun several years before to secure the match between Prince Arthur and Katherine of Aragon, a daughter of the Spanish king and queen, Ferdinand and Isabella. Although the agreement had been in place for several years, the Spanish rulers were reportedly unhappy at the existence of this young man who had declared himself Richard IV and according to Hall, were unwilling to commit to sending their daughter to a land where there was tension and potential for trouble. Hall recorded that the King of Spain would never make a full conclusion of the matrimony between Prince Arthur and the Lady Katherine, his daughter, nor send her into England as long as the threat from any remaining Yorkists remained.[14]

Elizabeth was understandably keen to secure her children's futures and a letter from her to Queen Isabella exists from 1497, expressing how much they are looking forward to the joining of the two royal houses. The letter is addressed: 'To the most serene and potent princess the Lady Elizabeth, by God's grace queen of Castile, Leon, Aragon, Sicily, Granada, &c., our cousin and dearest kinswoman' [note she addresses her as Elizabeth, as the names Isabella and Elizabeth were sometimes intertwined]:

> To the most serene and potent princess the Lady Elizabeth, by God's grace queen of Castile, Leon, Aragon, Sicily, Granada, &c., our cousin and dearest relation, Elizabeth, by the same grace queen of England and France, and lady of Ireland, wishes health and the most prosperous

increase of her desires. Although we before entertained singular love and regard to your highness above all other queens in a the world, as well for the consanguinity and necessary intercourse which mutually take place between us, as also for the eminent dignity and virtue by which your said majesty so shines and excels that your most celebrated name is noised abroad and diffused everywhere; yet much more has this our love increased and accumulated by the accession of the most noble affinity which has recently been celebrated between the most illustrious Lord Arthur prince of Wales, our eldest son, and the most illustrious princess the Lady Catherine, the infanta, your daughter. Hence it is that, amongst our other cares and cogitations, first and foremost we wish and desire from our heart that we may often and speedily hear of the health and safety of your serenity, and of the health and safety of the aforesaid most illustrious Lady Catherine, whom we think of and esteem as our own daughter, than which nothing can be more grateful and acceptable to us. Therefore we request your serenity to certify of your estate, and of that of the aforesaid most illustrious Lady Catherine our common daughter. And if there be any thing in our power which would be grateful or pleasant to your majesty, use us and ours as freely as you would your own; for, with most willing mind, we offer all that we have to you, and wish to have all in common with you. We should have written you the news of our state, and of that of this kingdom, but the most serene lord the king, our husband, will have written at length of these things to your majesties. For the rest may your majesty fare most happily according to your wishes. From our palace of Westminster, 3d day of December, 1497. ELIZABETH R[15]

As 1499 dawned, Elizabeth and Henry would have hoped to put the events of the previous year behind them and to finally seal the treaty that would one day see Katherine arrive on English shores and take up her place as Arthur's wife and England's future queen. But before then, Elizabeth, who was expecting once again, had a child to deliver. She entered confinement in February and on Thursday 21 February 1499, she gave birth to a baby boy at Greenwich, whom they named Edmund. Once again, Elizabeth experienced what may have been a difficult birth. It was reported by the Spanish ambassador at the time that there was 'much fear for her life'.[16] Thankfully, she survived the delivery but baby Edmund would not live longer than fifteen months, departing this life on 19 June 1500. He too was buried in Westminster Abbey next to his sister, Elizabeth.

A few months after the birth, on 19 May 1499, a proxy wedding took place between Arthur and Katherine at Tickenhall Palace, Bewdley. The Spanish ambassador, Dr Rodrigo de Puebla, stood proxy for Katherine. Then just under a year later, King Henry wrote to John Paston, announcing that Katherine would soon be on her way to England and that he would like Sir John to greet her on her arrival.

To our trusty and welbeloved knight, Sir John Paston.
By the Kinge.
1500 March 20

TRUSTY and welbeloved, we grete yow well, letting yow wete that our derest cousins, the Kinge and Queene of Spaine, have signified unto us by their sundry letters that the right excellent Princesse, the Lady Katherine, ther daughter, shal be transported from the parties of Spaine aforesaid to this our Realme, about the moneth of Maye next comeinge, for the solempnization of matrimony betweene our deerest sonne the Prince and the said Princesse. Wherfore we, consideringe that it is right fittinge and necessarye, as well for the honor of us as for the lawde and praise of our said Realme, to have the said Princesse honourably received at her arriveall, have appointed yow to be one amonge others to yeve attendance for the receivinge of the said Princesse; willinge and desiringe yow to prepare yourselfe for that intent, and so to continue in redynesse upon an houres warninge, till that by our other letters we shall advertise yow of the day and time of her arrivall, and where ye shall yeve your said attendance; and not to fayle therin, as ye tender our pleasure, the honor of yourselfe, and of this our foresaid Realme.

Yeven under our signet at our manner of Richmount, the xx[ty] day of Marche.

Later that year, on 22 November 1500, Arthur signed a formal agreement at Ludlow that would make the match unbreakable. The document was drawn up in the chapel at Ludlow Castle by two apostolic notaries and signed and sealed by the prince. Copies were sent to Katherine's parents in Spain and it was agreed that she would leave for England the following year.[17]

By the turn of the century, Elizabeth was now in her mid-thirties and it had been eight years since the death of her mother. Time had moved on as it is prone to do, and both Henry and Elizabeth were now well into middle age, with the average life expectancy of those living in 1500 being between thirty and forty. Henry was certainly feeling the passage of time, with his eyesight beginning to fail him, as he declared in a letter written to his mother: 'Verily, madame, my sight is nothing so perfect as it has been, and, I know well it will appear daily wherefore I trust that you will not be displeased, though I write not so often with mine own hand, for on my faith I have been three days ere I could make an end to this letter'.[18] Elizabeth had also had her fair share of sickness and ailments, particularly during and after childbirth, but as the first year of the new century ended, they must both have been looking forward to seeing their eldest son settle into his new life with the arrival of his new bride.

The date for Katherine to set off from Spain was set as 15 May 1501 but her departure had been delayed another week as both she and her mother, Isabella were suffering from an ague. The Spanish king and queen had written to inform their ambassador in England, Dr Roderigo De Puebla, that Katherine had been delayed a week and would begin her journey on 21 May, when she would say farewell to her family and depart Granada for her new life in England.[19]

They wrote again to De Puebla on 29 May, issuing instructions for the receiving of their daughter onto English shores. Twelve days after her arrival, the nuptials between her and Arthur were to be solemnised. De Puebla was also instructed to ensure she was endowed by the king with certain estates and that a proper acknowledgement was received of the jewels and plate that she was bringing as payment of her marriage portion. They were also keen for him to advise them of a list of her household staff.[20]

But Katherine's journey made much slower progress than was expected and on 5 July, De Puebla was informed by letter from Ferdinand and Isabella that although Katherine was travelling as quickly as possible, the heat was so great that long journeys were impossible. By 5 July, she had arrived at Guadalupe and by 20 July at the latest, they hoped she would have arrived at Coruña on the coast of north Spain. Her journey from Granada to Spain's northern coastline was some 630 miles.

Whilst they were waiting for Katherine to arrive, the queen would receive the terrible news that her half-brother, Thomas, Marquis of Dorset had died at the age of just forty-six. His young daughter, Elizabeth Grey, was just nine years old, still only a child but old enough to appreciate and understand the loss of her father. He was in London at the time, presumably ailing, as on 30 August 1501 he made his will. Just three weeks later he was dead.

Dorset was buried in the collegiate church of Astley in Warwickshire near Astley Castle, one of their family homes and the house where he had most likely been born. His wife, Cecily, was named as his executor alongside a neighbouring Leicestershire gentleman, Sir William Skeffington. Dorset left provision for the young Elizabeth and the rest of her female siblings that each of his unmarried daughters were to receive £1000 towards their dowry. The bulk of his estate and his title of Marquis went to his eldest son, also named Thomas. His manor of Astley was left to Elizabeth's mother, Cecily, as her dower and the young Elizabeth Grey would have continued living with her mother either at Astley or at Shute Manor, which was her mother's property from her Bonville inheritance.

It is unlikely that the queen attended Dorset's funeral, tradition dictated that the funeral would have been primarily a male affair. But like the rest of her siblings, there is evidence that she remained close to him throughout their life, and she would have mourned his loss. Meanwhile, as Dorset was being laid to rest, it was reported that the young Spanish princess had set sail for England but had been forced to turn back. In a letter from September 1501, written by Henry to the Archbishop of Santiago and the Count of Cabra, he writes how sorry he is that the princess has had such a terrible sea journey and has been forced to return to Spain. Reportedly storms and hurricanes had forced the ships to return to shore. He informed them he had sent one of his best sea captains, Stephen Butt, to convey the princess safely across the sea.[21]

Finally, after many years of planning, Katherine of Aragon finally arrived on English shores on Saturday 2 October, at 3 pm in the afternoon, docking at Plymouth Harbour. As she took her first steps onto English soil, she was received by the people with great joy and celebration. Upon hearing the good news, Henry and Arthur set out from London to meet her en route. The Spanish and English parties met up at Dogmerfield, where Henry and Arthur were informed that it was the wishes of Katherine's parents that the princess was not to converse with them until the finalisation of their marriage. Henry immediately overruled this and went to meet his new daughter-in-law. Arthur, accompanying him, would have had his first glimpse of his new bride. Father and son then returned to London so they could be there to officially receive Katherine upon her entry into London.

What their first impressions of each other were we cannot know, but we do know that Henry wrote to Katherine's parents to assure them of her safe arrival, informing them how much he and his son admired Katherine's beauty and dignified manners.

With Katherine left to make her progress towards London, the king made his way back to Elizabeth at Richmond, no doubt regaling her of his first impressions of their new daughter-in-law. Elizabeth and Henry remained at Richmond until 10 November, when he rode to Paris Garden in Southwark and then set off in the royal barge to Baynards Castle.[22]

Katherine and her Spanish retinue eventually reached the capital on 12 November, when she made her formal entrance. Approaching London from St George's fields, she was formerly met by the eleven-year-old Prince Harry, who was to escort her into the capital. The Spanish princess was riding a large mule and was accompanied by the Legate of Rome on her left. Prince Harry rode on the right of her. All across London Bridge, she was entreated to elaborate pageants. She was dressed in the Spanish style, with a broad round hat, the shape of a cardinal's hat upon her head, which was tied with a lace of gold to keep it in place. Underneath the hat, she wore a carnation-coloured coif and her hair streamed loose over her shoulders. Behind her, four of her Spanish ladies also rode on mules. The herald recorded his amusement that each Spanish lady was accompanied by an English lady, dressed in cloth of gold and riding a palfrey, but because of the different riding styles between the two countries, the English ladies sat on a different side to their Spanish counterparts and therefore each pair seemed to ride back-to-back!

Katherine's final destination that day was the Bishop's Palace, close to the cathedral where she would soon be married.[23] The people of the city came out in their masses to welcome this beautiful foreign princess and meanwhile the king and queen, alongside Prince Arthur and the king's mother watched from a merchant's house on the strand.

Queen Elizabeth would finally meet her future daughter-in-law face-to-face the next day when the pair spent the evening together at Baynards Castle. Then, on 14 November, Arthur and Katherine were properly wed at St Paul's Cathedral.

St Paul's had been appropriately prepared for the occasion. Within the body of the church, a long timber bridge had been erected, extending from the west door of the church to the step at the entrance to the choir. The bridge was to act as a stage and upon this was a mount for eight people to stand on, with steps to ascend and descend, covered in a fine red worsted.[24]

Both the fifteen-year-old groom and his sixteen-year-old bride wore white, although it was not yet tradition for the bride to be dressed in white; this would only take root in the Victorian era. Katherine wore a white satin bodice and skirt folded with pleats in the Spanish style and her hair hung loose under a veil of white silk, embroidered with gold thread and pearls. Arthur was also dressed in white satin. Prince Henry was awarded the honour of giving the bride away and it must have been with immense pride that Elizabeth and Henry watched proceedings from behind a screen.

When the formal ceremony was over and Mass had been said, the Duke of York once again accompanied his new sister-in-law to the Bishop's Palace, where the wedding feast would take place. Hall, in his exuberant way, writes that if he attempted to report the value of the tableware and plate that day, or declare the richness of the hangings, canopies, and cloth of estate, or set forth the number of dishes and courses served, he would surely fail to describe the abundance and honour.[25]

Once the feasting was over, it was time for the ritual of the bedding ceremony. Designed to bless the couple in their marriage and in their production of heirs, the ritual could be both religious and lewd. First, the bed and bedchamber were blessed by the priests and the bishop before Arthur climbed into bed next to Katherine in front of the gathered well-wishers. They were then both blessed and wine and spices were then served to the guests before they all departed and left the newly married couple in peace. No one could have possibly predicted at this point that this would become one of the most disputed wedding nights in history.

According to Hall, when Prince Arthur left the chamber in the morning, he uttered perhaps one of history's best-known phrases. Requesting a drink, he declared that he had 'been that night in the midst of Spain', a declaration that would be called into question nearly two decades later when what happened on their wedding night would become a matter for the courts.[26]

Whatever did or did not happen that night, the wedding celebrations continued for several weeks. The king and queen, along with Arthur and his new bride travelled by water back to Westminster, where there were more feasts and jousting. The space in front of Westminster Hall had been gravelled and smoothed, and a tilt had been set up. The Duke of Buckingham was the chief challenger and the new Marquis of Dorset, the queen's nephew, Thomas Grey, the chief defender.

To watch the sport, a stage had been erected, hung with cloth of gold and furnished with cushions of the same. The king and his lords would occupy the right side and the queen, the bride and their ladies the left. Dorset had borne over him a rich pavilion of cloth of gold and even more spectacularly Lord William Courtenay, who was married to Elizabeth's sister, Katherine of York, made his appearance riding on a red dragon led by a giant with a great tree in his hand. After the jousting, at dusk, the party moved inside to the comfortable atmosphere of Westminster Hall. At the upper end of the hall, the royal dais had been erected and the queen, Katherine of Aragon and the king's mother took their places at the king's left hand, with their ladies and the royal children sat next to them. Prince Arthur sat at his father's righthand side. The nobility of England present sat in the hall, men on the king's side and women on the queen's. When any dancing was required, a lady and a knight would proceed to the dancing space before the royal platform, one from each side of the hall. Prince Arthur danced two bass dances with his aunt, Cecily of York, and the court was also entertained by the young Prince Henry who danced with his sister, Princess Margaret, with Henry throwing off his robe and dancing in his jacket when it became too cumbersome.[27]

Finally, towards the end of November, the celebrations culminated at the new palace of Richmond before Arthur and Katherine set off to start their married life together in Ludlow.

Before they departed, both the king and Prince Arthur wrote to Ferdinand and Isabella. The king, writing from Richmond on 28 November, warmly assured them that 'although they cannot see the gentle face of their beloved daughter, they may be sure she has found a second father who will forever watch over her happiness'.[28] Arthur also wrote from Richmond two days later, declaring he had never felt so much joy in his life as when he beheld the sweet face of his bride, promising them he would make her a good husband.[29]

With Arthur and Katherine settled in Ludlow, it would not be long before Elizabeth would see the plans for the second of her children come to fruition. The following year, in January, Princess Margaret, was married in a proxy wedding to the Scottish King James IV. The ceremony itself took place in the Palace of Richmond, with the Earl of Bothwell standing proxy for James IV, although the actual wedding would not take place until the following year when the fourteen-year-old princess would set off for her new life in Scotland. After the ceremony, Elizabeth and Margaret, mother and daughter queens, dined together. Later that day the celebrations continued with jousting, feasting, wine and bonfires. We know that Cecily Grey was in attendance, perhaps the ten-year-old Elizabeth Grey also travelled to court with her mother for this family occasion, watching her eldest brother in the jousts and celebrating the wedding of her cousin alongside the rest of her siblings.

A proud king and queen had secured the fortune of their two eldest children and all must have seemed well that January. But the wheel of fortune kept on turning and just a few short weeks later, in February 1502, terrible news reached the court that Arthur was sick. Queen Elizabeth no doubt received the news with shock. With what must have been a terrible sense of helplessness that Arthur was too far away for her to care for him personally, she paid two priests to make offerings at thirty-five important religious shrines, praying to God that all would be well, then all she could do was wait. Finally, the most awful news reached them that on 2 April, Arthur had succumbed to his illness and died. Both the king and queen were stricken with grief.

An account of Prince Arthur's death and interment was recorded by Leland in his *De Rebus Britannicis Collectanea* and is a striking example of how close the king and queen had become during their sixteen-year marriage. Leland tells us that when the king was delivered the news of the death of his eldest son, he sent for the queen, so they could share in each other's grief. Finding the king in 'naturall and painefull sorrowe', the queen comforted him as best she could with wise words, reminding him that his Lady Mother 'had never no more children but him onely, and that God by his Grace had ever preserved him, and bought him that he was'. She also reminded him that 'God had left him yet a fayre Prince

[and] Two fayre princesses' and that God was where he was and they were both young enough to have more children. On hearing her words, the king was duly comforted and the queen departed to her chamber, where she broke down in such sorrow that her ladies called for the king, who in turn came and comforted her.[30]

Katherine too had fallen ill at Ludlow but unlike her husband, she had recovered. The distraught queen sent a litter of black velvet to bring her daughter-in-law home, a payment that is detailed in her one set of extant accounts for the year 1502–3, to a London tailor, John Cope:

> John Cope of London Taillour for the lynyng and covering
> of a lytture of blake velvet with blake cloth for the Quene,
> wherin the princes was brought from Ludlowe to London,
> frynged aboute with blake valance and the twoo hed peces
> of the same bounden aboute with blake rebyn and frynged
> abowte with blake valance[31]

What was to be the last year of Elizabeth's life is the one we get the best glimpse of her through her privy purse expenses which have survived for that year. Since their marriage, the king and queen had seemingly not spent much time apart, another indication that a real relationship had grown between them. But in 1502, Elizabeth decided to go off on a solo progress. Reasons behind this can only be guessed at, but the death of her son may almost certainly have been a factor. Not only that, but she had recently lost the company of her sister, Cecily of York, who had been banished from court by the king for marrying without his permission. Cecily's first husband had died in 1499, and in early 1502, she had fallen in love with and married a man named Thomas Kyme, a mere gentleman. Henry had been furious and sent her from court, his displeasure ringing in her ears. A third factor that could also have affected Elizabeth's frame of mind at the time occurred just before she set off on progress. According to Thomas More, a man named James Tyrell, who was being held in the Tower on charges of treason, allegedly claimed during his interrogation that he had murdered the two York princes. His confession has never been proven and he was unable to provide evidence of where the bodies lay, claiming they had been moved. How this supposed confession affected Elizabeth would depend on what she already knew or believed was the fate of her brothers. But this, coupled with the death of her son and the loss of her sister's company, perhaps meant she felt the need to leave her life behind for a while, to take some time to heal and reflect.

Elizabeth began her progress at Windsor on 12 July. Her first destination was to be Woodstock, perhaps a place that was filled with happy memories of spent summers. She was accompanied on her journey by her younger sister Katherine. It seems she fell ill at Woodstock, as her accounts detail a payment for an offering to Our Lady of Northampton for the queen's malady. She may have been sickening for a while as a payment was also made the previous April to the queen's apothecary for certain stuff for her use, although coming around the time of Arthur's death, this may have been grief that made her feel unwell. But she must have recovered enough to continue her journey, as from here she journeyed west into Wales, where on 19 August she arrived at Raglan Castle. Raglan Castle had been the home of her aunt Mary Woodville, who had been married to William Herbert. It was now in the possession of her cousin, Lady Elizabeth Somerset (née Herbert) and her husband, Charles Somerset. While she was in Wales, Elizabeth remained in touch with her grieving daughter-in-law, Katherine, with a payment made on the last day of August to 'my Lady Anne Percy for money by hire geven in reward to a Spanyarde that camme from the Princesse to the Quene into Walys'.

After Raglan, Elizabeth continued onto Chepstow, also owned by the Herbert and Somerset families, before returning slowly back towards London. In September, she was still suffering from some sort of illness as another payment was made to the queen's apothecary, although by this time she may have been aware that she was in the early stages of pregnancy and may well have been experiencing some kind of morning sickness. By 6 October, she had reached Minster Lovell, in Oxfordshire, once home to another of her aunt's, Katherine Woodville, and her husband, Jasper Tudor. After Jasper's death, Minster Lovell came into the Crown's possession.

Her progress destinations may perhaps reflect her state of mind that summer; many of them were places belonging to relatives on her mother's side of the family and places she may have visited as a young woman. She was mourning her eldest son and during those months, she may have needed some quiet contemplation; to look back at her life and her memories. As well as being able to follow this progress through her accounts, we also get a real glimpse into how Elizabeth cared deeply about her family, through the payments she made to support them. She had always remained close to her blood family and was extremely loyal to them all. Many of her sisters had been with her at court at some point during her queenship, and in 1501, Elizabeth even took her half-brother Arthur Plantagenet into her service as her carver.[32] Arthur was a bastard child of her father's. Two items in her accounts also illustrate a fondness towards her early life, as she makes payment to a gentleman who supposedly sheltered her uncle Anthony in Pontefract, many years before, and towards an old servant of her father's. These payments to people who were perhaps strangers to the queen herself highlight her strong bond and sense of responsibility towards her kin:

> Itm. To a man of Poynfreyt sayeng himself to lodge in his house Therl Ryvers in tyme of his deth in almous … xij d. December. (To a person in whose house Earl Anthony lodged at the time of his death in 1483.)

> Itm. the sixth day of Decembre to Henry Langton an olde servaunt of King Edwardes.

Her youngest sister, Bridget, was a nun at Dartford Priory and Elizabeth's accounts also detail payments made towards her upkeep. On top of that, she would also often buy clothes for her sisters, at the same time as ordering for herself, such as in May 1502 when she ordered a black satin and velvet for a gown for herself (presumably her mourning wear after Arthur's death), and at the same time she ordered seven yards of green satin 'for a kirtle for my Lady Anne'.[33]

Her kindness also showed no bounds when her sister Katherine found herself in strife when her husband was arrested and thrown into the Tower on charges of suspected treason. Although this must have put Elizabeth herself into a difficult position, not only did she step in to support her sister and her children, but she also paid for clothing to be sent to Katherine's husband in the Tower, paying for some shirts, a fur gown and a night cap.[34]

Katherine was chosen to accompany her on progress, and Elizabeth paid for her saddle to be covered out of her privy purse. While the two women were away, tragedy struck for Katherine when in July, whilst they were staying at the Abbot's House at Notley Abbey in Buckinghamshire, she received the sad news of the death of her little son, Edward. Elizabeth had arranged for Katherine's children to be housed at Havering under the care of Dame Margaret Cotton, and her privy purse accounts show that the news arrived via a servant of Dame Cotton's who was paid for his costs in coming from Havering to Notley to ask the queen where Lord Edward should be buried (the accounts call him Lord Edmund, which is evidently a scribe's error). The queen immediately wrote to the Abbot of Westminster and paid for all his funeral costs, as detailed in her accounts, as well as gifts for his nurse and rocker:

> March 1503. Itm. to Thomas Eldreton for the costs and charges of the burying of the young Lord Edmund (sic) Courtenay, son to the Lady Katherine, sister to the queen. And for money by him given at the commandment of the queen at the departure of the nurse and rocker of the same Lord[35]

The care of her sister's children at Havering is a prime example of Elizabeth's generosity, particularly as their father was languishing in the tower accused of plotting against Elizabeth's family, a charge he was later acquitted of. Her surviving accounts detail several payments throughout the year to Dame Cotton for their clothing, hose and shoelaces, and to a Mistress Cheyne for items bought for their chamber such as candlesticks. She also paid for all their food and an item in June 1502 shows a payment 'delivered to Dame Margaret Cotton for the diets of Lord Henry and Edward Courtenay and my Lady Margaret, their sister, two women servants and a groom'. Two more payments for food costs are made on 15 November 1502, the first identical to the May one for the diets of all three children from the last day of May to 13 July, and then a second payment made for the period 13 July to 2 November that sadly omits little Edward from the list.

Elizabeth was back in Richmond by 25 November, after which she then travelled by river to Westminster, ready to spend the Christmas season with her husband – maybe some time apart had been just what she needed. Her sister Katherine and her two remaining children joined her sister and the court at Christmas that year with the queen's accounts from December detailing a payment to Lawrance Travice for carrying 'stuff belonging to Lord Henry Courtenay and his sister Margaret from

Havering to London'. There is also another payment to John Staunton the Younger for money laid out by him for horsemeat and the expenses of 'certain personnes' that bought Lord Henry and Lady Margaret his sister from Essex to London, and for his costs – a journey that took two days'.

As the celebrations began for that Christmas 1502, Elizabeth hopefully felt a bit more refreshed after what had perhaps been one of her most difficult years. But as well as being reunited with her husband, she also had the birth of a baby to look forward to in the coming months. During her childbirths, Elizabeth favoured The Girdle of Our Lady, which belonged to Westminster Abbey and her accounts show this was bought to her in December: 'Itm. To a monke that brought our Lady gyrdelle to the Quene in rewarde'. The girdle would have been kept on an altar until it was needed, which was installed in her private chamber and contained any other relics that were kept for use in her private devotions. Then, during labour, the girdle would have been placed over her stomach, in the hope that the pains of childbirth would be eased by the aid and blessings of the Virgin Mary. So far, the Virgin Mary had seen her safely through the births of six children, would she see her safely through her seventh?

Chapter 8

Taken Too Soon

Whilst Queen Elizabeth was celebrating the Christmas period in London, her niece, the young Elizabeth Grey, now ten years old, would have been preparing for the advent celebrations with her mother and siblings. Sadly, much of the early years of her life are also lost to us, but like all young children, she was no doubt excitedly preparing for the twelve days of Christmas. Christmas in the early 1500s was the longest holiday of the year, and a time for families to spend together. The great hall, the centre of family life, was made even more impressive with festive garlands of holly, ivy and other evergreens. Although the Christmas we celebrate today has more of its origins in the Victorian era, the medieval Christmas was, like many other aspects of medieval life, a fusion of religion and pagan traditions. Once again magic and religion co-existed in the celebration of winter with pagan customs such as the dragging in of a Yule log to burn in the grate sitting happily alongside the celebration of Christianity and Christs' birth which included the singing of hymns and attendance at church on Christmas morning.

From the queen's household accounts, we can trace Elizabeth Grey's mother, Cecily, to the manor of Multon in Lincolnshire towards the end of 1502, perhaps to be closer to her mother, Katherine Neville, who by this time was sixty years old and may have been in poor health. An item in the queen's accounts for 11 November 1502 details a payment to William Pole, Elizabeth's Groom of the Chamber 'for his costs riding from Langley to the Lady Marquess into Lincolnshire by the space of 5 days'. The accounts do not detail the reason for the trip, but perhaps he was taking her a gift of venison as was reflected in the other payments made to him that day.[1] So perhaps Christmas this year for Elizabeth Grey and her family was spent in Lincolnshire rather than their preferred homes of Shute and Astley.

Much as today, the Christmas celebrations involved the giving of gifts and although some were exchanged on Christmas Day itself, the tradition of New Year gifts was of importance in the 1500s. Queen Elizabeth's household accounts detail some of her New Year gifts for January 1503, including payments to Thomas Hunt of the Confectionary, money paid out to servants of the Archbishops of Canterbury, and York and the Bishops of Bath, Exeter, Ely and others for their bringing of new years' gifts from their masters to the queen. The queen also generously gave gifts to her minstrels and those of the king, as well as the pages of the queen's chamber, and the children of the privy kitchen, the Lord of Misrule and the Lord Privy Seal's fool.[2]

As the Christmas celebrations ended, Queen Elizabeth's thoughts would have turned to the preparations for the birth of her new baby. At the end of January, she travelled by boat to the Tower in order to spend Candlemas with Henry and then enter her confinement. As she journeyed down the Thames, the heavily pregnant queen reclined on cushions, seated by burning braziers, filled with sweet herbs, trying to keep as comfortable as she could against the chilly winter air.[3]

But this time things did not go to plan. A few days later, on the occasion of Candlemas itself, 2 February 1503, Elizabeth was delivered suddenly of a girl. It seems the queen had unexpectedly gone into labour and the baby arrived much earlier than anticipated.

The king and queen named their new baby daughter Katherine, perhaps in honour of Elizabeth's sister Katherine who had been her recent companion on her travels. But just a few days after the birth, Elizabeth fell seriously ill and Henry sent into Kent for a Dr Aylsworth, a physician.[4] But even with medical help, she was unable to beat whatever ailed her. She had been ill after several of her births, but this time she was not strong enough. Her sands of time had run out and she died on the anniversary of her birth, 11 February 1503, her thirty-seventh birthday. Her accounts give us the details of her final days, and that of baby, Katherine, who also appeared in the accounts on 14 February but sadly followed her mother to the grave soon after.

> Itm. To James Nattres for his costs going into Kent for Doctor Hallyswurth physician to come to the Queen by the King's commandment. First for his boat hire from the Tower to Gravesend and again 3s. 4d.
>
> Itm. To two watermen abiding at Gravesend unto such time the said James came again for their expenses 4d.

Itm. For horse hire and two guides by night and day 2s. 4d. and for his own expenses 16d.

Itm. To Robert Lanston for 4 yards of flanell by him bought for my Lady Kateryn the King's daughter.

Understandably, the queen's family were all devastated by her death and her husband, King Henry, was heartbroken. Their union, which had been planned by their mothers in the darkest days of the 1480s, became a marriage of mutual respect and very possibly love. Never an exuberant personality anyway, the king retreated from public life for several weeks and when he re-emerged, it was undoubtedly as a dourer and much sterner version of himself. Her son, Henry, who would go on to become the great Henry VIII, reportedly said that the news of his mother's death was the worst news he ever received.

The royal family's grief at her passing is illustrated in an illuminated manuscript that is once thought to have belonged to Henry VII and is now held in the National Library of Wales. Known as the Vaux Passional, the manuscript is illustrated with thirty-four splendid Flemish-style miniatures. The first miniature is of a man presenting a book to a sovereign, thought to be Henry VII. In the background sits a young man in mourning, believed to be a young Prince Henry. He is sitting beside an empty, black-covered bed and nearby are two girls sitting by a fireplace wearing black head-dresses, most likely portraying the thirteen-year-old Princess Margaret and the seven-year-old Princess Mary.[5]

During her lifetime Elizabeth had been bound by her queenly duties, but her innate kindness and generosity of spirit ensured that she was also a particularly good mother to her children, all who would have experienced her loss keenly. Although the very role of queenship would have prevented her from being a completely hands-on mother, it is certainly believed that she had much influence over her children's upbringing and oversaw many aspects of her children's education. The historian, David Starkey, notes it was most probably Elizabeth that taught her children to write. In his comparison of extant handwritten letters by Princess Mary and Prince Henry, he observes that their handwriting is remarkably similar to the few extant examples of their mother's handwriting. She would also, of course, have ensured that they were raised in the Catholic tradition, and a payment in her privy purse accounts records a payment of twelve pence for a letter of pardon for Mary.[6]

Although never seen as the most influential of queens, Elizabeth's legacy was arguably her personal attributes; the kindness she bestowed on everyone and the love that her subjects and her family felt for her. Without her, it is highly unlikely that Henry VII would have been accepted on the throne as easily as he was. Henry was described by Hall as 'a man of body but lean and spare…, with a fair complexion, a merry countenance, his eyes grey, with a quick wit and princely courage'[7] and it seems that their marriage, which could have gone spectacularly wrong as many did, was a success because they made it so through their joint respect for each other.

Elizabeth's funeral was a much grander affair than that of her mother. On Sunday 12 February, the day after her death, Elizabeth's coffin was carried to the Church of St Peter ad Vincula within the Tower, where she remained for the next eleven days. The coffin was carried under a canopy, held by four knights of the realm. Behind the coffin, the queen's household walked in procession. The stained-glass windows of the church were lined with black crepe and the walls hung with black silk damask and light was provided by 500 tall candles. The honour of chief mourner should have been awarded to Elizabeth's sister, Cecily, who was next to her in age, but after her recent banishment, the role was given to Katherine of York. As chief mourner she entered the chapel, accompanied by her brother-in-law, Sir Thomas Howard, and took her place at the head of her sister's body. She remained there during Mass and for the next eleven days, the coffin would be watched over at all times by six ladies in rotation. Other gentlewomen would give way to their betters, but Katherine herself was a constant presence kneeling at the head alone. As the queen's death had been unexpected, the ladies wore the simplest clothing that they had, with kerchiefs on their heads until their mourning clothes were made.[8]

On the day of the funeral, 24 February 1503, the queen's procession from the Tower to Westminster followed the same route that she had taken for her coronation. Katherine was joined by her three sisters, Anne, Bridget and Cecily, who was allowed back for the occasion, all wearing mourning gowns with sweeping trains. Together they followed the chariot bearing the body of their sister and their queen. After the service in Westminster Abbey, their nephew, the Marquis of Dorset, escorted Katherine, her sisters and all the lords and ladies to the queen's great chamber in the Palace of Westminster where Katherine presided over a supper of fish.[9] Elizabeth was interred next to her children, Elizabeth and Edmund.

Her death was a personal loss to her family but outside of the court, Elizabeth was also mourned by the people. Thomas More wrote *A Rueful Lamentation* about her death, and his was one of many poems and eulogies written for England's beloved first Tudor queen:

> That tow'r that was so fatal once
> To princes of degree,
> Prov'd fatal to this noble queen,
> For therein died she.
> In childbed lost she her sweet life,
> Her life esteem'd so dear;
> Which had been England's loving queen
> Full many a happy year.
> The king herewith possess'd with grief,
> Spent many months in moan;
> And daily sigh'd and said,
> that he, Like her, could find out none;
> Nor none could he in fancy chuse
> To make his wedded wife;
> Therefore a widow'r would remain
> The remnant of his life.[10]

Elizabeth was fully represented at her funeral by all her living sisters and it is highly likely that her sister-in-law Cecily Grey, would also have been in attendance. Perhaps the eleven-year-old Elizabeth Grey also donned her black mourning robes and accompanied her mother, to support her cousins as they laid their mother to rest and to mourn her aunt and England's queen.

The subject of death was not an unfamiliar one to children living in the Middle Ages. At a time where medicine was not as advanced and life expectancy was much lower than nowadays, death was very much a part of life. But during this early period of her life, the young Elizabeth Grey was certainly being reminded of how fleeting life could be. Her aunt's death, coming just two years after the death of her father, would have been a period of sadness for all the family, and then just a few months later, Elizabeth was to experience loss once again when one of her elder sisters, Lady Eleanor Arundell, died aged around twenty-three, leaving behind several young children. Eleanor was the eldest Grey daughter, a full decade older than Elizabeth, so she may have married and left the family home whilst Elizabeth was still a small child. But she was still her sister and they may have been close. This family loss was followed just over a year later by the loss of her grandmother, Cecily's mother, Katherine Neville.

Katherine Neville, a daughter of the great Neville family and sister to the Earl of Warwick, kingmaker to Edward IV, was around sixty-two years old when she died. She had been married as a young woman to William Bonville, Elizabeth's maternal grandfather and her mother Cecily's father. William had died when Cecily was still a baby, and her mother had remarried William Hastings, Chamberlain to Edward IV. Hastings had of course been murdered by Richard III in 1483 so Elizabeth would never have met her step-grandfather. After Hastings death, Katherine had remained a widow for the remaining twenty years of her life. She had written her will on 22 November 1503, perhaps signalling that she knew her health was declining. Cecily certainly seemed to have remained close to her mother, and her children, including Elizabeth, may have had a real love and fondness for their grandmother,

Cecily Grey had also now been a widow for several years since the death of the marquis in 1501, but in 1504, a year after the queen's death, she announced her intention to take a second husband; Elizabeth, on the cusp of her teenage years, was to gain a new stepfather. Cecily's chosen spouse was Lord Henry Stafford, a younger son of Harry Stafford, the 2nd Duke of Buckingham and his wife, Katherine Woodville. There was a considerable age gap between them – Henry was around twenty-five years of age, with a birth date of 1479, to Cecily's forty-five.

The exact date of their marriage is unknown but it most likely took place sometime in mid-1505, as an indenture was made in April that year between Cecily, Marchioness of Dorset and Lord Harry Stafford 'in consideration that he has troth plighted and promised to take her to wife'.[11] The couple needed royal permission to marry and the king gave it, although at a cost of £2000. £1000 was payable immediately, as a guarantee of Stafford's good behaviour towards his king and the second was payable over the next five years. Stafford was appointed a Knight of the Order of the Garter (K.G.) the same year, perhaps intended to elevate him in status to marry Cecily. As the younger Buckingham brother, he did not have any fortune or status of his own.

But what did Elizabeth think of her mother's new husband? By the time of their likely nuptials, she would have been around thirteen years old. Perhaps she could see her mother was happy and was happy for her, but if so, this was not a view shared by all of her family, particularly her elder brother, Thomas. It seems that Thomas Dorset was hugely concerned that his mother's second marriage to a much younger man would considerably diminish his inheritance and was therefore completely against the match.

This could be seen as a selfish viewpoint from her eldest son, concerned only about his own financial dealings. That may be true and perhaps he was the greedy elder son, concerned only with his own inheritance. But there may also have been an element of concern for his mother, worried perhaps that although his mother may have developed an attraction for this younger man, perhaps it was not reciprocated to the same extent by Stafford. Indeed, Thomas may have suspected, rightly or wrongly, that Stafford's primary motive for marrying his mother was financial. But whatever the truth, their intended nuptials led to Thomas objecting that by their marriage, his inheritance could be diluted amongst any children that his mother and her new husband may have together. Consequently, the pair dramatically fell out and in November 1504, Thomas challenged her right to continue as his father's executor.

Tensions escalated to such a height that the king and council were forced to step in to resolve the dispute. Unfortunately, the legal wrangling between Thomas Dorset and Stafford would eventually result in Cecily's daughters becoming the biggest losers in these arguments between mother and son. When it became Elizabeth's time to marry, some fifteen years later, she too would be affected by these legal and financial disputes between her mother, her new stepfather and her elder brother.

Sadly, not much is known of Elizabeth's early life, including her teenage years. When Queen Elizabeth died, her household was disbanded and the king's mother, Lady Margaret Beaufort, took over the supervision of the bringing up of the royal children. Princess

Margaret had travelled to Scotland in 1504, so just Prince Henry and Princess Mary remained behind in London. Whether Elizabeth Grey and her family ever visited the court to visit her cousins in the few years after the queen's death is unknown. Without the queen, there was less of a reason for the Grey family to be involved in court life, and in fact in 1508 whatever closeness they had had to the king was damaged when Elizabeth's eldest brother, the Marquis of Dorset was arrested and thrown into prison.

By the mid-1500s, Henry VII had been king for nearly two decades. He was infinitely securer on his throne than he had been at the start of his reign, but the threat from the House of York had never completely gone away. Towards the end of Henry's rule, there was a much smaller pool of males still associated with the House of York to cause him trouble. But one, Edmund de la Pole, a younger brother of the Earl of Lincoln and son of Edward IV's sister, Elizabeth of York, Duchess of Suffolk, was becoming a thorn in Henry's side. Edmund had rebelled against the king when Henry VII had refused to grant him the dukedom upon the death of his father, the Duke of Suffolk. Instead, he was only granted the lesser title of Earl of Suffolk, and Edmund had been resentful ever since. In 1498, he had been indicted of murder in a fight and fled overseas, although he was later pardoned for the offence. Returning to England for a short while, he had fled again in 1501 without royal leave, to his Aunt Margaret's court in Burgundy. In the summer of that year in what was obviously designed to be a clear threat to Henry, he began calling himself the 'White Rose'. In response to this threat, Edmund was declared an outlaw and in February 1502, many of his close associates were arrested and imprisoned, suspected of their involvement in the conspiracy. These men included William de la Pole (Edmund's younger brother) and William Courtenay, husband to Katherine of York.

Although Thomas Dorset was also a close associate of this group of men, he had managed to remain clear of suspicion and had retained his freedom. However, he had clearly come under Henry's suspicion by 1508, as in that year Sir Richard Carew, Lieutenant of Calais, transported William Courtenay and Thomas Dorset across the sea to the Calais prison by commandment of the king. According to the writer of the Chronicle of Calais, on 18 October 1508, the pair were brought across the sea after 'they had bene in the towre of London a greate season'.[12]

Elizabeth's brother, Thomas, and William Courtenay were still imprisoned in 1509 when King Henry VII died. After a reign of nearly twenty-five years, England's first Tudor king died on 12 April in his favourite Palace of Richmond. According to Hall, he may have been ill for some time 'he was so consumed with his long malady that nature could no longer sustain his life'.[13] He was buried in Westminster Abbey next to his wife, and it was now turn for his son, Prince Harry, to take the throne. The Grey family may have hoped that Henry's death would secure Dorset's release but things would get worse before they got better. Immediately upon Henry's accession, Elizabeth's stepfather, Stafford was also arrested and thrown into the Tower, more on a suspicion of anything he might do than on anything he had actually done.

Whilst Dorset and Stafford were incarcerated, the coronation of England's new king took place. After Prince Arthur's death, his widow, Katherine of Aragon, had not returned to her Spanish homeland but had remained in England where she had lived in much poverty and strife after the death of Queen Elizabeth. It seems she had been somewhat neglected by Henry VII after the death of the queen and she had spent a miserable few years. Her position as England's future queen had disappeared with Arthur's death and no new position had been found for her. However, upon Henry's death in 1509, it was decided that she would still make a suitable queen for England and England's new king, Henry, had no reservations in making her his wife. In a joint coronation that took place on Midsummers Day, 24 June 1509, a newly married Henry VIII and his beautiful Spanish queen brought joy to the country. The streets of London were hung with tapestries and cloth of gold and Londoners gathered to watch this new young Tudor king take the helm of England. Henry rode to his coronation at Westminster Abbey, and following behind him in the procession was Katherine, her long auburn hair loose, reclining in a litter. With the air still tinged with the smell of smoke from the Midsummer's eve bonfires, upon reaching the abbey, Henry and Katherine proceeded on foot through the great hall of the abbey towards the abbey church. The formal proceedings were followed by feasting and a great tournament that night, and the festivities then continued for two more days after. Elizabeth's stepfather and brother missed the whole event. The suspicion that had fallen on both men presumably did not stretch to the whole family as some of the Grey family were welcome at court; Elizabeth's brothers, Richard,

John and Anthony Grey certainly attended the coronation celebrations. Elizabeth by this time was seventeen so she too may have joined other members of her family in celebrating the rise of her cousin to the throne.

It would be another month before King Henry finally sent to Calais for Dorset's release and he returned back across the channel and back into royal favour. According to the Calais chronicler, both Thomas Dorset and William Courtenay had only narrowly escaped with their lives; they had been facing execution and only survived because Henry VII had died before he could give the order.[14] Elizabeth's stepfather was also released and he was created Earl of Wiltshire on 27 January 1510.

After Elizabeth of York's death in 1503, the court had become a more solemn place. The king, too caught up in his grief, had become withdrawn, focusing solely on the business of running the country. But this new court, under the rule of Henry VIII, was young, vibrant and fun and both the king and queen and Henry's younger sister, Princess Mary were the centre of attention, revelling in masques, jousts and lavish entertainment. Perhaps Elizabeth frequented these court entertainments as she became older; we do know that her brothers were involved in the life of the court, particularly Richard and John Grey although they were a whole decade older than Elizabeth. Our first real glimpse of Elizabeth Grey however comes in 1514, when she accompanied her cousin, the king's younger sister Mary, across the sea to her new life as Queen of France.

During her father's lifetime, Princess Mary had been betrothed to Charles of Castille, the son of Juana of Spain and her husband, Philip and therefore a nephew of Katherine of Aragon's. On 21 December 1507, a treaty had been signed in Calais confirming the betrothal of Mary and Charles, then eleven and seven years old respectively, and it was agreed that when Charles turned fourteen in 1514, Mary would be sent to live in his household; until that time, she would continue to live in England.

After her brother Henry had succeeded to the English throne, he continued with the discussions to marry Mary to Charles but as 1514 drew near, negotiations began to stall. As the talks became increasingly delayed, the French ambassador, Louis d'Orléans, Duke of Longueville, who was in England at the time, took the opportunity to further his master's cause in French/Anglo relations. When King Louis's queen died on 9 January 1514, Longueville broached the idea of a union between Louis and Mary. Henry listened. On 30 July 1514, Mary formally renounced her marriage with Charles in front of witnesses and just under two weeks later, on 13 August, she celebrated her marriage to Louis. The ceremony took place at Greenwich, in the presence of her brother, the king and Queen Katherine. The Duke of Longueville acted as proxy for King Louis and after the ceremony, all those present proceeded to Mass. Nicolò Di Favri of Treviso, in his dispatches home to Venice, gives us a vivid description of the wedding party that day. King Henry was wearing a gown of cloth of gold and ash-coloured satin, in chequers, with jewelled embroidery and a costly collar around his neck. Alongside him, the Duke of Longueville also wore a gown of cloth of gold and purple satin in chequers, whilst Queen Katherine, who was pregnant, was clad in ash-coloured satin, with chains and jewels; upon her head, she wore a cap of cloth of gold. Princess Mary, now the new French queen, also wore a petticoat of ash-coloured satin, and a gown of purple satin and cloth of gold in chequers and also wore a cap of cloth of gold and chains and jewels like the queen.[15] She was accompanied by many ladies, and it is just possible that one of them might have been Elizabeth Grey. After Mass, the party returned to a great banquet and dancing, with the ball lasting nearly two hours before further refreshments were served and they all retired back to their homes.

King Louis of France was thirty-four years older than Mary and at the time of their nuptials, he was fifty-two years old to Mary's eighteen. As well as cementing a peaceful union with England, Louis greatly desired a son and he was hopeful that this marriage to a young Princess of England would provide him with one. In 1514, the heir to the French throne was Duke Francis, the husband of Louis's eldest daughter, Claude. Although Francis was now currently known as the dauphin, Louis was keen to have a son who could take the place of the ambitious Francis in the succession.

Having never met the King of France but obviously aware of the significant age gap, we can only guess at Mary's feelings towards the husband that had been chosen for her. However, she had an exceptionally good and close relationship with her brother, Henry, and upon consenting to the French marriage, she negotiated with Henry and persuaded him to agree that should she ever be in a position to take a second husband, she could choose that person for herself. Henry gave his beloved younger sister his word and Mary excitedly began her preparations for her journey to France; if nothing else she was now a queen and this was a role she knew she could excel at. As well as sorting her personal belongings, Mary also required a group of ladies that would travel with her and serve her in France. These were honoured positions, much sought after, and King Louis required that the names of her companions should be sent to him in advance. As the women of England jostled for available positions, a full list of names was sent to Louis for his approval during the last week of September.[16]

One of the criteria for Mary's companions was that they must be competent in French and it was reported by the Venetian ambassador, Pasqualigo, writing home on 23 September 1514, that in the hope of securing a place in her entourage, the whole court now speaks French and English. Pasqualigo also provides us with a description of Mary, declaring her as 'very beautiful, and has not her match in all England ... tall, fair, and of a light complexion, with a colour, and most affable and graceful'.[17]

Elizabeth Grey was successful in gaining a position as one of Mary's ladies, perhaps due to her family ties. That she was selected indicates that she must have been fairly well educated and had some mastery over the French language. Education and learning were almost certainly important to the Grey family as it had been to the Woodvilles. At least four of Elizabeth's brothers had attended Magdalen College in Oxford as they grew up and Elizabeth's father had left a bequest to the scholars of Oxford and Cambridge in his will.

As Henry was sending a member of his family to the French court, it afforded him the opportunity to make a good impression on Louis, to illustrate the richness and opulence of the English court. That, coupled with his affection for his beloved younger sister, guaranteed that he made sure she was well provided for in her new life in France. Reports detail the wardrobe that he had made for her, which included fifteen gowns in the French fashion, six gowns in the Milan fashion and seven gowns in English fashion as well as thirteen kirtles in all of these styles. These were made for her in a myriad of colours – crimson, green, yellow, purple and black – and a multitude of fabrics, including cloth of gold, velvet, and satin. Many of the gowns were lined with fur and elaborately embroidered.[18] She also was equipped with jackets for her footmen, altar cloths, cushions and many other items for her comfort. Her trousseau was completed with her lavish jewels; bracelets, rings, necklaces and girdles made of diamonds, pearls, rubies and gold.

No doubt similar preparations, albeit on a smaller scale, were also taking place in the Grey household as Elizabeth would have needed several gowns to fill her own trunk, ready to make the journey to France. All who travelled with her on her journey across the sea would receive twenty days wages in hand. Many of Elizabeth's brothers were also to accompany Mary, including her elder brother, the Marquis of Dorset alongside his wife, and Lords Edward, Richard, John and Leonard Grey. The gentlemen would return to England but the gentlewomen that were appointed to accompany Mary were due to remain with her in France. They were named in the official records as Lady Guildford, who was Mary's main Lady of Honour, Elizabeth Ferrers, Ann Devereux, M. Wotton, Alice Denys, Anne Jerningham and an M. Boleyne, who is believed to have been Mary Boleyn. The more famous Boleyn, Anne, would later join the party in France as she was currently residing at the Austrian court. Elizabeth Grey and her sister Anne Grey were also named amongst these ladies.[19]

For his part, Louis, like Henry, was also keen to make a good impression and sent Mary opulent gifts before she left England, which illustrated not only his esteem for her but were designed to show off the power and might of France. One such present was accessories for her headwear in the French style, which he sent with an accompanying note to Wolsey asking for Henry's permission for a French gentlewoman to travel to England to dress Mary's hair and show her how to wear them.[20] The most spectacular gift he sent her was a piece of jewellery known as the Mirror of Naples: 'a jewelled diamond as large and as broad as a full-sized finger with a pear-shaped pearl beneath it, the size of a pigeon's egg' which Henry had valued at 60,000 crowns.[21]

By the middle of September, Mary was finally deemed ready to depart for her new life. As she left London, she was accompanied by the king and queen, her extensive retinue and many other members of the court who would travel with her to Dover. The fact that many members of the court also brought their retainers and servants, and accompanying merchants bought along their wives and families, meant that this was quite a parade. Her retinue that travelled from the capital to the coast was estimated at over 400 knights and barons and 200 gentlemen and squires, all accompanied by their wives and damsels. They travelled on 1000 palfreys and in 100 carriages and must have provided quite a sight to the inhabitants of the towns and villages they passed through, lucky to get a glimpse of this exciting event.[22] Elizabeth and her Grey siblings must have truly felt that they were setting off on a great adventure.

The party eventually arrived in Dover, where the king and queen would end their journey, waving Mary farewell before returning to London. Henry initially intended to accompany Mary ten miles out to sea in the *Henry Grace à Dieu*, his great flagship, but found 'the wynde was troublous and the wether foule'. Not only did this prevent Henry's plan to sail some of the way with his sister, but the bad weather also halted Mary's departure for several days. Finally, as dusk was breaking on the morning of 2 October, Mary's ship left the dock on her journey across the English Channel. She bade a pregnant Katherine farewell from her rooms in Dover castle, then Henry escorted her to the waterside to see her and her ladies safely aboard. For Elizabeth, making what was likely her first trip across the sea and potentially the first time spent away from her family, this early morning boarding of the wooden ship on the choppy seas must have been both hugely exhilarating and yet slightly daunting due to the stormy weather.

Several ships set sail that morning to carry Mary's extensive retinue across the sea, and we can only assume that as one of Mary's ladies, Elizabeth was on the same ship as the princess. During the rough crossing, the ships became separated. Mary's ship was courageously steered by the ship's captain into Boulogne Harbour in the ensuing storm. A landing craft was sent out to meet her but the water was too choppy for the small craft to reach the jetty so a gallant gentleman, Sir Christopher Garnyshe, reportedly jumped into the water and carried her to shore.[23] How Elizabeth and the other ladies made it to land, we can only guess at, but they likely arrived on French shores cold and wet, and yet relieved to be back on firm ground. Several of the other ships made land further along the coast, although one unfortunate craft, named the *Great Elizabeth*, was shipwrecked off the coast of Calais.

Mary arrived in Boulogne at ten in the morning and had to borrow horses from the town as hers were on one of the other ships that had been forced to dock elsewhere. She was greeted by a procession of monks from the church of Notre Dame who accompanied her to a bridge that was the entrance to the city. Above the bridge was hoisted a ship painted with fleurs-de-lis and roses. When Mary approached, the mechanical ship descended before her. She and her retinue remained in Boulogne to rest after the long and treacherous journey. It must have been with some relief that Elizabeth and the other ladies laid their heads on their pillows that night, offering a prayer of thanks that they had survived the perilous sea crossing.

After a good night's rest, Mary and her party set off towards Abbeville, where Louis and the rest of the court were waiting to receive her. In a planned charade, the English party stopped at a village just outside town, while the dauphin, Francis, rode into Abbeville to inform Louis that his bride was nearby. The French king mounted his horse and rode to meet her carrying a hawk, so that he might pretend to encounter Mary 'accidentally' while hunting. Mary and Louis even coordinated their clothing, both wearing crimson velvet and cloth of gold. When Louis arrived, Mary attempted to dismount and curtsey to him, but before she could he embraced and kissed her before spurring his horse and returning to Abbeville by a different route. Mary and her English contingent, Elizabeth included, then continued their journey into the town. Once again it was a magnificent procession comprising over 400 archers, musketeers, and gentlemen at the front, followed by clergy carrying relics, then over eighty sumptuously dressed English lords. The Scotch guard surrounded their new monarch and Mary's ladies travelled on horseback directly behind their mistress, no doubt marvelling at the reception they were receiving all along the route. The citizens of Abbeville had spared no expense to welcome their new queen and had built several wonderful structures to line the route, including a serpent with seven heads that spouted white wine and a lily surrounded by roses with jets of white and red wine streaming out.[24]

The next morning, 9 October, was Mary's official wedding day. At seven-thirty in the morning, Mary was escorted to the king's lodgings by her English retinue, all dressed in their finery. Elizabeth would almost certainly have been one of the fine ladies that accompanied her, perhaps in a new gown of her own made especially for the occasion. Wearing her hair loose under an expensively decorated hat, Mary was dressed in a gown of gold brocade in the English fashion. Upon reaching the king's hall, Mary made a deep curtsey and Louis greeted her with a kiss. Seated next to Louis, their union was consecrated by Cardinal de

Prie, whilst the Dukes of Angoulême, Alençon, and Vendôme, and the Count of Guise, held an expensive canopy over their heads. When the ceremony was over, Mary and Louis returned to their own chambers to dine and rest awhile before returning to the hall later in the day for dancing and entertainment.

Whether Mary genuinely developed a fondness for her ageing husband or whether she was just a very able actress, she spent most of her time in the company of her husband and king. The chroniclers reported that Louis had intended to leave Abbeville shortly after the wedding but had been prevented by his gout, and that 'The Quene is continually with hym, of whom he maketh as much, as she reporteth to us herself, as it is possible for any man to make of a Lady'. When they finally did depart from Abbeville, they travelled to Beauvais, where Charles Brandon, who had been sent to France as one of Henry's new ambassadors, caught up with them.

Charles Brandon was Henry VIII's closest friend and Mary had therefore spent much time in his company. The second but only surviving son of Henry VII's standard-bearer at Bosworth, William Brandon, Charles was brought up at court alongside Henry. With the privilege of hindsight that Brandon would become her second husband, it is interesting to wonder what Mary's thoughts were at seeing him again in France. As one of her brother's closest friends, Mary knew him of old and most likely already harboured feelings for him. Now she was a married woman, she would have to bury those feelings in the presence of her husband. Did she confide in her English ladies at all, including Elizabeth, or did they suspect that their mistress loved another other than her husband?

Shortly after the wedding Louis, for reasons unknown, dismissed many of Mary's English retinue. His motives for this are unclear, as he had agreed to the names by signing a list of Mary's principal retainers before her arrival. Mary was particularly upset at losing many of her English ladies, particularly her chief lady of honour Lady Guildford, and she wrote immediately to Wolsey begging him to intercede. Fortunately, as one of the younger girls in Mary's train, Elizabeth was permitted to stay alongside her sister Anne. Wolsey attempted to get the women reinstated but failed, and Mary was obliged to have certain French ladies instead, including Madame D'Aumont as her chief lady in place of Lady Guildford. The king's daughter, Claude and Marguerite d'Angoulême, the sister of the dauphin were also appointed to attend the queen. The six English ladies she was allowed to retain were Elizabeth and Anne Grey, Anne Jernyngham, Mary Fiennes, Mary Boleyn and Elizabeth Ferrers. Anne Boleyn would also shortly join this group, fresh from the court of Margaret of Austria.[25]

Undoubtedly Elizabeth would also have been there to witness Mary's coronation in the abbey church at St Denis, just outside Paris, on Sunday 5 November. Brandon and Elizabeth's brother Dorset were also there to watch the king's sister become the official Queen of France, two among just a handful of English ambassadors who had remained in France to see her crowned. Mary was escorted to the church by the dauphin and the formalities were once again performed by Cardinal René de Prie.

The following day, 6 November, France's new queen made her formal entrance into Paris at midday. Travelling in a beautifully decorated litter, and wearing a gown of cloth of gold, adorned with precious stones, Mary was accompanied by the dauphin riding at her side. They were followed by several other French dukes, as well as Brandon and Dorset. Approaching the entrance to the city, she was met by some of the dignitaries of Paris, who accompanied her on her journey, holding a canopy of cloth of gold embroidered with fleurs-de-lis and red roses above her head. The people of Paris had spared no expense in decorating the streets and the welcome she received was incredibly warm and welcoming. That evening she returned to the Palais Royal for the banqueting, where she was seated with Claude, Marguerite, and Louise of Savoy, the dauphin's mother, as well as other nobles. All those gathered, Elizabeth no doubt included, dined in a hall decked with rich tapestries on the most sumptuous food that Paris could provide.

Just over a week later, the dauphin organised a tournament in Mary's honour at the Parc des Tournelles. King Henry was anxious that his knights should uphold the honour of England, and Brandon and Dorset headed a carefully selected team of some of the best jousters the English could provide. Elizabeth's brothers took part in this event and it was noted that Dorset and his young brother Edward, especially, had much success.

France had certainly welcomed its new queen with open arms and everyone was keen to meet Mary. In fact, a banquet held for her at the Hotel de Ville, to celebrate the coronation, caused quite a commotion. When Mary arrived, accompanied by Brandon, Francis, Claude and her

English ladies amongst others, her party was unable to enter by the front door because of the crush of people waiting to catch a glimpse of her. Eventually, they made their way in through a back door but even inside, so many women of the city had come to honour her, that some of the dishes could not reach the tables.[26]

Aged just twenty-two, Elizabeth Grey suddenly found herself in a world of pomp and splendour. She was no stranger to court life, having been the niece and granddaughter of English queens, but this was a new world, a foreign court resplendent in its own culture and customs. Travelling with Mary, she would have been witness to most if not all of the events put on to welcome her mistress to France, and certainly the first few weeks she spent on French soil must have passed in a whirlwind of activity. Her mistress was a young bride, and Elizabeth would have no doubt been looking forward to many more months of service at the French court and the experiences that would bring. But then, just three months after their wedding, the French king Louis was dead. He died on New Year's Day, 1515 and suddenly, just 140 days after she had married, Mary was a widow queen in a foreign country.

Upon Louis's death, the throne immediately passed to Francis, with Louis' daughter Claude as his queen. However, before it could be officially confirmed, they had to be completely sure that Mary was not pregnant. If she were with child and that child was a boy, the French throne would be his. With no early way of detecting a pregnancy, all Mary could do was wait until her courses began as proof that she was not carrying the heir of France. The day after Louis's death, 2 January 1515, Mary and her ladies withdrew to the Hôtel de Cluny where she would remain for a period of forty days of official mourning, and where she would earn the name that she would become known for: La Reine Blanche – The White Queen, so named because she wore mourning garments all in white. Secluded in the hotel, she cut a forlorn figure, shut away from the world and unsure of her future. Tradition dictated her rooms should remain dark with the curtains drawn, lit only by candlelight. To make matters worse, it seems that she was only allowed the company of some of her French ladies; her English companions were kept away. Elizabeth and the other young English women may have found themselves in a period of limbo, unable to be with their mistress and without a queen to serve.

Although Mary had to remain in seclusion for the required period of mourning, she had regular visits from Francis and was able to write to Wolsey and her brother, which she immediately set about doing, requesting she be allowed to return home. King Henry, for his part, was keen to have his sister back on home shores and he dispatched Charles Brandon to negotiate her return and bring her home.

With her official period of mourning ending on 11 February, it was clear that she was not pregnant and Francis was then able to make his official entry into Paris as the new King of France. This he did on 15 February, and Mary watched his parade from a window at Cluny, before attending a banquet at the palace with the new French king and queen. And it was now that Mary decided to take her future into her own hands. The arrival of Brandon in Paris gave her the opportunity she needed. Headstrong and determined to keep her brother to his word that she be allowed to now choose the man she wished to marry, when the man she adored arrived at her side, she convinced him to marry her in secret.

According to Spinelly, once Mary heard of Brandon's arrival in France, she dismissed the French servants appointed to wait on her and re-engaged her English attendants, ensuring that her entourage was loyal to her, much to Francis' displeasure.[27] Elizabeth would have suddenly found herself called back to her mistress's side. The date that Brandon and Mary wed has never been established but it was likely sometime towards the end of February. Once the deed had been done, the newlywed couple knew that they would have to break the news to Henry. Unsure of his reaction, they used Wolsey as a potential mediator, and Brandon wrote to Wolsey on 5 March stating: 'And the Queen would never let me [be] in rest till I had granted her to be married; and so, to be plain with you, I have married her harettylle and has lyen wyet her, in soo moche [as] I fyer me lyes that sche by wyet chyld'.[28]

But it was only right that the couple also wrote directly to the king to confess and in Brandon's letter to Henry, in which he apologises for acting without the king's consent, he writes of the ceremony and notes that only ten people were present. It is highly probable that Elizabeth could have been one of those ten witnesses. For the next couple of weeks, Mary and Brandon remained in France but they knew that they would have to return to England to face the wrath of Henry face-to-face. At some point before April, they journeyed back across the English Channel. Many of Mary's entourage returned with her including Mary Boleyn and Elizabeth's sister, Anne Grey. Elizabeth however chose to remain in France; at some point in early 1515, it seems she had transferred into the service of Queen Claude. She was not the only English woman to remain behind, both Mary Fiennes and Anne Boleyn also stayed on in France to serve the new French queen, Claude.[29] The reasons behind Elizabeth's decision to stay at the French court we cannot know; perhaps it was as simple as she was enjoying her time in France and keen to stay longer. Opportunities may have arisen to serve in Claude's household and she may have jumped at the chance to experience more of the French culture. Claude was also said to have been a gentle and kind woman so perhaps Elizabeth liked her and wanted to spend some more time in her household. Whatever her reasons, in April 1515, she waved her sister Anne farewell and remained with a pregnant Queen Claude in Paris, whilst King Francis travelled to Rheims.

Life at the French court under Queen Claude would likely have been a more sedate and gentle experience than it would have been under the fun-loving Mary. Born in 1499, Claude was seven years younger than Elizabeth. Small in stature, she was born with a deformity, most likely scoliosis, and it was thought that she would be unable to bear children, although she proved everyone wrong, giving birth eight times. Claude's primary residence and the place where Elizabeth probably spent the majority of her time whilst in France was the Chateau of Blois, her childhood home. This beautiful fairytale castle in the Loire Valley was just twenty miles away from her husband's main residence at Amboise. Both nestled beside the river, the journey was a relatively simple boat ride between the two. The chateau boasts the oldest grand hall in France, as well as each of its wings displaying a different period of architecture from across the centuries. During his time as king, Francis redeveloped the north wing of the chateau, which opened up onto the beautiful gardens.[30]

Francis' household was mostly based at Amboise and Elizabeth would also have spent some of her time there, travelling there with her mistress perhaps for the first time in August 1515 for the birth of Claude's first child, a girl whom they named Louise after Francis' mother. Amboise was a picturesque castle, set on top of a promontory with panoramic views across the Loire. It was here that King Francis employed and housed the Italian artist, Leonardo da Vinci. It is often written in the life story of Anne Boleyn that it was possible that she met da Vinci whilst in Claude's service and if that was the case, there is every reason to believe that Elizabeth may have met him too during her time at Amboise. Da Vinci's grave is located in the chapel next to the chateau.

Elizabeth's time at the French court would have been a great experience for her. Claude spent much time away from her husband and as a devout woman with a strict moral code, her court would have been much simpler and less raucous than that of her husband's. Often unwell, she preferred the quiet of the countryside, and Elizabeth would have spent some idyllic time in the magnificent French landscape gardens of the chateau or the beautiful countryside around it. But she would also have been able to experience the busier and more vibrant court of the French king when the two households merged, as they would have done at times. Brantome describes Claude as 'very good, very charitable and very gentle to all, never doing any unkindness or harm to anyone, either at court or in the kingdom' and it is likely that she was a kind mistress.[31] Her husband, Francis, was almost the complete opposite of her – tall and athletic and a notorious womaniser, with many mistresses. A comment made by him in later years has led to speculation that Mary Boleyn may at one point have been one of his conquests. But even though Claude and Francis were polar opposites, he had great respect for his wife and was reportedly genuinely fond of her. Francis had been crowned officially in 1515, and although he was a strong character, the dominant female influence at the French court was not Claude, but his formidable mother, Louise of Savoy, who acted as regent in his absence, including for the first time in 1515 when he went off to fight in Italy. Claude, it seemed, played a more sedentary role in her queenship, living in relative peace, bearing Francis' children and staying out of the politics of the French court. She did not even receive her official coronation until May 1517, by which point it is understood that Elizabeth had ended her time in Claude's service and had decided to return to England.

Elizabeth's destination when she eventually arrived back on English shores is unknown, but it is possible that she went back into the Brandon household, returning to her position alongside her sister. Upon their return to England in 1515, Mary and Brandon had weathered Henry's anger and were relatively quickly forgiven and welcomed back as part of the royal circle. Their first child had been born in 1516, a son named Henry in honour of the king, and Elizabeth's sister, Anne Grey, who had remained in Mary's household herself, had been given the honour of carrying the baby into the christening. Anne had been assisted during the ceremony by Lord Dacres, Mary's chamberlain, and Elizabeth's brother, Lord Edward Grey.[32]

So, it is a distinct possibility that Elizabeth did return to Mary's service. Mary was her cousin, and in her book, *The French Queen's Letters*, Erin Sadlack records that Mary retained many of the young nobles who had attended her in France. She specifically names Elizabeth Grey, although she could be confused with her sister Anne who we know did remain in Mary's service, travelling back to England with her in 1514. Other's names who remained with Mary are George Brooke, the son of Thomas, Lord Cobham, Richard Manners, the younger son of George, Lord Roos, Anne Jerningham and Humphrey Berners.[33]

Although Elizabeth and Mary were cousins, Elizabeth would not have considered it below her status working for her cousin, in fact, a position as a lady-in-waiting or a young lady to the queen or the king's sister was a much sought-after position and was considered to be a mark of high social standing. As part of the *Domus Regie Magnificencie*, the courtiers and staff who worked above stairs in the court (as opposed to the menial 'below stairs' staff such as the kitchen hands), young ladies would also hope that positions in a royal household would put them into the sphere of eligible gentlemen in the hope of one day securing themselves a good match.

Elizabeth was certainly back in England by July 1517, when she attended a banquet at Greenwich held in Mary's honour. The banquet took place on 7 July and at least three members of her own family were present, Richard and Leonard Grey who carried the king's towels and basins and Lord Edward Grey who was a gentleman usher. A diagram of their placement at the table still survives and Lady Elizabeth Grey was placed next to the Duke of Suffolk (Brandon) and the Venetian ambassador. Her brother the marquis and his wife were also seated at the same table, as was Elizabeth Boleyn, mother of Mary and Anne.[34]

At the time of the gathering, Mary was in the late stages of pregnancy. Wanting to remain at court, but aware that the time for her confinement was drawing near, she left court shortly after the banquet. However, her decision to visit Walsingham Priory on the way home put her in strife as she was forced to stop at nearby Hatfield House when she went into labour en route. It was here that she gave birth to her daughter on 16 July 1517 between 2 am and 3 am in the morning. The new baby girl was named Frances, after the saint on whose day she was born (St Francis). Elizabeth may have been travelling with her as she was chosen to be one of the stand-in godmothers, attending in proxy for the queen and Princess Mary.[35]

Baby Frances was christened on the Saturday following the birth. The road to the church was strewn with rushes and the church porch hung with rich cloth of gold and needlework in honour of their unexpected guests. The procession to the church was headed up by yeomen bearing eighty torches; another eight were carried by attending gentlemen. The other deputy godmother alongside Elizabeth was Elizabeth Boleyn whilst the Abbot of St. Alban's stood as godfather. The font used to christen baby Frances was hung with a canopy of crimson satin, decorated with red and white roses, with the sun shining, and fleur-de-lis gold and Mary's arms were displayed in fine needlework. Baby Frances was carried to the church by a Mrs Dorothy Verney, who was assisted by the Lord Powes and Sir Roger Pelston and accompanied by sixty ladies and gentlemen.[36]

After her presence at the christening of Mary's daughter, Elizabeth is once again hard to trace over the next few years. She very possibly remained in Mary's service or she may have switched to the household of Katherine of Aragon. Some reports suggest that the queen sent Elizabeth Grey and Elizabeth Boleyn as her representatives to the christening of Mary's daughter, so she may already have been in the queen's service at that point, rather than the assumption that she was travelling with Mary as one of her ladies. But we do know that in 1520 she travelled with the court back across the sea once again to France and she is listed as travelling in the queen's retinue. This may indicate that she was in service to the queen, but perhaps also as a close relation to Henry and involved in court life, she was selected to travel as part of the queen's party. Her destination was a French valley between Guisnes and Ardres and the event was arguably the most spectacular meeting of kings and courts in history: The Field of the Cloth of Gold. Several other members of her family also travelled across the sea with the English retinue, including her stepfather, Wiltshire.

The Field of the Cloth of Gold, an event that had been in the planning since 1515, took place between 7-24 June 1520. Apart from the grandeur of the concept itself, it was a magnificent display of planning on behalf of the English contingent as some 5,800 people and 3,200 horses collectively travelled across the sea to meet with those from the court of France. As this huge entourage crossed the channel on 31 May 1520, the palaces of Westminster, Greenwich, Sheen and Eltham fell empty and silent. As well as the king and queen, the dukes and the earls and the ladies and the prelates who travelled, each of those was entitled to bring their own personal attendants. Wolsey alone took with him 300 servants. With the purpose of replicating the comfort and efficiency of the English court in France, members of all the household departments, such as the bakehouse and the pantry, the spicery and the confectionery were transported across the channel to resume their duties in France. Numbers were regulated according to position; an earl for example was entitled to bring thirty people, including six gentlemen, two chaplains and thirty horses. The queen's retinue was considerably higher, numbering 1,260 persons, which included fifty-four chaplains, four barons, thirty-one knights and twenty-five gentlewomen, of which Elizabeth was one.

Not unlike the last time Elizabeth had crossed the channel in the train of the Princess Mary in 1514, the journey across to France was to prove tempestuous as Henry's ship and the accompanying flotilla crossed from Dover to Calais in the midst of a fierce storm. They arrived close to midnight and the battered English travellers needed an extra day to recover, the king sending a message to Francis that they would be delayed whilst they recovered from the journey. Eventually, on Tuesday 5 June the English party departed Calais and travelled the seven miles to Guisnes. Katherine rode beside the king on a palfrey, accompanied by her gold litter and followed by her ladies and the wagons carrying their belongings.

As the English party met up with the French party, who made their camp at Ardres, one of the ladies travelling alongside Elizabeth, Mary Boleyn, was reunited with her sister, Anne, who attended the celebrations in the train of Queen Claude of France. Elizabeth may also have greeted the woman whom she once served with at the French court.

Arriving in the French valley, a magnificent sight would have greeted them. Golden tents, decorated with roses and dragons, stood side by side with the tiltyards and the fountains. Henry's temporary residence was a two-storey pavilion, with stone foundations and brick and wood walls. On the ground floor were offices, a cellar and the kitchens and a banqueting hall. A great staircase led to the upper rooms, which was full of large and airy chambers, decorated with tapestries and silks and cloth of gold. Mary, the French queen, had two chambers in the pavilion which she shared with her husband, and the king and queen also had lodgings there.

Elizabeth is likely to have been housed in one of the many tents constructed on the site of varying sizes and colours, some plain white, others in the Tudor colours of green and white and some of the bigger tents decorated with gold and divided into several rooms within. All the halls, tents and pavilions were identified by names such as Pomegarnet, Mounteyne, The Lyon, The Manshe of Golld and The Blew Shelld.[37]

During the next two weeks, Elizabeth would have been caught up in a whirlwind of masques and jousts, food and drink, glitz and splendour. She almost certainly would have accompanied the queen and Mary when they met the French queen, Claude, for the first time on Monday 11 June, and Elizabeth too may have received a warm welcome from her one-time mistress. Reportedly Katherine arrived at the pre-arranged meeting place first in a litter covered in crimson satin and embroidered in gold. Mary also travelled by litter, decorated in cloth of gold and lilies and in respect to her first husband, his porcupine motif and the letters L & M emblazoned on the sides. Behind them three wagons followed, one gold, one crimson and one azure to transport the ladies, some of whom travelled in the litter, others riding on palfreys. The two queens spent time together taking refreshments with their ladies before the two kings arrived on horseback and the planned jousting tournament began.

It was during these two glorious weeks in the countryside of rural France that Elizabeth may have begun her relationship with the man who would become her husband. The man in question was Gerald Fitzgerald, the young lad who had spent time at the English court in the 1490s, and who was now the 9th Earl of Kildare. Whether they remembered each other from their childhood years or whether they had never met before, it was around this time that romance between them began to blossom. Perhaps as the English camp departed once more for Calais on Monday 25 June, Elizabeth's heart had been given to the man she would love for the rest of her life.

As a teenager, Gerald had returned to Ireland in 1503 at the age of sixteen. He returned to his land of birth a married man, having married Henry VII's cousin Elizabeth Zouche. Ten years after Gerald's return, in 1513, his father, the great Earl of Kildare died. Taken ill on a march to invade Ely, he was taken back to Kildare and died in September of that year. Gerald, aged twenty-six, succeeded his father and became the 9th Earl of Kildare. The powerful and highly respected 8th earl was buried in St Mary's chapel, in the choir of Christ Church, Dublin and the council nominated his son Gerald as Lord Justice to continue his father's role. Later Henry VIII also made him Lord Deputy of Ireland.

The new earl had inherited much of his father's spirit and bravery and consequently would find himself, on many occasions, in trouble like his father had been before him.[38]

By 1519, having been Lord Deputy for just over six years, the earl had found himself summoned back to England when his enemies, with the support of the king's advisor, Cardinal Wolsey, had made charges against him for maladministration. Henry demanded his presence across the channel in London to answer the charges. Before he left for England, Kildare appointed a knight from his own family, Sir Thomas FitzGerald of Laccagh, to act as deputy during his absence. Whilst he was on his way to England to answer to his king, Wolsey advised the king that the government of Ireland should be in the hands of an Englishman, someone separate from all the warring factions and families that inhabited the troubled lands across the Irish sea. Taking his advice the king appointed Thomas Howard, Earl of Surrey, to act as Lord Lieutenant and dispatched him across the sea with 100 men of the king's guard. The Earl of Surrey was the brother of Elizabeth Boleyn, and therefore uncle to Mary and Anne Boleyn. He was also the first husband of Princess Anne of York, daughter of Elizabeth Woodville and Edward IV, who had died sometime around 1512. Later on in his career, he would become better known as the infamous Duke of Norfolk.

One of Surrey's first tasks on arriving in Ireland was issued to him by Wolsey and that was to collect evidence against the Earl of Kildare from his servants and followers. Wolsey was desperate to locate a letter that Kildare had apparently sent upon his arrival in England that urged his supporters to 'Keep good peace to the Englishmen in Ireland until an English deputy come there. But when any English deputy shall come thither, then do your best to make war upon the English'.[39]

It seems the king may have had a soft spot towards the Earl of Kildare, in the same way his father Henry VII did towards Kildare's father. During his time in England, he was not kept as a prisoner but gained himself a place in the retinue of the distinguished noblemen who accompanied the king across the sea to France.

We have no contemporary description of Elizabeth but aged twenty-eight, the Field of the Cloth of Gold would have been an exciting time for her, involving herself in the pomp and splendour of the whole event and also romancing and falling in love with the man she would marry. The Earl of Kildare was famed for his handsome good looks and affable character and Holinshed describes him as 'a wise, deep, and far-reaching man; in war valiant and without rashness; and politic without treachery: such a suppressor of rebels in his government, as they durst not bear armour to the annoyance of any subject. His great hospitality is to this day rather of each man commended than of any followed. He was so religiously addicted unto the serving of God, as what time soever he travelled to any part of the country, such as were of his chapel should be sure to follow him'.[40] After the magnificent display of politics and power, gaiety and celebration that the Field of Cloth of Gold provided, the whole court was back in England by 20 September. On 6 September the Earl of Surrey wrote to Wolsey to inform him he was still unable to get his hands on the letter from Kildare that could have been construed as an act of treason if it had been located, with its instructions to his fellow countrymen to make war on the English. Elizabeth and Kildare's relationship had seemingly become common knowledge by then as Surrey reports in his letter 'It is reported that the Earl shall marry the king's kinswoman and return to his place; of which the Irish are much afraid'.[41]

Henry replied to Surrey himself in September, advising him that he had liberated Kildare but under surety not to leave England. He requested that Surrey continue in his post there and on a separate matter asked him to ascertain whether the Earl of Ormond was of a mind to marry his son to the daughter of Sir Thomas Boleyn. The Earl of Ormond's son was James Butler and the daughter of Thomas Boleyn being referred to was Anne Boleyn. Anne was at this time still at the French court but as Thomas Boleyn's only unmarried daughter a union was being explored for her with James Butler in order to solve an inheritance dispute. Piers Butler, the 8th Earl of Ormond, had inherited the title upon the death of his father in August 1515. But Thomas Boleyn's mother was also a Butler and he felt he also had a rightful claim to the Ormond estates. The king had become involved and was hoping to solve the dispute by bringing about a marriage between Pier's son, James Butler, who was serving in Wolsey's household in 1520 and Anne Boleyn.

It seems that by October 1520 Elizabeth and Kildare had married as in his reply to the king's last letter, the Earl of Surrey tells him that the prospect of the return of the Earl of Kildare, who had married 'the Kinges kyneswoman' agitated the whole island. But as Elizabeth and Kildare were beginning their married life together, it seems there were signs that perhaps all was not well with the king's marriage.

By 1520, Henry VIII had been on the throne for over a decade and during that time Queen Katherine had been unable to provide the king with his much-desired heir. After several miscarriages and stillbirths, Katherine had given birth to a healthy living girl in February 1516, whom they named Mary. But a further pregnancy in 1518 had culminated in the birth of another baby girl who died after only a few short hours. It is also thought that it was sometime during this year that the king started his affair with Mary Boleyn. Whether Mary had ever succumbed to the advances of the French king is a matter of debate, but she did catch the eye of King Henry and subsequently became his mistress. Mary was married in February 1520 to a courtier, William Carey, and the king had been a guest at their wedding. Whether their affair began before or after her wedding is unknown.

No details are recorded of where Elizabeth and Kildare lived during their first months of marriage, but perhaps they resided in rooms at court, so the king could keep the troublesome earl close. Across the sea, Surrey was having a miserable time in Ireland and he and his men were hugely troubled by bouts of fever and diarrhoea as well as not having the financial means to make their life comfortable. His return to England could not come soon enough for him and in 1521, he was recalled home, much to his relief. It seems King Henry had too much respect for Surrey's opinion to place Kildare back in charge immediately but needed someone across the sea with some degree of authority. The man the king appointed to the task was none other than Sir Piers Butler, who also was, by marriage to his sister Lady Margaret Fitzgerald, Kildare's brother-in-law. Surrey retained the position of Lord Lieutenant even though he was back in England and the Earl of Ormond was appointed as his deputy.

But Kildare could not remain in England forever. Before too long he and Elizabeth would cross the Irish sea and return to Ireland together.

Chapter 9

The Wilds of Ireland and the Wives of England

Like many of the strong women in her family who came before her, Elizabeth Grey took her fate into her own hands and married for love. That she did not gain permission from her family beforehand is referenced in a later letter from her mother who states that Elizabeth has married 'without the assent of her friends, contrary to the will of the lord marquess her father'.[1] Her father of course had died many years before but had obviously left strict instructions for the marriages of his daughters. But it seems the charismatic earl was able to win around his new family quite quickly as Elizabeth's mother and four brothers all put up bonds for Kildare's appearance before the king in 1521.[2]

The newly married couple would remain at the English court until 1523, when Kildare was 'released' by King Henry and given permission to return back home. As the Countess of Kildare, in January 1523, Elizabeth once again boarded a ship, but this time she was not sailing south, but west across the Irish Sea to her new home. Her destination in Ireland was the Fitzgerald stronghold of Maynooth Castle.

Constructed in the early thirteenth century by an ancestor of the Earl of Kildare, Maurice Fitzgerald, the beautiful Castle at Maynooth was built at the meeting of two streams, the Lyreen and the Joan Slade. Maurice Fitzgerald's son became the first Baron of Offaly; the district around Maynooth was anciently know as Ui Faelain or Offelan and by the fourteenth century, the castle was the principal residence of the Kildare branch of the Geraldines. The first Earl of Kildare died there in 1316.

Elizabeth's new home at Maynooth was, like the houses of many of the Irish nobility, both a domestic dwelling and a military fortress. Built of stone, the entrance to the castle grounds was through two gates, one leading to the town and the other to the garden, which extended down to the river. The castle keep, which played the most vital role in keeping its inhabitants safe was completed by about 1200. In one of the two vaulted rooms on the ground floor of the keep, there was a well, which was the main water supply for the castle residents and meant that if under attack, they would not have to venture outside of the castle walls.

The great hall which would have been used by the earl and his family was situated on the first floor of the keep. Divided into two rooms, the hall occupied one side whilst on the other side was the private quarters for the family. Inside the walls of the private quarters, there were three small rooms that were used as bedrooms. The second floor of the keep, a later addition, housed the extensive library of Gerald's father, the 8th earl, which contained books written in English, French, Latin and Irish. It is believed that there may also have been a second home on the site by the fifteenth century which Elizabeth may also have lived in. That also possibly contained a great hall but none of that building remains today.

An extant rental book compiled by the earl in 1518 gives us an insight into the inhabitants of Maynooth and those who would become Elizabeth's tenants and neighbours when she took up residence as countess of the manor some four years after the book was compiled. The Earl of Kildare was an astute businessman, highly capable of running his estates and managing his rents and Elizabeth, upon her arrival in 1523, may also have assisted as Mistress of Maynooth. In 1518, the recorded number of houses in the town was sixty-four, which included a respectable property that belonged to Sir Nicholas Brassel, the parish priest. Other tenants included Master Miaghe, the miller of Maynooth and Fenlagh Albanagh who inhabited the Earl's general post-house, where he was able to dispatch his messengers to all parts. The town also contained numerous cottages, occupied by those such as John Fowler, whose occupation it was to snare wildfowl, William Turner, Owen Carter, Dermot Tanner, Richard Baker, Walter Glover, and Dennis Carpenter, all whose surnames in most instances described their trade. Another cottage inhabitant and known to the earl and his family was Thomas Kerde, who lived rent-free in exchange for mending his lord's gear. Some of the female inhabitants of the town who Elizabeth may have met during her time at Maynooth were named as Meg Crese, Margery Brenane and Katherine Moran.[3]

As for Maynooth Castle itself, the place Elizabeth was to make her home, as well as the keep and the domestic quarters, it had its own brewhouse, cooper's chamber, bolting house, hall, and parlour and great chamber. Some thirty years later after the siege of Maynooth, Holinshed wrote of the riches that were found within the castle: 'Great and rich was the spoile, such store of beds, so manie goodlie hangings, so rich a wardrobe, such brave furniture, as trulie it was accounted (for household stuffe and utensils) one of the richest earle his houses under the crowne of England.[4] Amongst those great riches were tapestries, beds, arras hangings, Turkey carpets, cushions and within 'the greate chamber next the galerie' could be found 'chaires of velvet yellow, chaires of velvet grene and blew; stooles of velvet blew and grene, chaires of grene clothe and crewel, stooles of crewel'.[5] The plate belonging to the Kildares was valued at £1000 and it was reported that the earl had more than one thousand horses in his stud.

Arriving at her new home in Ireland, Elizabeth found herself living in what had become known as the English Pale. Maurice Fitzgerald had been in command of the first group of Normans to arrive in Ireland after their invasion of England in 1066. The new landowners built fortified castles against the raids of the Gaelic Irish and the Kildares quickly became one of the most powerful Anglo-Norman families. Elizabeth's new family had properties across the Pale, which covered Kildare, Louth and Meath, a region of around twenty miles centred around Dublin. The inhabitants of the Pale lived a similar life to that which Elizabeth would have known in England. Beyond the Pale, the Gaelic Irish kept their own language, customs and laws. The origin of the famous saying 'beyond the pale', meaning outside the bounds of acceptable behaviour, may have originated from the Pale in Ireland. As Earl of Kildare, Gerald Fitzgerald had the difficult role of being a subject of the English king, whilst living amongst the people of Ireland, and it is considered that perhaps more so than his forebears, he was in favour of Irish unity – Ireland for the Irish. In 1531, a visiting Ambassador, Lodovico Falier, sent back a report of his observations of England and in it, he described the situation in Ireland at the time:

> His Majesty's rule also extends to the island of Ireland, where he possesses the sea coast (*le maritime parti estreme*) and is master there. The island is large and populous, the natives warlike and wild, especially inland, where under the doublet (*corsetto*) they wear a shirt steeped in saffron (*zafferanata*) on account of the lice, and half-hose from the

knee downwards. The government used to be in the hands
of prelates, so that well nigh the whole island is divided into
abbacies and temporal bishoprics, and the Pope even now
has his collector there[6]

By the time of her arrival in Ireland, Elizabeth had been married for
around three years and there was still no sign of her dowry being paid.
The arguments that had begun in 1504 between her elder brother the
Marquis and her mother and stepfather were now having a direct effect
on her as her marriage portion was tied up in their legal squabbling. In
an extant letter from Elizabeth written to Wolsey in 1523 (discussed
later in the chapter), she requests Wolsey 'To remember me to my lady
my mother, as touching my marriage-money, when she was before your
grace' and continues 'for as yet my sayd lord and husband hat not had
enny gret proffyt by me, yet I find hym as good and kynd unto me alwes,
as eny man may be to hys wyf'.[7]

She was not the only Grey sibling to be affected either, just a few
months previous in December 1522 her brother-in-law, John Dudley,
who was married to her sister Cecily Grey, had also complained to
the king that Wiltshire was still withholding Cecily's dowry. The
financial disputes in her blood family had now been going on for nearly
twenty years, but were soon to be partly resolved, for in April 1523,
Elizabeth was to receive the news of the death of her stepfather; he died
on 6 April 1523, aged forty-four. With no sons to inherit his Earl of
Wiltshire title (he and Cecily Grey had no children together), it would
be held in abeyance until December 1529 when it would be awarded
to Thomas Boleyn. Whether Elizabeth mourned him greatly we cannot
know. She had been around thirteen years of age when he came into her
life and was old enough to remember her real father and he, therefore,
may not have taken a prominent place in her affections. Although she
may have spent a period of around nine years in his household before
she had left for France, it is likely he was away at court for long periods
of time so their relationship can only be guessed at.

His death meant that Elizabeth's mother, Cecily, was now left to pay
her husband's debts and she became tied into financial arrangements
in an agreement brokered by Wolsey that she would pay her daughter's
dowries out of her lands. Stafford had, in the end, proved himself terrible
at managing his own finances and was even in debt to the king who had

loaned him a considerable amount of money over the years; by 1521 he owed the Crown £4407 4s. Elizabeth would now have to rely on her mother to pay her what she had been promised by her father towards her marriage portion.

As Elizabeth settled into her new home in Ireland, she may have quickly come to realise that she was not going to lead a quiet and peaceful life in this new land. Trouble was never far away from the Earls of Kildare and now her husband was back in his homeland, the quarrels continued between Kildare and the new Irish Deputy, Piers Butler, the Earl of Ormond. Back on Irish soil, Kildare was without an official position but he was not going to let that stop him. As the pair squabbled, the Earl of Ormond accused Kildare of treason.

In a letter written from Maynooth in 1523, perhaps after hearing of the death of her stepfather, Elizabeth complains angrily to Wolsey about the harassment of the Earl of Ormond towards her husband and his allies. Attempting to bring about some peace and resolution to the troubles, she writes that she suspects some of this has come about because her husband has refused to get involved in the monetary disputes between the Earl of Ormond and the Boleyn family. In the letter she asks Wolsey:

> To remember me to my lady my mother, as touching my marriage-money, when she was before your grace. Asserting (certifying) your grace that I am in continual fear; and thogha of the king's deputy's sore and unfavourable demeanour unto my said lord. It is commonly noised here, that if the said deputy might have my said lord at any advantage that he would utterly destroy him; of the which I have known him twice in one morning warned ere he rose out of his bed. As I hear say, the cause why that he is so cruel disposed towards him is, for that my said lord refused to indent to have taken part with him against the heirs of the late earl of Ormond, which pretendeth title to the said earldom, in case the king's grace had willed my said lord to the contrary; which clause in no wise he would be contented withal, but would have had my said lord bound, without any exception. For the which he doth not only oppress my, said lord's friends and servants to the extremity, but also maintaineth the king's Irish rebels against him continually. And now of late, since

May last past, the said deputy hath broken divers castles longing to my said lord and to his friends, which castles was among the king's Irish rebels, and were a great defence for the king's English subjects; not only these, but divers other injuries and wrongs, daily to my said lord, his friends and servants, too long to me to write of unto your grace. And my said lord suffereth patiently the same, fearing the king's displeasure; and if it were not therefore, little would he suffer such wrongs as the said deputy doth unto him, his friends and servants. My lord complains to the king's council here still thereof, and the deputy will not be ruled by them, neither my said lord dare not stir himself, for fear of the king's displeasure; so that he hath no remedy, unless it be by the king and your grace. And it feareth me full sore that my said lord is like to take great harm in the meanwhile; beseeching your grace, for the love of God, to help for the expedition of the redress hereof, which is needful both to my said lord and to most part of all the king's subjects in this land. As knoweth God, who have your noble grace in his blessed keeping.

From my lord's manor of Maynooth, the 25th day of May. Yours, ELIZABETH KILDARE. To my Lord Cardinal's grace[8].

This letter from Elizabeth, and there may have been others, seemingly had the desired effect. Wolsey took the complaints to the king, who for his part endeavoured to bring about a reconciliation between the earls. An official order was drawn up on 28 November 1523, between Piers, Earl of Ormond and the Earl of Kildare. The arbiters were the Archbishops of Dublin and Armagh, the Prior of Kilmainham and the Chief Justice of the King's Bench and the four men were tasked to hear the evidence of both parties. They subsequently agreed, amongst other things, that 'Sir Peter [Piers] Butler, Erle of Ormound, now being the King's Deputie in his land of Ireland aforesaid, and Sir Geralde FitzGarrald, Erle of Kildayre should not make war or peace without the King's license or that of his Deputy'. That they 'should not levy coin and livery within the four obeysant shires, Meth, Urgell, Dublin, and Kildayre' and that the two earls should persuade their kinsmen to submit to the laws. Also, that neither of the earls should allow the Irish enemies of the other to remain in his castles or allow the Irish enemies of the other to remain in his castles on the borders of the other's country.

For a while, both men kept their part of the bargain, but an incident that occurred between associates of the two men soon brought the peace to an end. James Talbot, a favourite ally of the Earl of Ormond was on his way to spend Christmas with Ormond at Kilkenny Castle, when he came across James Fitzgerald, one of Kildare's men. Whatever transpired between Fitzgerald and Talbot, Talbot ended up dead. A furious Ormond took out an impeachment against Kildare in England and was backed by his countess who, also furious with her brother, took active steps to have him punished by producing a letter that Kildare had written to the rebel Earl of Desmond requesting a meeting with him. Desmond was wanted by the English for 'misdemeanours against the king.' The Countess of Ormond had apparently stolen the letter from one of Kildare's messengers while he was staying in their house.

Elizabeth, keen to defend her husband, turned to her brother, the Marquis of Dorset for help. Dorset managed to persuade the king that the matter should be dealt with by an enquiry in Ireland. The king obliged and ordered his commissioners, Sir Ralph Egerton, Sir Anthony Fitzherbert, Justice of the Common Pleas, and James Denton, Dean of Litchfield to look into the matter. If the charges against Kildare were not proven, the king ordered that the Earl of Ormond should be removed from office and Kildare should be appointed Lord Deputy instead.

In his defence, Kildare argued that he had written the letter to Desmond on his arrival in Ireland in early 1523 and was ignorant of Desmond's misdemeanours. The commissioners decided in Kildare's favour and on 28 July 1524, a further indenture was drawn up between the two men and they agreed to forgive each other of any wrongs they had committed, to be friendly to each other and to side with each other against the king's enemies. A week later, on 4 August 1524, Kildare was restored as Lord Deputy.[9] Much to Elizabeth's relief her cousin, the king, like his father before him, had reached the conclusion that the English needed Kildare in a position of power as much as Ireland did. The earl and countess celebrated by throwing a splendid banquet for the commissioners.

During the enquiry, Elizabeth may have been in the initial stages of pregnancy as in 1525 she gave birth to their first son together, a son whom they named Gerald after his father. It is possible that Gerald was not their first child; during their marriage the couple would have two boys and three girls together. One of their daughters, Cecily, whose birth date is unknown may actually, for reasons discussed later in the book, have been their first child and therefore born somewhere between 1520 and 1524. It is possible, or even probable that Elizabeth and Gerald made their first trip across the sea to Maynooth in 1523 with Cecily, a toddler, in tow. The earl also had several children from his first marriage: Thomas Fitzgerald who by then was twelve years old and his sisters, Alice and Mary, who would have been slightly younger. Elizabeth would have become their stepmother upon her arrival in Ireland and the whole blended family would no doubt have celebrated the birth of the newest addition in 1525.

With her husband now restored to his position as deputy, Elizabeth may have hoped that things would be less turbulent going forward and as 1526 came around the troubles had abated a little, perhaps allowing them some peaceful family life. As the king's representative in Ireland, Kildare had a key role that required him to keep the king's castles in good repair and to do his best to make the people of the Pale speak, dress, and shave like Englishmen. He was the king's trusted servant across the sea and in that prominent position he had to behave himself.

But by the end of summer 1526, Kildare was once again forced to write to the king to apologise. Writing from Maynooth on 17 August, he says that he had received the king's instructions, dated 20 May, instructing him to pay within twenty days his due half of the subsidy and other revenues, which amounted to 800 pounds. He tells the king that he had not received his letter until St Laurence's Eve (9 August) and had already paid the Earl of Ormond all that he had received but it did not amount to that much. He hoped that Henry would not listen to the lies of his enemies and implored the king that he was bound to him, not only by his oath of allegiance, but because, after being brought up in his service, King Henry made him treasurer, and gave him lands worth 100 marks a year. He also wrote 'My first wife was your poor kinswoman and my wife now in like manner; and in all my troubles before this, by untrue surmises against me, ye were good and gracious unto me.' The letter was delivered to the king by Elizabeth's brother, Lord Leonard Grey, who also showed the king articles on the earl's behalf detailing the Earl of Ormond's misdemeanours since the commissioners had left.[10]

It seems once again though the Earl of Ormond had been complaining to the king of Kildare's behaviour. His accusations were that scarcely a word of English could be heard in the county of Kildare and that its inhabitants wore Irish garments so that they could not be distinguished from Irishmen. Ormond accused Kildare of tolerating this behaviour and even went as far as to accuse him of wanting to take the Pale away from English rule. To further push his complaints, Ormond travelled to England personally in September 1526 to gain a personal audience with the king. Arriving at court with his list of complaints, he also accused Kildare of conspiring with his Irish enemies to help the Earl of Desmond and of neglecting to arrest him when ordered to do so by special letters from the king. Kildare's pleas to Henry to ignore his enemies' accusations and to remember his allegiance to him failed and the earl was once again summoned to London. Elizabeth must have received the news with horror, especially as around this time she was likely pregnant again. Upon his arrival in London, Kildare was sent straight to the Tower.

Called before the council to answer the charges against him, it seems that Wolsey, Henry's chief advisor, was not going to be his ally. Wolsey is said to have berated him during the hearing, calling him 'King of Ireland' and questioning why he was unable to arrest Desmond who had acted against the Crown of England. The earl, in his defence, likened Wolsey to being 'as much a King in England' as he was in Ireland and queried why the Earl of Desmond's capture rested solely on his shoulders.

Having taken a dressing down, the earl angrily challenged Wolsey, stating that he would willingly change places for a month. In a passionate plea he argued: 'I slumber in a hard cabin, when you sleep in a soft bed of down; I serve under the King his cope of heaven, when you are served under a canopy; I drink water out of my skull, when you drink wine out of golden cups; my courser is trained to the field, when your genet is taught to amble; when you are begraced and belorded, and crouched and kneeled unto, then find I small grace with our Irish borderers, except I cut them off by the knees'.[11]

This impassioned defence clearly illustrates the difficult position Kildare was often in in trying to maintain a part of Ireland for the English Crown. The earl was clearly no saint, but the challenge of representing a faceless king to the people in Ireland cannot have been easy. The Council was adjourned and Kildare was sent back to the Tower until such time that further evidence that Wolsey was apparently seeking could arrive from Ireland. That evidence would have not been easily forthcoming as allegedly before leaving Dublin, Kildare had taken the precaution of meeting with each councillor separately and binding him by oath to write in his defence.

It had now come down to a battle of wills between the king's closest advisor and the man who officially or unofficially held the power to rule over Ireland. It is alleged that Wolsey at that time, took it upon himself to send a death warrant to the Governor of the Tower, which arrived while the governor was playing shovelboard with his prisoner. With his charisma and likeability, Kildare had even charmed the governor and upon reading the contents of the message, Kildare begged the governor to go straight to the king at Whitehall to ascertain his intentions. Unwilling to disobey Wolsey, but even more unwilling to disobey Kildare, the governor did just that and was admitted into the king's presence, even though it was ten o'clock at night. The gamble paid off and the king immediately overturned the execution, using strong language to reprimand Wolsey and threatening him with unpleasant consequences.[12]

Elizabeth must have been hugely relieved, particularly if she had heard how close her husband came to meeting his end. Wolsey, having been berated by the king, tried to persuade Henry that at the very least Kildare should be removed from government and that the deputyship should be returned to the Earl of Ormond, but with his son actually taking over the reins. Henry refused astutely stating that the young James Butler was far too inexperienced to rule Ireland and that the noblemen of the Pale would never follow the rule of one younger than they. And although Kildare had escaped death, he did not completely escape punishment, with Henry declaring that Kildare should remain imprisoned. His stay in the Tower would last for the next four years.

Back in Ireland, Elizabeth gave birth to their third child, a girl whom they named Elizabeth. It is believed she was born in Maynooth in 1527 so presumably, Elizabeth had not travelled to London with her husband, conceivably due to her pregnancy. However, at some point after her daughter's birth, she must have made her way to England, perhaps even to introduce her husband to their new baby girl. Even though he was confined to the Tower, Elizabeth was seemingly given visitation rights as their fourth child, a boy whom they named Edward, was said to have been eight years old in 1536, giving him a birth date of 1528. He must therefore have been conceived during Kildare's imprisonment.

But even with access to her husband, it must have been a worrying time for Elizabeth and she no doubt tried to intercede on his behalf with her cousin, the king. But Henry around this time had other things on his mind. A few years earlier, Elizabeth had been followed back to the English court by another of her fellow English ladies who had remained to serve Queen Claude. That lady was Anne Boleyn. Anne had returned back to English shores several years after Elizabeth, sometime around 1522, and had secured a place in the service of Katherine of Aragon, alongside her sister Mary Boleyn. And like her sister, Mary, she too had caught the eye of the king, eventually replacing her sister Mary in his affections. But unlike Mary, Anne was prepared to play the long game and had refused to become the king's mistress. By 1526 when the king began paying court to Anne, he had been married to Queen Katherine for seventeen years. They still had only the one daughter, Princess Mary, although Katherine had gone through five further pregnancies, all of which had resulted in stillbirths or infant death. Her last pregnancy had been 1518 and it was now clear that she would no longer be able to provide him with any more children. Yet Henry desperately wanted a son and heir. He had already fathered a boy in 1519 but by his then mistress Elizabeth (Bessie) Blount, but this was not enough, he needed a legitimate heir. So when Anne Boleyn entered his orbit, raven-haired, exotic and full of wit and intelligence, yet refusing to succumb to his charms, Henry wanted her, both as his lover and as time went on and she would continue to refuse to be just his mistress, as a potential second wife who may just be able to provide him with a legitimate son. The only problem was what to do with his first wife and queen?

Whether Elizabeth remained in England during the whole of Kildare's imprisonment or whether she travelled between London and her estates in Ireland is unknown. But if she were in or around the court in the late 1520s, she almost certainly would have heard the gossip about the king's attraction to Anne and may even have witnessed herself their growing relationship. She obviously knew Anne Boleyn; whether she liked her or not is impossible to tell. But having herself served both the queen and the king's sister, Mary, who came out fully in support of her sister-in-law the queen, Elizabeth would later prove to be fully against Henry's new relationship, as she too joined the growing number of women throwing their support behind Queen Katherine.

Whilst her husband was incarcerated, Elizabeth did receive some good news when in 1527 she finally received payment of her dowry. Comments made by her mother at the time give credence to the fact that Elizabeth's marriage was a love match and that her family had forgiven her for marrying without permission. Cecily Grey declared that she had paid all her daughter's dowries, including to her daughter, Elizabeth, Countess of Kildare, even though she married 'without the assent of her friends, contrary to the will of the lord marquess her father, by reason whereof the said £1000 ought not to be paid'. Cecily explained she was giving Elizabeth the money nonetheless 'forasmuch as the said marriage is honourable, and I and all her friends have cause to be content with the same'.[13]

Even whilst imprisoned the Earl of Kildare was still able to cause trouble and in 1528, from his prison cell, he managed to stir up rebellion in Ireland by making himself chief governor for life. His eldest son Thomas Fitzgerald, by Kildare's first wife, was by then a young lad of fifteen. In 1528, he declared his allegiance to his father and much of the Pale had followed suit. Consequently, Henry soon found himself in a situation where the allegiance of much of Ireland was to the Earl of Kildare rather than himself. Realising the situation, Henry thought it prudent to give the earl his liberty, once again appreciating that he needed the earl as his only hope in controlling the wild men of Ireland. But still reluctant to relinquish all power to Kildare, he was determined to have an English man in charge, even if in name only, to hold Ireland for the Crown and to that end, he appointed his nine-year-old bastard son, Henry Fitzroy, as Lord Lieutenant.[14]

As he was still a child, the Duke of Richmond did not travel to Ireland in person, meaning Kildare was effectively the powerhouse in his homelands. But for a short time after his release from prison, Henry demanded he remained at the English court. We have no evidence as to whether Elizabeth remained with him or whether she had returned to Ireland and the family estates.

As 1528 turned into 1529, the marriage of the king and queen was irretrievably breaking down. Henry was desperate to achieve an annulment of his marriage to Katherine so he could marry Anne and had set Wolsey the task of finding a way to bring this about. By 1529, the king's great matter as it became known had been rumbling on for several years. Henry believed that his lack of children by Katherine was punishment from God for marrying his brother's wife and felt this was a good reason why their marriage should be ended. His relationship and desire to marry Anne was now public knowledge. But the queen, with her strong Catholic beliefs in the sanctity of marriage and queenship was not going to go quietly. She believed with all her heart that her marriage was legal, as was her position as queen, and she had appealed to her nephew, Holy Roman Emperor Charles V and the Pope to defend her case.

As the Pope's permission was required for Henry to obtain his divorce, Wolsey had managed to succeed in getting the Pope to send a representative to England. The man who would hear the case was one Cardinal Campeggio, who had arrived in England under the instructions from the Pope to hear Henry's case for a divorce but to ensure the matter was not brought to a speedy conclusion. On 1 May 1529, the proceedings began at Blackfriars. Henry's evidence was that he believed that marrying his brother's wife was a sin in the eyes of God. Katherine's defence was that she and Arthur had never consummated their marriage so in the eyes of God, she was Henry's true wife. As a young lad who had been residing at the English court at the time of the marriage between Prince Arthur and Katherine, Kildare was called as a witness alongside Elizabeth's brother, the Marquis of Dorset. In November 1501 after Katherine and Arthur's wedding, both Dorset and Gerald Fitzgerald had been part of the bedding ceremony, escorting the prince to his chamber where the young couple would have been put to bed and blessed in their union, with the expectation that they would bear healthy children together. Dorset told the court how he recalled having seen Katherine awaiting Arthur under the bedclothes during the bedding ceremony and how he had noted Arthur's healthy complexion the next day. Another courtier, Sir Anthony Willoughby also testified that the morning after his wedding, Arthur emerged from Catherine's bedchamber to say, 'Willoughby, bring me a cup of ale, for I have been this night in the midst of Spain'.

On 29ᵗ June, the queen was called to Blackfriars and she knew this was her chance to fight for her rights as a wife, a queen and a woman. Refusing to abide by the etiquette of the court, she entered the building and walked up to the king. Kneeling in front of him, she gave the speech of her life, announcing herself as his true wife, she declared 'This twenty years have I been your true wife, or more, and by me ye have had divers children, although it hath pleased God to call them out of the world, which has been no fault of mine. And when ye had me at the first, I take God to be my judge, I was a true maid without touch of man; and whether it be true or no, I put it to your conscience'. When she had finished her impassioned plea, she rose and walked back out the way she had come, ignoring the calls for her to return and declaring she would accept no judgement from this court who were no friends of hers and would commit her case to God himself.

The legatine court at Blackfriars closed shortly after, with the Pope recalling Campeggio back to Rome where they would decide the case, although the Pope had no intention of permitting Henry an annulment or divorce. With Henry's great matter rumbling on, Kildare was finally released and permitted to return to Ireland in 1530. Filled with relief at having her husband home, Elizabeth must have been keen to settle back into family life in Maynooth. But clearly the shock of the last four years living without her husband by her side had made Elizabeth anxious about her future and that of her children. To secure herself some sort of financial stability, unbeknownst to her husband it seems, she wrote directly to the most powerful man she felt could give her assistance, her cousin, the king. In the letter she is clearly anxious that her husband's inheritance upon his death would go to the children of his first marriage rather than her own children:

> After my most humble recommendation, please it to your Grace to be advertised that I am your poor oratrice and kinswoman, advanced by your grace and married to your faithful and true subject the earl of Kildare, who hath fair issue by his first wife; and by reason of former assurances made by the said earl my husband, long time before my marriage, of all his lands in effect to the use of his said former issue, which lawfully cannot be dissolved or broken; and such of his lands not comprised within the said assurances being but of little value and profit, and also being amongst the wild Irish, and by the same continually wasted and destroyed, so that the same is of very little profit, and also far from the succour of the English pale, and the residence of my said lord's lands, if need should require; whereof my said husband is contented to insure such issue male as is betwixt him and me, which I think little or none advancement to my children, being of your most royal blood. In consideration whereof I most humbly beseech your grace to be so good and gracious lord unto me and my poor children, that it may please the same to

grant unto me and to my son, Gerald Fitzgerald, in farm for term of sixty-one years, the manors of Rathwin, Castle Ricard, Rathcoure, Balsheagh, and Balrayn, in the county of Meath. I and my said son paying unto your grace and to your heirs yearly, during the said term, for the said manors in your exchequer here, like as your grace hath had for them in times past, according the extent of the same, appearing of record in the said exchequer; which shall be no hinderance to your grace in your revenues, and yet the same shall be a great commodity for me and my said son, whereby he may hereafter be the more able to do you noble service in this your land of Ireland. As knoweth God, &c. ELIZABETH KILDARE[15]

Referencing her family ties to the king and that her children are of the same royal blood, she appeals directly to his sense of family. Her closeness to her brother, Leonard Grey, is also clear at this point as he also wrote to Cromwell at the same time pressing her suit, enclosing a copy of Elizabeth's letter to the king. In his letter, Leonard added 'Sir, my sister Kildare would have you labour this as secretly as you can, because my lord her husband should not know of her suit, for she supposeth he would be more gladder to get these manors unto his eldest son than unto this son that he hath by my sister'.

This addition from Leonard is interesting. Undoubtedly Elizabeth and Kildare had married for love, and were presumably still very much in love, but it seems that for whatever reason she did not wish him to know about her letter to the king. Perhaps he was as headstrong in their relationship as he was in life. That Elizabeth was prepared to go behind his back to try and secure the future of her own children illustrates that she also had strength of character and an ardent desire to do whatever was needed to protect her children. Henry did agree to help his cousin and she afterwards received an annual pension of 200 marks from Henry VIII, to be paid quarterly as detailed in the king's accounts in 1532 when she received a payment of 33l 6s 8d.[16]

Later in 1530, Elizabeth was to receive devastating news when in October that year her mother died. Cecily Grey was sixty-one when she passed away on 10 October 1530. It is believed she may have been in London at the time of her death so perhaps Elizabeth had been able to spend some time with her fairly recently. She was buried in the church at Astley, alongside Elizabeth's father. Her vast Bonville inheritance that she had received from her father mostly passed into the hands of Elizabeth's eldest brother, Thomas, Marquis of Dorset, although her other living brothers received several of her manors and her daughters, Elizabeth included, were left money. During the latter years of her life, after the death of Stafford, Cecily had spent her time designing the Dorset aisle in the church of Ottery St Mary and it is one of her most beautiful legacies. Steeped in her family connections, the Staffords and the Hastings families are all represented, alongside heraldic details such as the Bourchier knot and the Wake knot, representing the families of two of her daughter's husbands. Also featured is the crest of Fitzgerald, representing Elizabeth's marriage and the joining of the Grey family with that of the Earls of Kildare. Sadly, more unwelcome news would follow just a few months later when Elizabeth's eldest brother, Thomas, also died. He barely had time to enjoy his mother's vast estates, and upon his death, they passed to his eldest son, the then thirteen-year-old Henry Grey, Elizabeth's nephew, who inherited all his properties and his title of marquis.

Perhaps with the financial security of his family also now on the earl's mind after the death of two of Elizabeth's family members in 1531, Kildare secured a private act of parliament assuring Elizabeth an annual income of £200 for life from his estates, with a clause allowing her possession of the manor of Portlester after his death if she chose to live in Ireland. The manor of Portlester had been given to the earl in an indenture of 1502/3 when he married his first wife, Elizabeth Zouche. It was drawn up between the then king (Henry VII) and Gerald's father, the 8th Earl of Kildare. The earl assented to the marriage of his son Gerald, 'who was brought up in his yought and tender age at the king's court, to Elizabeth Zouche, kinswoman to Margaret the king's mother, to be solemnized before 1 Aug. next at Margaret's manor of Colyweston, where she now kepith her honorable houshold'. The king agreed to bear the cost of their clothes and of the ceremonies and the earl was 'to make estate before Whitsuntide next to his son and Elizabeth and the heirs male of their two bodies of the lordships and manors of Moylaghe co. Meath and Rathamghan co. Kildare of the clear yearly value of 100 m., of which they shall take the issues from the date of this indenture, and also of the lordships or manors of Portlester and Moynalwey co. Meath of the same yearly value, of which the earl will take the issues during his life'.[17]

Perhaps in his eagerness to consider the future of his wife and children, it seems that for a while Kildare was also keen to make an effort to keep on the good side of the king. An item in the king's accounts for 10 June 1532 detail a payment to a servant of Kildare's in reward for presenting a couple of 'hobyes' (horses or ponies) to the king at Greenwich. That same year he also made a trip to London to the court, where he apparently stayed for six months, returning back to Ireland with the legal as well as the real power of Chief Governor.[18] Given the closeness of their relationship, it is likely that Elizabeth travelled with him. This time during their trip to England they would have found the court a vastly different place. Unable to procure the king's divorce for him, an infuriated Henry had had Wolsey arrested, although he had died in 1530 before he could be tried and sentenced. Then in 1531, Queen Katherine had been banished from court and her rooms had been given over to Anne and it had been left to Henry's new chief minister, Thomas Cromwell, to find a way to secure Henry's divorce. This he had done by passing several acts through parliament recognising royal supremacy over the church, effectively putting Henry as head of his own Church of England and therefore able to make his own decisions on divorce and marriage and all but paving the way for the king to divorce the queen under his own authority. This bold and momentous plan, put together by Cromwell and supported by the Boleyns, removed England from the jurisdiction of the Pope and the Catholic church and heralded the beginning of the Church of England.

If Elizabeth did spend some time at court in 1532, it may have been an awkward time for her with Anne in so prominent a position. Many women in England at the time supported Katherine and her rights as a wife to not be cast aside at the whim of her husband. Du Bellay, a French ambassador writing to his master King Francis in 1529 after Katherine's appearance at the Blackfriars court wrote that 'If the matter [of Henry's divorce] was to be decided by women, he would lose the battle; for they did not fail to encourage the queen at her entrance and departure [to the court] by their cries, telling her to care for nothing, and other such words'.[19]

One of Queen Katherine's most ardent supporters was Elizabeth's former mistress, the king's sister, Mary. Once an integral part of court life, she all but refused to come to court once Anne had taken the queen's place. Like many aristocratic women, she felt strong enough in her defence of Katherine as a wronged wife to defy not just her brother's wishes but to question the actions of the king. Many others such as the Duchess of Norfolk, the Marchioness of Exeter and the Countess of Salisbury made it clear that they were also willing to disobey patriarchal authority to champion a queen. Elizabeth may have found herself in a difficult position if she had once been friends with Anne, but it seems that she too was a supporter of the woman she had likely known for many years. And it was not only women of the gentry class that made their feelings clear, the common women of London were also, seemingly, not afraid to make their opinions known. Lodovico Favalier in November 1531 recorded a rather frightening incident that had happened in late 1531 when Anne was dining at a house by the river. The king was not with her and upon hearing news of her whereabouts, a mob of some 7-8000 women turned up at the house in demonstration. Anne, having received notice of their approach, managed to escape through the gardens that ran down to the river and away by boat. According to Favalier, the women had intended to kill her. Even more frightening for Anne, amongst the mob were several men dressed as women. Surprisingly the king, on hearing the news, decided not to issue any retribution because, according to Favalier, he considered it 'a thing done by women'.[20]

Favalier, in his report of England, also gives us an incredibly detailed description of the country during the 1530s, the England that would have been so familiar to Elizabeth. He begins by describing the king and queen, writing that Queen Katherine 'is of low stature, rather stout with a modest countenance; she is virtuous, just, replete with goodness and religion; she speaks Spanish, Flemish, French, and English; she is beloved by the islanders more than any queen that ever reigned; she is about forty-five years old, having lived thirty years in England, from the time of her first marriage'. He then goes on to describe Henry: 'In this eighth Henry, God combined such corporal and mental beauty, as not merely to surprise but to astound all men. Who could fail to be struck with admiration on perceiving the lofty position of so glorious a Prince to be in such accordance with his stature, giving manifest proof of that intrinsic mental superiority which is inherent to him? His face is angelic rather than handsome; his head imperial and bald, and he wears a beard, contrary to English custom'. The French queen, Mary, and her husband also get a mention: 'The Lord Suffolk [Charles Brandon] ... is 61 years of age, very robust, and although not of very noble lineage, yet as he has for wife his Majesty's sister, widow of King Lewis of France, much honour and respect are paid him; and he has the second seat in his Majesty's Privy Council, which he rarely enters, save for the discussion of matters of a certain importance, passing his time more pleasantly in other amusements'.

He then switches his attention to describing England itself and his report of its climate would perhaps be of no surprise to us today: 'The climate is neither warm nor cold, but very damp. In the northern parts [of England] the longest day is of nineteen hours, and of sixteen and a half to the southward'. Describing the land: 'The soil is reddish, and sufficiently cultivated for their maintenance, with wheat, barley, and spelt, the rest is laid out in very beautiful meadows and most profitable pasturages for cattle and innumerable flocks of sheep, which remain the whole year in the open air; so that the English are extremely well supplied with the best wool, which they convert into every sort of superfine cloth; and their amount of hides is incredible. The olive and the vine have, however, been denied them, instead of which they use malt liquor, made with crab-apples and hops, and other ingredients, from which, by boiling them, they obtain a drink as intoxicating as the strongest wine. The island is ennobled by 22 cathedral cities; 50 towns, some walled and some open; and 1300 villages, the whole being divided into 35 counties'.

Describing the well-known landmarks of London Bridge and the Tower, he writes: 'The city of London has a most noble bridge, on which are lofty edifices, with shops containing goods of all sorts, and in its centre a most beautiful church, to be seen rather than described'. And of the Tower: 'The Tower, although washed by the Thames, and surrounded by walls, is not a strong fortress. The king keeps his artillery and ammunition there; and there he coins his money, which is of much lower standard than it used to be. The Tower is garrisoned by a captain with a few foot soldiers, and their retainers. All criminals of importance are confined there. The English say that the castle was built by Julius Caesar, and on this they pride themselves'. Elizabeth's nephew, Henry Grey, the new Marquis of Dorset also gets a mention: 'There are also two marquises. One of Exeter ... the other is the Marquis of Dorset, a youth eighteen years of age, with a revenue of 15,000 ducats. He is under charge of the Court of Wards, which requires feudatories to remain dependent on his Majesty, if orphans, until their twentieth year, after which age no one can prosecute them'.[21]

The Earl of Kildare finally returned to Ireland in late 1532. Assuming Elizabeth to have travelled with him, she too would have returned, perhaps ready for the Christmas season. But it was to turn out to be a fateful decision. On 21 December 1532, Walter Cowley, the Principal Solicitor of Ireland wrote to Thomas Cromwell and reported that 'My Lord of Kildare, for the mayntenaunce of his son- in-law, Fergenanym O'Karroll, besedged a castell which appertayned to the adversaries of his said son-in-law, with whom they were in strife for the name and Lordship of O'Karroll, and that there then my said Lord of Kildare was shott with a hand gon thorow the syde , under the ribbes , and so lyeth in great daunger'.

Fergenanym was the illegitimate but favourite son of Mulroney the Great, the head of the O'Carroll clan and when Mulroney died in 1532, Fergenanym relied on Kildare to enforce his claims against his uncles. The earl, it seems, offered his support as Fergenanym was his son-in-law. Who Fergenanym was married to is not clear, but it is possible that he was married to Cecily, as the earl's daughters from his first marriage seem to have been married elsewhere. If so, it would indicate that Cecily was most likely Elizabeth and Gerald's eldest child. She would have been wed at quite a young age; if she was born in 1521 for instance, she must have been married by 1532, but this in itself was not unusual and her marriage may have been arranged to bring about an alliance between the Kildares and the O'Carrolls. Indeed, Fergenanym would later support the earl's son Thomas in his rebellion.

Christmas 1532 must have been a solemn affair at Maynooth. Kildare was lying seriously ill from the bullet wound and Elizabeth would have been concerned for his life, praying for his survival as she nursed him as best she could. With the earl injured and perhaps facing death, his enemies seized on the opportunity to bring about his downfall. Several of them journeyed to England to make their complaints directly to the king. In early 1533, the Council reported that there was such antagonism between the Earls of Kildare and Ormond, that it would be impossible to reconcile them. In another report sent to Cromwell which he took to the king, it was claimed the Irish were committing many outrages. Kildare's enemies claimed that a son of the Earl of Ormond had been killed and that John, Kildare's brother, had attacked the McMahons, where he himself was wounded and thirty of his men were killed. Allegedly Thomas, Kildare's son and heir had also been involved in violence against the O'Reylys. Perhaps the last straw was a report to Cromwell that the council in Ireland were hugely corrupted with their affection to the Earl of Kildare and yet in such dread of him that they dare not act against him. Once again Kildare was summoned to England to answer the charges.

Perhaps due to his injury and also because possibly he sensed that his chances were running out, Kildare sent Elizabeth over to see her cousin, the king, to intercede on his behalf. Once again Elizabeth would have boarded a ship to cross the Irish sea, this time with her mind full of worry but with a determination to persuade the king to ignore her husband's enemies. It is believed that she took her two daughters with her on her journey to England, Elizabeth who would have been around six years old and her youngest Margaret, whose birth date is unknown but she would have been a toddler in 1533. She reached the English court in October of that year and requested an audience with her cousin, the king. Whatever transpired between them, she was unsuccessful in her suit and the king demanded that Kildare attend him in person. Back home in Ireland, Kildare received letters brought to him at Maynooth from the king and from Elizabeth herself by a manservant, Robert Reyley, who was in Kildare's service. Seemingly Elizabeth delayed these letters as long as she could. Perhaps Elizabeth also feared that her husband had used too many of his nine lives and this time he may not emerge from another spell in the Tower. But even with her efforts to delay the letters, she had to follow the king's orders and eventually her husband was advised by this correspondence of the news that he had no choice but was required in England to defend himself against the charges. He was permitted to name any person he wanted as deputy during his absence and before embarking at Drogheda, Kildare delivered his sword to his eldest son, Thomas, in the presence of several members of Council. Also known as Silken Thomas because of the silken trimmings around his helmet, Kildare's son was by then about twenty years old. His father advised him to be guided in all things by his uncle, Sir James Fitzgerald; his cousin, Sir Thomas Eustace; his great-aunt, Lady Janet Eustace, and her husband and son, Walter and James Delahide. He reportedly told his son that 'his youth should be guided by age; his ignorance by experience' and urged him to defer to the Council, 'for albeit in authority you rule them, yet in counsel they must rule you'.[22]

Holinshed's account records the speech that Kildare allegedly made when handing over the reins of power to his son:

> Sonne Thomas, I doubt not but you know that my sovereign Lord, the King, hath sent for me to Englande, and what shall betyde me, God knoweth, for I know not. But howsoever it falleth, both you and I know, that I am well steped in years; and as I may shortly die, for that I am mortal, so must I in haste decease, bicause I am old. Wherefore, in so much as my wynter is well neare ended and the spring of your age now buddeth, my will is that you behave yourselfe so wisely in these your greene yeares, as that to the comfort of your friends, you may enjoy the pleasure of sommer, gleane and reape the fruit of your harvest, that with honour you may growe to the catching of that hoarie winter, on which you see me, your father, fast pricking. And whereas it pleaseth the King, his Majestie, that upon my departure hence, I should substitute in my roome such one, for whose government I would answere; albeit I know that your yeares are tender, your wit not settled, your judgment not fully rectified and therefore I myght bee with good cause re claymed from putting a naked sworde in a young man's hande, yet notwithstanding, for as much as I am your father, and you my sonne, I am well assured to beare that stroke with you in steering your ship, as that upon any information I may commande you as your father, and correct you as my sonne, for the wrong handling of your helme. There be here that set at this bourde far more sufficient personages for so great a charge than you are. But what then? If I should cast this burthen on their shoulders, it might bee that hereafter they woulde be so farre with envie carryed, as they would percase hazard the losse of one of their owne eyes, to be assured that I should be deprived of both mine eyes. But forasmuch as the case toucheth your skinne as neare as mine, and in one respect nigher than mine, bycause, as I sayde before, I rest in the winter and you in the spring of your yeares; and nowe I am resolved, day by day, to learn rather how to die in the fear of God, than to live in the pompe of the worlde, I thinke you will not be so brain.

Then no doubt hugging his son goodbye, he and Reyley set off on their journey to the English court, no doubt with the thought in his mind that this may well be the last time he saw his son, his manor and his homeland.

Whilst waiting for her husband to arrive in England, Elizabeth may have had time to mourn and reflect on the loss of her former mistress, Mary, the French queen, who died in June of that year. In early 1533, their two families had been brought even closer together when Elizabeth's nephew, Henry Grey, had married the Brandon's daughter, Frances, to whom Elizabeth had acted as a deputy godmother at her christening sixteen years before. Frances was the same age as her husband and their first daughter, Jane Grey, would be born three years later. Even though both Mary and Brandon were in London to celebrate the wedding, neither attended a banquet organised by Henry and Anne for the French ambassadors on 8 March 1533. The exact cause of Mary's death is unknown although she had been ailing for a while – in the days leading up to the Field of Cloth of Gold in 1520, Brandon had written to Wolsey that he had not attended council recently as Mary had had several physicians for a disease in her side. Shortly before Mary died, on 23 June, she wrote to her brother to say she had been very sick and ill at ease. She had sent for Master Peter the physician but was rather worse than better although she hoped that she could come to London soon with her husband to see the king 'as she had been a great while out of his sight and hopes not to be so long again'.[23] Sadly, she likely never got to see him as she died between the hours of seven and eight o'clock in the morning of 25 June at her home at Westhorpe and was interred in Bury St Edmunds Abbey, her body later being moved to St Mary's Church, Bury St Edmunds in the eighteenth century. She was thirty-seven years old.

The Earl of Kildare finally arrived in England to answer his summons sometime around April 1534. In a letter from Chapuys, the Spanish Ambassador, writing to his master, Holy Roman Emperor Charles V, he wrote:

> I have not been able to learn more about the earl of Desmond than I formerly wrote. The earl of Kildare is here, sick both in body and brain by the shot of a harquebus, which he received long ago, and there is no hope of his recovery, so that he must not be counted among those who will serve your majesty. I am told he has brothers, who are good enough

fellows, but they have no power. He has a son who is said to be a likely fellow for his age, but his father being here, I know not if he would give ear to it. Some think that if the Pope were to send someone to Ireland, or the censures of his Holiness were duly executed and published, there would be some commotion, for they hold themselves entirely subject to the Apostolic See. I send the statutes made against the Pope, the Queen and Princess. London, 22 April 1534.[24]

By April 1534, Queen Katherine, still banished from court, was living at the Bishop of Lincoln's Palace at Buckden. Chapuys was working hard for her cause, acting as a messenger between her and nephew Charles and doing his best to protect her interest and that of her daughter, Princess Mary. The king had made the break from Rome and seemingly the Spanish were looking to see if they could make alliances with the Irish. By July 1534, Kildare had appeared before the council. As the charges were brought against him, this time he felt their full wrath. One of the most serious charges against him was that he had fortified his own castles using the king's weapons. He could only answer that he had intended to defend the Pale against the Irish. He was still suffering from his injury and no longer the young gallant cavalier who could charm his accusers and defend the charges against him in the charismatic way he would have done previously. After giving his evidence, he was thrown into the Tower. And this time Elizabeth was prevented from visiting him.

A further letter from Chapuys written in July 1534 tells of Kildare's fate and the trouble brewing across the sea in Ireland.

Although the earl of Kildare is so ill, both in brain and body, that he can do nothing either good or evil, he was apprehended eight days ago and taken prisoner to the Tower, where I am told he would have been put long ago as soon as he arrived here, had it not been that the king always hoped to bring over and entrap his son, a young man of bold and valiant spirit, who has great influence in Ireland; but he has not only refused to come, but has even mustered men and seized artillery belonging to this king, besides other things, of which your majesty will be more surely informed by the person you have sent into Ireland, who I am told had arrived

200

10 days ago. It is reported that the earl of Desmond has
joined the said son of Kildare. ..... They have news in Court
that the said son of Kildare, or some of his men, had boasted
they would have the aid of 12,000 Spaniards; at which, I am
told, the king and his Council were much troubled, and some
think if these tumults be not appeased, the interview will be
broken off; in which case the king might take offence, even at
warlike appearances in Spain. It is incredible what pleasure
all the people would have at such news. It is some time since
the king appointed master Skeffington, master of the artillery,
to be governor of Ireland in place of Kildare. He formerly
had some charge in Ireland, but some think he will not go
thither, for his secretary three days since was committed to
the Tower on account of some letters from Ireland[25]

Chapuys' account refers correctly to the actions of Kildare's son, as
indeed back across the Irish sea the hot-tempered Thomas Fitzgerald
was making no secret of his dislike of the king's policy and his treatment
of his father and had indeed sought an alliance with Desmond. Not
long after his father's imprisonment, a report had reached Ireland that
Kildare was to be beheaded, and his son and brothers arrested. The letter
containing the news was discovered by a retainer James Delahide, an
ally of the Kildares. Delahide was one of those whose advice Kildare
had directed his son to take: he now counselled him to avenge his
father's death although in truth Thomas did not need much persuading.
He resigned his position as Lord Deputy, ready to rebel against the
Crown. But the news was false; Kildare was extremely ill but was still
languishing in the Tower. As his condition worsened, Elizabeth was
finally granted permission to visit him. As soon as she could she hurried
to his side, refusing to leave him.

Meanwhile, back in Ireland, Thomas was preparing for war. On
St. Barnabas' Day, he rode through Dublin with 140 armed retainers and
at a council meeting at St Mary's Abbey he declared himself no longer
an officer of King Henry and called upon all who hated tyranny to join
him. Resigning his post as Lord Deputy, it meant he was now a subject
and the Council immediately ordered his arrest. Sensing the danger,
the archbishop and Chief Baron, still loyal to Henry, immediately took
refuge in the castle and wrote to Cromwell for help.

As Thomas and his band of supporters began terrorising the English Pale, the archbishop took the opportunity to escape the castle, whilst the attention of the rebels was centred on Dublin. Putting his trust in his servant, Bartholomew Fitzgerald, he tried to escape in a small boat. But the wind sent them off course and he made land at Artane, seeking refuge in the house of a gentleman there. Hearing of his escape, Thomas and his followers tracked him there. The archbishop was dragged from the house begging for mercy. Thomas ignored his pleas, ordering two of his men to 'take away the churl'. The men immediately killed him. When he was later captured and questioned, Thomas always maintained that his intention was to detain and not to kill and that his men had misunderstood his orders.

After the death of the archbishop, Thomas and his followers were excommunicated from the Catholic See. Leprosy and madness, hunger and thirst were invoked upon them in this life, and eternal damnation in the life to come. No house was to shelter them, no church to give them sanctuary, no kind Christian to bestow on them a morsel of bread when starving, nor a cup of cold water when dying of thirst, on pain of being considered accessories to their crime and accursed like them.[26]

As Elizabeth continued to nurse her dying husband in the Tower at the end of 1534, Thomas had attempted to take Dublin. But the citizens, fearing punishment from the king, refused to help. After a failed attempt to acquire money and weapons, he was left with little choice but to retreat to his stronghold of Maynooth to regroup. Proclaiming Thomas and his uncles and supporters as traitors, the king dispatched a man named William Skeffington, whom he had reinstated as Lord Deputy of Ireland (after a short stint some years previously) to capture the rebels and bring them to London to face justice. Skeffington sailed from North Wales with his men, heading for Waterford, whilst Sir William Brereton and Captain Salisbury were sent with 400 men to protect the citizens of Dublin.

Hearing the news of his son's rebellion from his prison cell, the earl was fearful for his son and brothers, although part of the great man was surely proud of his son. As the year drew to an end, it was clear the earl was not going to recover. Elizabeth, distraught, remained with the man she loved until his death which occurred on 12 December 1534. The earl was buried in the Chapel of St Peter ad Vincula within the Tower grounds and in 1580 the following inscription was found on a chest under the earth 'Here lieth the corpes of the L. Gerald Fitz Gerald, Earle of Kyldare, who deceased the 12th December, in the year of Our Lord MCCCCCXXXIIII . , on whose sole Jesu have mercey'.[27]

Elizabeth would have been heartbroken. Unlike so many of her contemporaries, it seems she really did find a marriage based on love and attraction. Doyne C. Bell in his book detailing the burials within the chapel writes 'He [Kildare] was also so well affected to his wife as he would not at any time buy a suit of apparel for himself, but he would suit her with the same stuff: which gentleness she recompensed with equal kindness; for after that he deceased in the Tower, she did not only ever after live a chaste and honourable widow, but also nightly, before she went to bed, she would resort to his picture, and there, with a solemn congé, she would bid her lord good night.[28]

Elizabeth was now a widow, aged forty-two years old and back home in the country of her birth. She had lost the man she loved and she now had to decide what to do with the rest of her life, and not only that but how she could protect her family, particularly her sons who were still on Irish soil.

Chapter 10

A Widow in England as Maynooth Burned

Elizabeth's whereabouts immediately after Kildare's death are unknown. She must have had lodgings where the couple had stayed during the periods spent in England or perhaps she went to stay with family, who could comfort and support her during this time. Her two daughters were still with her but as well as mourning her husband, she must have been hugely worried about her two sons across the sea in Ireland. Her eldest son, ten-year-old Gerald, was believed to have been sick in Ireland at the time of his father's death and in the care of the family priest; the whereabouts of young Edward Fitzgerald, just seven years old, is unclear.

Out of all her five children, Cecily and Margaret are the most mysterious. It seems that Elizabeth's eldest daughter Cecily had also remained in Ireland, and if she has been married by 1534 that would make sense. Later on in 1535, some of the hangings from Maynooth along with the Earl of Kildare's parliament robes were left with a 'Lady Cecily' by Thomas, presumably to keep them safe as he waged war across the Pale. The existence of Cecily in a later appeal made to Queen Elizabeth lists Cecily alongside Gerald and his siblings, Edward, Elizabeth and Margaret (discussed in the next chapter) which points to the fact that Cecily was indeed Elizabeth's daughter and not a product of her father's first marriage. As a first-born daughter, the name Cecily would also make sense as a tribute to Elizabeth's mother.

Whilst Elizabeth was mourning her husband, back across the Irish sea her stepson was even more determined to avenge his father's death. Elizabeth's decision to remain in England kept her out of suspicion of involvement in the Kildare rebellion, and in fact when it was thought that she was considering returning to Ireland in late 1535 a warning to Cromwell given by an old adversary of the earl cautioned that this could do no good, a warning that was presumably also conveyed directly to Elizabeth herself.

Elizabeth was seemingly still in favour with her cousin, the king, despite the fact that her stepson was now a wanted man and that her husband had died a prisoner in the tower. On 16 January 1535, Cromwell wrote to a James Boys in Ireland conveying the king's order for him to deliver to Elizabeth, or to her attorney Thomas Houthe, all her clothing that remained in his custody. He also requested a report on behalf of the king of all the other goods belonging to the Earl of Kildare. Boys replied that shortly after Elizabeth's stepson had surrendered the constableship of Maynooth, he had moved all her clothing and their property to the Castle of Ley. Ley (or Lea) Castle was near Portarlington in Leinster and belonged to the Kildare family.[1] As well as allowing Cromwell to recover her belongings from Ireland, the king also continued to pay her jointure, as detailed in a payment from May that year: To the late Countess of Kildare, part of her jointure, 133l. 6s. 8d.[2]

Over in Ireland, Thomas Fitzgerald was continuing to garner as much support as he could against the English. Upon his arrival in Ireland in December 1534, Skeffington had been taken ill and he and his men had remained in Dublin until he was well enough to proceed. This had given Thomas the time he needed to regroup. It was around this time that he dispatched a man named Dominick Power across the sea to Europe on a mission to enlist the support of the Emperor. Taking gifts of a dozen hawks and fourteen hobbies (Irish palfreys), Power was instructed to enlist Spain's backing for the rebellion. As well as the gifts, he also sent documents reminding the Emperor that King Henry had committed heresy by denying the Pope's authority and marrying Anne Boleyn whereas Ireland was a fief of the Holy See and would remain loyal. He, Kildare, he wrote, was ready to hold the country for the Pope and the Emperor if they would send men to fight against the English.[3] By February, Skeffington was still indisposed, and in a letter sent to Cromwell dated 16 February 1536, John Alen, the king's Chancellor in Ireland, informed Cromwell that Skeffington had been unwell for twelve or thirteen weeks, never once leaving the house. In the meantime, he wrote, the rebel Thomas Kildare had burnt most of the country, turning the English Pale to waste. Alen also advised Cromwell that they were holding an aunt of Kildare's in the castle of Dublin, one Janet Eustace who was married to Sir Walter Delahide. Accompanying her was a woman named Rose Eustace, who had been one of Elizabeth's waiting-women at Maynooth. He ended the letter requesting more money to pay

205

the soldiers so they could continue with the planned siege on the Kildare stronghold of Maynooth.[4]

Once Skeffington had finally recovered, the English army left Dublin and set off towards Maynooth. As they marched, they discovered that indeed many of the Geraldine villages en route had been burnt, with the village of Maynooth itself being no exception. Thomas can only have realised that the time where he would be left alone to live in peace as master of his own lands had passed, so rather than have them fall to the English, he destroyed them as he went. The residents of Maynooth, those such as Master Miaghe, the miller, John Fowler and Meg Crese, were no doubt horrified at this turn of events and the destruction of their properties.

Arriving at the castle of Maynooth in March, Skeffington and his men were met by the sight of an imposing and impenetrable castle, furnished with royal ammunition. Thomas, however, was not within its walls; he had left it under the command of his foster brother, Christopher Parys, who had been bought up with him at Maynooth. The English had little choice but to set about their planned siege, surrounding the castle in an attempt to starve its occupants out. However just over a week into the siege, Parys, for whatever reason, perhaps panic, decided to save his own skin. Sending a letter out to the English commander, he offered him a deal – he would turn the situation to their advantage if his life were spared. Skeffington accepted and Parys proceeded to supply the men within the castle with plentiful amounts of alcohol, eventually rendering them drunk and incapable. The next morning when they were all still asleep, he gave a sign and the English army threw ladders up against the walls of the keep and scaled the walls with little to no resistance. In the end, it was all over in a relatively short space of time.

But Parys was not to be rewarded as he had thought. When Skeffington arrived inside the castle and thanked him, he asked him how well he had been treated by his adopted family, to which Parys answered that he had always been treated well. Skeffington then replied that if he could be so disloyal to those who had treated him with such love and kindness then the English, who did not deserve his loyalty, could never believe he would be true to them. He was then summarily executed.[5] Alongside Parys, twenty-five other inhabitants of the castle were also executed and as a warning, the heads of the main rebels were displayed on the turrets of Maynooth. A priest from within the castle walls who was captured allegedly revealed that the Emperor had promised to send 10,000 men by 1 May and that the King of Scots had also promised aid.

The taking of Maynooth castle became one of history's noticeable events, and the pardon and subsequent execution of Parys coined the saying 'the pardon of Maynooth' or 'the Maynooth pardon'. A ballad entitled 'The Siege of Maynooth' describes Parys' traitorous actions to his adopted family that day and was founded on a fuller account of the siege in Holinshed's *Chronicles of Ireland*. Fifteen verses in its entirety, the ballad gives us an overview of Thomas' rebellion, the loss of his family stronghold, and the treacherous actions of his foster brother:

Crom, Crom-a-boo! The Geraldine rebels from proud Maynooth,

And with him are leagued four hundred, the flower of Leinster's youth.

Take heart once more, O Erin! The great God gives thee hope;

And thro' the mists of Time and Woe thy true Life's portals ope!

Earl Thomas of the Silken Robes! – here doubtless burns thy soul?

Thou beamest here a Living Sun, round which thy planets roll?

0! would the Eternal Powers above that this were only so!

Then had our land, now scorned and banned, been saved a world of woe!

No more! — no more! it maddeneth so! —But rampart, keep, and tower,

At least are still — long may they be — a part of Ireland's power!

But — who looks 'mid his warriors from the walls, as gleams a pearl

'Mid meaner stones? ' Tis Parez – foster – brother of the Earl.

Enough! we shall hear more of him! Amid the hundred shafts,

Which campward towards the Saxon host the wind upbears and wafts,

One strikes the earth at Brereton's feet, with somewhat white – a scroll

Impaled upon its barb – 0! how exults the leader's soul!

He grasps it – reads – "Now, by St. George, the day at last is ours!

Before to – morrow's sun arise we hold yon haughty towers!

The craven traitor! —but, 'tis well! he shall receive his hire,

And somewhat more to boot, God wot, than perchance he may desire!"

Alas! alas! — ' tis all too true! A thousand marks of gold

In Parez' hands, and Leinster's bands are basely bought and sold!

Earl Thomas loses fair Maynooth and a hundred of his clan –

But, worse! he loses half his hopes, for he loses trust in Man!

The morn is up; the gates lie wide; the foe pour in amain.

0! Parez, pride thee in thy plot, and hug thy golden chain!

There are cries of rage from battlements, and mellays beneath in court.

But Leinster's Brave, ere noon blaze high, shall mourn in donjon fort!

"Ho! Master Parez! thou?" So spake in the hall the Saxon chief

"How hast thou proved this tentless loon? But, come, we will stanch thy grief!

Count these broad pieces over well! " He flung a purse on the ground,

Which in wrathful silence Parez grasped, 'mid the gaze of all around.

So! – right?" "Yes, right, good Sir! Enough! I now depart
for home!"

"*Home*, sayest thou, Master Parez? Aye, and by my Halidome,

Mayest reach *that* sooner than thou dreamest. But before
we part,

I would a brief, blunt parle with thee. Nay, man, why dost
thou start?

"A sudden spasm, good Sir." — "Ay, ay! those sudden
spasms will shock,

As when, thou knowest, a traitor lays his head upon the
block!"

"Sir!" – "Silence, man, and answer me! Till then thou art
in bale

Till then mine enemy and thrall!" The trembling man turned
pale.

"Say, have I kept good faith with thee?" — "Thou hast –
good faith and true!

"I owe thee nought, then?" — "Not a mark; the gold lies
here to view."

"Thou art the Earl's own foster – brother?" — "Yes, and
bosom friend!"

"What?" — "Nay, good Sir, I need those pieces, and "Come,
there an end!"

"The Earl heaped favours on thee?" — "Never King heaped
more on Lord!"

"He loved thee? honoured thee?" — "I was his heart, his
arm, his sword!"

"He trusted thee?" — "Even as he trusted his own lofty soul!"

"AND THOU BETRAYEDST HIM? Base wretch! thou
knowest the traitor's goal!

"Ho! Provost – Marshal, hither! Take this losel caitiff hence

I mark, methinks, a scaffold under yonder stone defence,

Off with his head! By Heaven, the blood within me boils and seethes

To look on him! So vile a knave pollutes the air he breathes!"

'Twas but four days thereafter, of a stormy evening late,

When a horseman reared his charger in before the castle gate,

And gazing upwards, he descried by the light the pale moon shed,

Impaled upon an iron stake, a well – known gory head!

"So, Parez! thou hast met thy meed!" he said and turned away

"And was it a foe that thus avenged me on that fatal day?

Now, by my troth, albeit I hate the Saxon and his land,

I could, methinks, for one brief moment clasp Sir William's hand!"[6]

Presumably Elizabeth herself had raised Christopher Parys as he had grown up at Maynooth, she may even have been a mother figure to him, so we can only imagine her thoughts on hearing that her family had been betrayed by him. When the news spread that Maynooth had been taken by the English army, many of Thomas's supporters began to melt away, no doubt fearing for their own lives. With his remaining men, he journeyed to Clane, bumping into Skeffington en route who managed to capture over a hundred of his supporters. Thomas decided to dispatch more men to Spain to try and speed up the Spanish support he believed or hoped would come. This time it was James Delahide and Robert Walsh who set sail to try and muster up support. Thomas then continued to wander about his ancestral estates, attempting to avoid the English army until back up arrived, but under no illusion that Maynooth Castle, his family home, was going to be impossible to take back.

As the news of events in her adopted homeland slowly filtered back to her in England, Elizabeth must have suffered more misery at the destruction of the village she may have grown to love and the castle she called home. We can never know her feelings towards her stepson, whether she secretly wished him success or whether she disagreed with his actions; her innermost thoughts on what was happening across the sea were most likely only conveyed to those closest to her, if at all. It may have been some comfort to her that in July her brother, Lord Leonard Grey, was dispatched to Ireland by the king with an army. She may have had some hope that in him, she would have an ally and someone who would be considerate to both her family cause whilst doing his duty to the English king. Grey arrived at Maynooth Castle to discover that Skeffington was still in residence there and had become ill again. By now he was seventy years old, his age and his illness rendering him an old man. In a letter from Gerald Aylmer and John Alen to Cromwell they wrote of Skeffington that if he rose before ten or eleven o'clock in the morning, he was almost dead by noon![7]

At the time of Grey's arrival, Thomas was hiding out in a boggy wood near Rathangan, an area naturally fortified with earthworks and wet ditches. As soon as Skeffington felt well enough, he and Grey advanced to the borders of Offaly where one of Thomas's last remaining allies, Bryan O'Connor, married to Thomas' sister, Lady Mary Fitzgerald, gave himself up to the English, anxious to save his harvest. In the end, it was Leonard Grey who persuaded Thomas to surrender; he reportedly would give himself up to none other, perhaps hoping for leniency because of their family ties. Thomas wrote to Grey, confessing himself a rebel but stressing that he had done all by the advice of his father's advisors. In the letter, he pleaded for his lands and his life. Eventually captured alongside his Fitzgerald uncles, the men were taken to England as prisoners. The Duke of Norfolk, previously the Earl of Surrey, who had served in Ireland and therefore spoke from experience, advised that they should be held in the Tower until such time as Ireland had been bought back under English control. Their deaths, he advised, could cause even more trouble throughout the Pale with others taking up arms to revenge their cause. The king listened and in October 1535 Thomas and his uncles, James, Oliver, Richard, John and Walter Fitzgerald were dispatched to the Tower. The rebellion was over.

Although she was the king's cousin, Elizabeth may have received the news of the capture of her stepson and brothers-in-law with some sadness. But she now had to make a future for herself and her children. With her old home in Maynooth no longer available to her, occupied as it was by the English forces, Elizabeth needed somewhere to reside permanently. On the 10 September 1535, Sir William Brabazon, the Vice-Treasurer of Ireland, wrote to Cromwell requesting the Earl of Kildare's rental book be sent to him, which it seems Elizabeth had taken to England with her, perhaps to better keep an eye on the administration of her estates but also perhaps to keep it out of the hands of their enemies.[8] Whether it ever made its way to Ireland is unclear, but Herbert Francis Hore, during his examination of the manuscript for his publication *The Rental Book of Gerald, Ninth Earl of Kildare, A.D. 1518* observed that on the inside of the vellum cover there was a library ticket of John Clinton, Duke of Newcastle. This circumstance led him to believe that the rental book was later in the possession of Elizabeth's daughter, Lady Elizabeth Fitzgerald, who would later marry (as her second husband) Edward Clinton, Earl of Lincoln. It seems the book was then passed down through his family to his descendants. In which case it is likely that Elizabeth somehow managed to hold onto it. By the end of 1535, Elizabeth, perhaps with the rental book still in her possession, had gone to live at the house of her brother, Leonard, at Beaumanor in Leicestershire.

Situated deep in a vale on the eastern side of Charnwood Forest, the picturesque Beaumanor was an ideal location for Elizabeth to grieve and begin to rebuild her life. Close by were the manors of Bradgate and Groby and they, along with many of the surrounding estates, belonged to her nephew, the Marquis of Dorset, so she may have found some comfort being within her family lands. Believed to have been built by Geoffrey le Despenser in the thirteenth century, Beaumanor had come into the possession of the Crown in 1325 before passing into the hands of Henry de Beaumont who built a second mansion on the site and enclosed the surrounding parkland. The circumference of this Great Park was believed to have been some twenty miles and when Leland visited in 1536, most likely during Elizabeth's residence, he wrote of the house 'Riding a little farther, I left the parke of Bewmanor, closid with stone waulles and a pratie logge yn it, longging alate to Bellemonts.[9] When Henry de Beaumont was attained for fighting for Henry VI at Towton, the property passed into the hands of William Hastings, before transferring back to the Crown in 1483 upon his death. It then came into the hands of Leonard Grey who leased it from the Crown and he offered it up as a safe place for his sister to reside. A later description of Beaumanor from 1594 describes the property as 'an antient mansion house of great receipte, moted about with as large mote stored with fish, with a drawbridge, garden, orchard, hop yards &c, thereto belonging, all very convenient and answerable'. An even later survey in 1656 details 'this antient manour house standeth and is seated in the parke called Beaumanor Parke; the manour house is moated about with a faire cleare moare; about which said building is a second moat'. The house would later fall into the hands of the Herrick family who completely rebuilt the manor in the nineteenth century.[10]

The lives of Elizabeth and her brother Leonard would remain intertwined going forward, for while she was residing at his manor, he was made Lord Deputy of Ireland. He was given the appointment by the king in January 1536 after Skeffington had succumbed to his illness the previous month. In May 1536, in a letter to the king detailing what had become of the Kildare belongings, it is he who mentions Lady Cecily (Sislie). He writes that before Thomas' departure he delivered two standing cups, certain bolts and a nutte with a cover to Melyor Faye (likely a coconut shell used as a goblet or bowl), the White Freres of Kildare were given plate (although he did not have the exact details of how much) and Lady Cecily, he advised, was in possession of all the hangings of Maynooth as well as her father's parliament robes.

Grey had become aware of this information through the examination of one John Dyrram, an old servant of Thomas', who had newly returned from Spain. Along with those items already mentioned, a huge amount of household goods had also been left with a man named O'Breen, including some gilded pots, four ingots of silver, two silver candlesticks, a gilded mawdeling pot from which to drink water, two silver basins without ewers, twelve partially gilded spoons and eight standing cups with covers. O'Breen had also been left with clothing belonging to the late earl, which included a gown of cloth of gold, a gown of cloth of silver lined with cloth of gold, a gown of purple velvet lined with cloth of tissue (a silk fabric), a piece of orange-coloured damask and a counterpane of black satin. Giving us a glimpse into Elizabeth's wardrobe, O'Breen also came into possession of a gown of purple velvet lined with cloth of tissue and two crimson gowns belonging to the countess along with many other small items belonging to them both such as doublets, hose and capes.[11]

Later that year, Grey would also question Robert Reyley, the faithful servant of the Kildare's who had travelled to England with Elizabeth and later accompanied her husband to London for the last time. Although he eventually handed himself in to the English authorities, in his testimony it is noticeably clear that his loyalties still remained with the Kildares as he defends their actions as much as he can without landing himself in any further trouble. We learn from his deposition, given on 5 August 1536, that he was twenty-four years of age and had been brought up in the house of the Earl of Kildare. After travelling to England with Elizabeth, she had sent him back to Ireland to her husband with two letters, one from herself and one from the king; Reyley said he read neither. He stated that he received no other letters, tokens or message from Elizabeth to her husband or to her stepson Thomas and could only suppose that the letters summoned Kildare to England as that was what happened. If any other messages were sent, he claimed they must have been taken by an older servant by the name of Sexton who returned to Ireland before him. According to Reyley, Kildare received the letters with reverence and made no answer.[12]

Reyley continued his evidence with details of the earl's preparations to leave Ireland and his instructions to his son, Thomas, to be ruled by the advice and counsel of his uncle, James Fitzgerald, Thomas Eustace, Sir Walter Delahide and his wife Janet Eustace and their son James Delahide. Accompanying the earl to London, Reyley maintained that he remained with him for the next three months before returning to Ireland as the earl was sick and unlikely to live long. He travelled with two other of the earl's servants, Edward Rokes and Humfrey Sexton, and denied that any of them carried any letters. Upon arriving in Ireland, he went into the service of Thomas Fitzgerald, whom, he implied, began his rebellion after several letters from different people advising that if he was 'taken', he and all his uncles and any others of the Fitzgerald stock were in danger of being taken to England and put to death.

The rest of his evidence covers the movements of Thomas during the months of his rebellion, including the murder of the archbishop, which he admits to being aware of but said he had no knowledge of whether he was killed on Thomas' command or not. Once Thomas and his uncles had been captured, Reyley said he thought it best to give himself up and travelled to Bristowe where he handed himself in to a Mr Shurloke, an Irishman and a servant to the Lord Privy Seal. Together they travelled to London and yet he had been at liberty to leave the whole time, emphasising the point that he had chosen to hand himself in to the authorities, which he, assuredly, hoped would help his case. Reyley's eventual fate is undocumented but given that he was a servant, he hopefully was eventually released to return to his homeland and forge a life for himself. Perhaps he even found his way to Beaumanor in Leicestershire and back into the service of the countess he had served so faithfully.

During her early days residing at Beaumanor, Elizabeth would have heard the news of the death of Katherine of Aragon, who died on 7 January 1536 at Kimbolton Castle, the last of many places she had lived during her banishment from court. Katherine had spent her last few months with few visitors, only leaving her rooms to attend Mass. Back in London, King Henry and Queen Anne celebrated; with her death, there was now no impediment to their relationship. How close Elizabeth was to Katherine is uncertain but it is likely that she felt some sorrow at the news of her death. A few months later, in April 1536, we find Elizabeth dining with Chapuys, the Spanish ambassador, who fought so hard for Katherine's cause and that of her daughter Mary, perhaps illustrating that Elizabeth had maintained ties with Henry's first queen. In a letter to Charles V dated 1 April, Chapuys wrote that he had recently dined with the young marquis (Henry Grey), Elizabeth, Lord Montagu and other gentlemen. It seems that Henry and Anne's celebrations on Katherine's death had been short-lived and that by April 'some new marriage for the king was spoken of'. This new lady who had caught the king's eye was a Seymour daughter named Jane, one of Anne's ladies. Since their marriage in 1532/3, Anne had also been unable to provide Henry with his much longed-for heir, having given birth to a daughter, Elizabeth, in 1533 and then suffering several miscarriages. By spring 1536, Henry was tiring of all the qualities he had once found so engaging in Anne – she was certainly not the meek and obedient wife that Katherine had been. Anne Boleyn, the intelligent, passionate and fiery woman once so attractive to Henry, had now become an opinionated and difficult wife in his eyes. Chapuys also noted that 'the concubine' (as he referred to Anne) and Cromwell were on bad terms and she had reportedly told him that she would like to see his head cut off. No doubt this was one of the main topics of conversation around the table that evening.[13] Just over one month and a further miscarriage later, Queen Anne was arrested alongside her brother, George Boleyn, and four other gentlemen: Henry Norris, William Brereton, Francis Weston and Mark Smeaton. Accused of adultery with the men and incest with her brother, Anne was tried and executed on 19 May 1536 on charges that were undoubtedly engineered by Cromwell to bring about her downfall. Whether Henry believed the accusations or not, by the end of May he had married Jane Seymour, a young woman of Catholic sympathies and the antithesis of Anne in her personality and demeanour.

Few mourned the downfall of Anne Boleyn, although the speed that her demise came about coupled with the injustice of the accusations perhaps afforded her some sympathy even amongst her enemies. For Elizabeth, although it appears her allegiance lay with the old queen Katherine, she may have felt some sadness at Anne's tragic end, particularly after the time they spent together in their early years in France. As Elizabeth, along with the rest of the country, digested the shocking news from court, back in her adopted homeland of Ireland, her brother, Lord Leonard Grey, was making waves by causing an argument with Lady Skeffington over her husband's finances. Less than a month after her husband's death, Lady Skeffington had written to Anne Boleyn, declaring that she was overwhelmed with debt. It seems that Grey wanted Maynooth handing over to him as a pledge that Skeffington's debts would be paid, although Lady Skeffington pleaded that her money troubles were to do with the fact that her husband's salary during his time in the king's service had never arrived and that she had no money to return to England. Cromwell, it seems, heard her pleas and gave orders that her goods should be delivered to her and that she should be safely conveyed home to England. During the time that this correspondence was taking place, Grey had turned all her furniture and belongings out of Maynooth Castle before carts could be provided to carry it away. He arranged for it to be stored in a church and refused to let her have access to it until her debts had been paid, causing Lady Skeffington to be stuck in Ireland for the next eight or nine months until the issue was sorted.[14] Perhaps Elizabeth received some comfort that her old home was now in her brother's possession, although she may not have agreed with his methods!

From Beaumanor, Elizabeth was busy making attempts to secure the future of her sons who had been left behind in Ireland, perhaps calling upon the help of Leonard to do what he could for his nephews. Her sons had escaped arrest alongside their half-brother, Thomas, probably due to their age and also possibly with Lord Leonard's collusion. Somehow, by July 1536, her second youngest, Edward, had been smuggled across the sea and back to his mother. Elizabeth wrote to Cromwell that month to say that Edward, then aged eight, had been mysteriously left at Beaumanor during her absence with no word of who brought him there; she had returned (from wherever she had been) to delightedly discover him there. Wanting to remain on the right side of the king, Elizabeth wrote to Cromwell asking for his advice and asking to be allowed custody of him. In her letter, dated 16 July, she wrote:

> Please it your good Lordship to be advertised that, at my coming to Beaumanoir the 14th day of this present month, I found there my son Edward FitzGerald, of the age of eight years, whose bringers thither be of none acquaintance, nor no knowledge to none of mine, nor brought word who sent him, nor left token nor letter how he should be used. Wherefore I beseech your good lordship that I may know the pleasure of the king's highness, by your good lordship's advice, how he should be ordered; and if I durst be so bold I would desire the custody of him, because he is an innocent, to see him brought up in virtue; and let it please your good lordship to send me word by your writing, by this bearer, how you will have him ordered: your pleasure known it shall be done with all the diligence that I may. As knoweth God, who preserve you in long life with great increase in honour.
>
> Written at Beaumanoir, the 16th day of July, By your oratrice, ELIZABETH KILDARE[15]

Her wishes were granted and Elizabeth was allowed to keep custody of her son. Now her only worry was her eldest son, Gerald. After the imprisonment and later execution of his half-brother, Gerald, just eleven years old, became the sole heir to his father's forfeited estates and was also a potential magnate for all those who wished to see the Kildare family restored to power. During the next few years, he would be smuggled around Ireland by loyal family and friends and kept out of reach of the English authorities. Having been ill with smallpox during his father's imprisonment, once he had recovered, his tutor Thomas

Leverous, who was also his father's foster brother, had allegedly carried him off in a basket and conveyed him to his sister in Offaly (perhaps his half-sister, Lady Mary Fitzgerald, married to Bryan O'Connor?). A few months later he was transferred to Clare and placed with another of his father's allies, James Delahide. Refusing to give him up, Delahide and O'Breen (who also had custody of the Kildare plate and jewels) kept him safe and he eventually found his way to his aunt, Lady Eleanor MacCarthy, his father's sister.

Anxious to keep her young charge safe, it is reported that in 1538 Eleanor agreed to take as her second husband an Irishman by the name of Manus O'Donnell (having previously been married to Donnell MacCarthy Reagh). She had turned down his advances in the past but now agreed to marry him on the condition that he keep her and her young nephew safe. Accompanied by Leverous and Delahide, she travelled through Ireland to her new marital home, with many of the old families who were Fitzgerald supporters offering them food and shelter along the route.

The news of her marriage was widely reported to the English council. A letter to Gerald Aylmer on 5 June 1538 reported 'My brother Plunket will show you the news. Eleanor Fitzgerald, late wife to MacCarty Ryagh, has passed through Tomownd [Thomond] and Connaught into Ulster to marry Manus O'Downyll. With her went Gerrot, son to the late earl of Kildare. Fear he will, with the aid of the North and of Scotland, make war'. Another extant letter from William Brabazon, also dated 5th June 1538 notes: 'The late earl of Kildare's Sister is gone to be married to Manus O'Donell. Young Gerrot, Delahide and others have gone with her, which I like not' and in a missive from the Council of Ireland to Cromwell on 10th June 1538 they reported that 'Eleanor Fitzgerald, sister to the late earl of Kildare and late wife of McCarte Riaghe, has gone, accompanied by young Gerald Fitzgerald and two of James Fitzgerald's sons, to marry O'Donyll. A combination of O'Neill and O'Donyll is feared'.[16] Although the young Gerald was still only a boy, it seems there was a great fear, possibly with good reason, that those with a past loyalty to the Earls of Kildare would now throw their support behind Elizabeth's son and once again challenge English authority across the Pale.

During those years 1536–8 when her son was being moved around those trusty Irish families still loyal to the Kildares, Elizabeth would hopefully have been kept well-informed with news of Gerald's wellbeing and whereabouts by those who sheltered her son, although presumably, she would have denied any knowledge if questioned by the English authorities. She remained at Beaumanor and managed to stay in favour with the king, continuing to receive her full jointure from him as detailed in several payments in the king's accounts from 1537: Eliz. countess of Kildare, in full satisfaction of her jointure, 200l[17]; and 1539: The countess of Kildare, arrearages due for her jointure, 40l.[18] Not much is known of her life during these years. As a new widow, she presumably lived a fairly quiet life raising her children in the idyllic Leicestershire countryside. Her peaceful existence, however, was in stark contrast to her cousin, the king, during the late 1530s and early 1540s. His marriage to Jane Seymour had lasted just a mere seventeen months; the queen had died in October 1537 shortly after providing Henry with his much longed-for son, a prince whom they named Edward. His daughters from his first two marriages, the Princesses Mary and Elizabeth, had their own households and Elizabeth's daughter, Elizabeth Fitzgerald, by that time about twelve years old, was invited to be a companion of the princesses at Hunsdon. For a few years after the death of Queen Jane, Henry had remained a widower. Many believe that out of all of Henry's wives, Jane was the one he loved the most, and not only for the fact she had provided him with a son. But in an age where child death was common, and from his own experience of losing his older brother, Henry was well aware that a king needed as many sons as possible. His chief minister, Cromwell, had convinced him that England would benefit from an alliance with a foreign power and that for his next marriage, he should look to foreign shores. In January 1540, he married his fourth wife, Anne of Cleves, a German lady and daughter of the Duke of Cleves, in a marriage treaty arranged by Cromwell. By July 1540, finding Anne completely not to his taste, Henry had divorced her and moved on to his fifth wife, a younger daughter of the great Howard family by the name of Katherine. She was just seventeen or eighteen years old to his forty-nine but Henry was besotted.

Several weeks before their marriage, Princess Mary's privy purse expenses ceased and her household was broken up. Elizabeth Fitzgerald was moved from her service and transferred into the service of the new queen at Hampton Court. Elizabeth's daughter and namesake was growing into a lovely young woman and it was at Hampton Court that the young Elizabeth came to the notice of her cousin and poet, Henry Howard, Earl of Surrey. His poem, entitled 'The Fair Geraldine' is largely thought to have been written to enhance his cousin's chances of a good marriage.

> From Tuscane came my lady's worthy race;
> Fair Florence was sometime her ancient seat;
> The western isle whose pleasant shore doth face
> Wild Camber's cliffs, did give her lively heat.
> Foster'd she was with milk of Irish breast;
> Her sire an earl; her dame of princes blood.
> From tender years in Britain doth she rest
> With kinges child, where she tasteth costly food.
> Hunsdon did first present her to mine eye.
> Bright is her hue and Geraldine she hight,
> Hampton me taught to wish her first for mine;
> Windsor, alas! doth chase me from her sight.
> Her beauty of kind, her virtues from above,
> Happy is he that can obtain her love![19]

By 1540, Elizabeth's eldest son had been in the safekeeping of his aunt for the last few years, hidden from the English authorities, but Eleanor was becoming suspicious that her new husband could be bribed to give up her nephew. Determined to keep him safe, she arranged safe passage for him to France aboard an English ship bound for St Malo. Providing him with money and plate, she entrusted him to the care of the ship's captain. His faithful tutor, Leverous, and a man named Robert Walshe travelled with him. Gerald arrived safely at Morlaix and was received there by the military governor who agreed to keep him safe. Once her nephew was safely away, Eleanor, perhaps giving us a glimpse of her strong, steely character, reprimanded her husband for his disloyalty and promptly left him and returned to her homelands.

Henry's ambassador in France was aware of his arrival on French shores and immediately demanded his surrender. King Francis did not refuse outright, but at the same time, he secretly removed the boy to the imperial town of Valenciennes out of English reach. Leverous remained with him and the small Irish contingent eventually made their way to the Emperor at Brussels. Charles transferred him to the Prince-bishop of Liège, with an allowance of 100 crowns a month and for the next few years, Gerald remained on the continent. After living with the bishop for six months, Gerald's kinsman, Reginald Pole, requested his presence in Italy and provided him with an excellent education. Reginald was the son of Margaret Pole, daughter of George, Duke of Clarence.

It must have been with some relief that Elizabeth heard of her son's escape to foreign shores, although her worry for him as his mother would never end until he was back with her. Although he had committed no crime, he was, and continued to be, a magnet for anyone who wanted to support the family of Fitzgerald over the king and whilst Henry wanted him in his custody, the boy could not return. Over in Ireland, Elizabeth's brother, Leonard, was beginning to suffer the same fate as her husband; his power in Ireland, albeit on behalf of the Crown, had made him enemies. And whilst he was out of the king's earshot, his enemies complained to Cromwell and the king in an effort to bring him down. Grey requested leave to go to court and defend himself and in 1540 his request was granted.

Upon his arrival in England, however, an enormous number of charges were brought against him. Amongst those charges he was accused of corresponding with his nephew, Gerald, (which he admitted to, although he argued that all the letters were also shown to the council, bar one), of allowing his nephew to escape, of allowing insurrections and working with the king's enemies. It was alleged that 'his pillages and extortion would fill a book'.[20] Realising that he was in a lot of trouble, he pleaded guilty, perhaps hoping that an admission would bring mercy. But that mercy did not come and he was immediately sent to the Tower.

Elizabeth once again had a close member of her family in the Tower. With all the lessons learned from the past, Henry was counselled that he needed to take control of Ireland once and for all and when parliament met on Monday, 13 June 1541 and at the sitting of the House of Lords on the following day, it was proposed that Henry VIII should be proclaimed King of Ireland. A Bill to that effect was read in English and Irish and was received with approval. Just a few weeks later, on 28 July 1541, Elizabeth's brother Lord Leonard Grey was executed at the Tower of London. The news was reported by Chapuys in a letter to the Queen of Hungary who wrote: 'On St. Peter's eve lord Leonard, uncle of the Marquis of Osceter (Dorset) and of the Chancellor's wife, was beheaded in front of the Tower. Hears he was accused of letting his nephew, the young earl of Kildare, escape to France and thence to Liege'.[21]

His house at Beaumanor passed into the ownership of his nephew, Henry Grey, the Marquis of Dorset, who presumably allowed his aunt to continue living there. Elizabeth who had been particularly close to Leonard must have been once again grief-stricken that she had lost a man she loved to the Tower. With his death and with her son abroad, it must have felt like her connection to Ireland was irretrievably broken. With a lack of information on her daughter, Cecily, we can only assume that she may have been Elizabeth's last real contact in the land that she may have grown to love.

Grey's execution was followed just seven months later by that of Queen Katherine Howard, who was beheaded on 13 February 1542 after having been accused and found guilty of entering into a pre-contract with a young man named Francis Dereham and the even bigger crime, of being involved in an illicit liaison with one of the king's men, Thomas Culpepper, during her marriage to the king. Unlike her cousin, Anne Boleyn, the accusations against Katherine were not planned to bring about her downfall, and upon discovering her infidelity the king was heartbroken. Her household was broken up and the young Elizabeth Fitzgerald presumably returned to Beaumanor to live with her mother.

But she would not remain at Beaumanor for long, for just over a year later, Elizabeth celebrated the marriage of her daughter to Sir Anthony Browne. Twenty-seven years her senior, the young Elizabeth was just sixteen when she married Sir Anthony. Browne was a favourite courtier of Henry VIII and had been made a Knight of the Garter in 1540. It is likely that the king may even have been instrumental in arranging the match, Despite the age difference, it was a good marriage and Elizabeth would have been happy to see her daughter settled. The young Elizabeth became stepmother to Sir Anthony's eight children and a year after the wedding, in 1544, Henry gifted Anthony and Elizabeth the manor house at Hatchlands within the manor of East Clandon, Surrey.

In the same year that Elizabeth Fitzgerald married Anthony Browne, King Henry was to marry his last wife, Katherine Parr. Elizabeth herself was now in her early fifties and despite the transgressions of her husband and brother that led to their deaths, she had somehow managed to navigate the politics and dangers of the Tudor court and remain in the king's favour. By 1543, her daughter Cecily was presumably still living in Ireland, her second daughter Elizabeth had married well and her son, Edward, had recently been awarded a place in the household of Prince Edward and would be brought up with him as a childhood companion. Nothing is known of her youngest daughter, Margaret but reportedly deaf and unable to speak, she may have remained with her mother. Both Elizabeths, mother and daughter, had maintained a connection with Princess Mary, illustrated by payments made from Mary's accounts as early as December 1536 with a payment of 7s 6d given 'to my lady Kildare's woman' and again in January 1538 of five shillings to 'Lady Kildare's servant', right the way through to 1543 when both sent her New Year gifts. Elizabeth sent a comb-case set with pearls and the nature of her daughter's gift was not recorded but was listed under the designation of Lady Browne of London. The following year, 1544, Lady Browne sent Mary a silver fuming box.[22]

The only thing missing to bring Elizabeth peace of mind would surely have been a reunion with her eldest son. As 1544 dawned, rumours were surfacing about a possible invasion of Ireland in the name of Gerald of Kildare. But Gerald was not planning a war; he had left his cousin Reginald Pole and gone to serve with the Knights of Malta. How much Elizabeth was kept informed of his whereabouts we can only guess at, but with her advancing years, she must have feared that she may never see him again.

For the last few years of her life, Elizabeth is a very shadowy figure indeed and we can only catch glimpses of her. In 1545, she received 33l 6s and 8d at Christmas as detailed in the king's payments for that year. The payment is recorded as 'Quarter wagis at Cristemas anno r.r. Henr. Viii' and it is possible that she attended court as one of Katherine Parr's ladies, which would explain her receiving wages.[23] By 1547, Katherine had around forty-five women in attendance upon her. Some were in constant service, and Elizabeth's daughter was one of these women, listed as Elizabeth Browne as one of the queen's ladies and living at court alongside her new husband who closely served the king. In her master's thesis on the Household of Queen Katherine Parr, Dakota L. Hamilton has noted the existence of a Lady Garrett who was a member of the queen's household from 1545 through to late 1546/early 1547.[24] Although we have no evidence that this was Elizabeth, Garrett was an alternative name for Fitzgerald and with her children no longer needing her full attention, she may well have attended court in service to the queen. A letter, written in 1539 from John Husee to Lady Lisle, discusses placements in the household of Princess Elizabeth and in that letter, Elizabeth is indeed referred to as Lady Garret in reference to the placement of her daughter, Elizabeth Fitzgerald.

We also catch a glimpse of Elizabeth in August 1546 when during a meeting of the Privy Council it was discussed that the Countess of Kildare had declared that 121 mks. 8s. 6d. of her dower was still owed to her and hadn't yet been paid because the Vice-Treasurer in Ireland had needed the money for more necessary affairs.[25] That same year, in the Irish Patent Roll for 12 November 1546, 'Lady Cycylie, daughter of the Earl of Kildare, was authorised to retain her father's plate, as of the King's gift'.[26]

As the year 1546 drew to a close Elizabeth and her family had finally, it seems, reached a period of stability. But as England celebrated the Christmas festivities, no one could have predicted that the end of an era was just around the corner.

Chapter 11

An End always signals a new Beginning

On 28 January 1547, the country was rocked by the news of the death of King Henry VIII. He had been on the throne of England for nearly thirty-eight years. Larger than life, he had begun as the hope of England, a new, young energetic king and had ended his rule fearsome and tyrannical. Upon his death, the throne passed to the young boy he had dispatched two of his wives for – his young son and heir, Edward. Just nine years old when his reign began, his maternal uncle, Edward Seymour, brother of Queen Jane, became Lord Protector until Edward was of an age to rule independently.

Did Elizabeth mourn the death of her cousin and king? He had seemingly treated her fairly well given that her husband was considered a traitor, but perhaps she could not forgive him for the death of her husband in prison. Whatever her feelings towards Henry, his death would now give her hope that her son could now return home. By the time of Henry's death, Gerald had entered the service of Cosmo de Medici, Duke of Florence, as his Master of the Horse.

But it would take another year before Elizabeth could finally write to her son and tell him the good news that he would be welcome if he came back; presumably once she had received assurances from Somerset and the Privy Council that her son would not be harmed. It was in January 1548, therefore, that Elizabeth wrote to her son requesting him to come home. At the same time the council addressed a letter to a Mr Young in Venice, thanking him for speaking with FitzGerald 'whom, on account of his youth and penitence for his faults, the king is willing to pardon, at the intercession of the Countess of Kildare and others, who bear him natural affection, requesting that he may return by Germany into Flanders, where his pardon shall be sent'. Elizabeth's letter is shown below and illustrates just how much she felt his loss over the years they had not seen each other, although ever the diplomat, she was careful to remove all blame for his absence from the Crown, writing that Gerald must submit and ask forgiveness for his mistakes:

Son, I commend me, &c., letting you wit that, since your so long absence, being always desirous to hear of you, I have taken such care of you as never mother took greater for her child. God knoweth what sorrowful days I have led, and ever since, grace I find so good and merciful that I am well assured of your well doing if your towardness be answerable to his goodness. I have (seen) such great mercy and clemency showed to sundry persons of divers estates, that it encouraged me to be the bolder a suitor for you. And, albeit, I found my said lord protector's grace always well affected towards you; yet now, of very late, upon such report as hath been made by an English gentleman in Italy of your humble submission and good demeanour, his grace hath given ine so good words, as I account myself most assured of your well doing, if the fault shall not be in you yourself. Son, it cannot be excused but yours hath been the fault, and therefore to deserve grace it must proceed of yourself, which must be to make demonstration of humble submission to the king's majesty's mercy; whereof, if my said lord protector's grace might understand any argument in you, I assure you to be received into the king's majesty's and his good favour, and such estate of living as shall be honourable for you. And therefore, good son, I pray you and charge you of my blessing that you fail not to follow my advice, shewing yourself repentant for your former proceedings, and desirous to be received to the king's majesty's most gracious favour, wherein, when I shall perceive your good conformity (as I most heartily pray you I may do with all possible speed), I doubt not to find the means to send you your pardon, and besides that to devise for such stay of living for you as shall not only be to your own honour and great comfort, but also to me an end of much care and sorrow, and one of the most joyful tidings that may come to me, as knoweth the Almighty God, who send you his grace and me shortly to see you. And yet again I pray you let me hear shortly from

226

you; if you shall not now conform yourself, I fear me I shall
not hereafter be so able to help you as now I have been, but
rather in suspicion for your case[1]

Gerald took his mother's advice and assurances that it was safe to
return and arrived in England during the spring, conducted home by a
Mr Knight, Elizabeth's chaplain. Finally, the long-awaited reunion
between mother and son could take place. Elizabeth by now was fifty-
six years old. If she had spent some time at court in the service of
Katherine Parr, we could only assume that her main residence remained
Beaumanor and perhaps it was here that mother and son met for the first
time in over a decade. Sadly for us, with the return of Gerald, Elizabeth
once again fades into the shadows and other than a payment in 1549
listed in the Privy Council Acts to Lady Kildare's chaplain, Mr Knight,
for bringing Fitzgerald home[2] and a payment in May 1550, awarding
Lady Kildare an annuity of 100 marks granted for the term of her life
(perhaps a renewal or a reconfirmation of the grant awarded to her in
Henry VIII's reign)[3], this is the last trace of Elizabeth Kildare and it is
believed she died sometime around 1550/1551.

Elizabeth had outlived many of her other Grey siblings, although
perhaps unsurprisingly as she was one of the youngest (only Margaret
and Edward were younger). Out of her brothers, her eldest brother,
Thomas, who had inherited the title of Marquis of Dorset upon the death
of their father had of course died just a few short months after their
mother, Cecily. Richard Grey who was born c.1479 had served at court
and attended the funeral of Henry VII as well as the coronation festivities
of Henry VIII and had been very much a part of Henry VIII's court. He
had died in 1541 leaving all his possessions to his wife, Florence Pudsey,
who he married later in life in a marriage organised by the king. Sir John
Grey, born c.1481 had followed in his brother's footsteps and also became
part of the Henrician court. His second wife, Anne, is believed to have
remarried in 1530 so John must also have died shortly after his mother.[4]
As for her other brothers, Anthony, born c.1483, served at court with his
brothers and volunteered to be part of a band of knights sent to Spain
in 1511 to fight the Infidel alongside King Ferdinand. He disappears
from the records before his brothers and is not mentioned in his mother's
will, so it is probable that he died sometime in the 1520s. George, born
c.1486, graduated around 1511 with a Bachelor of Civil Law and then

took holy orders. He became Dean of the College of the Annunciation of St Mary in The Newarke, Leicester in 1517 and resigned from the post in 1530. Little is known of him after that and we have no record of his death. Similarly, there is no record of the death of the youngest Grey brother, Edward, born three years after Elizabeth. He accompanied her to France in the train of Princess Mary and he reportedly later served in Mary's household when she returned to England and married Charles Brandon, Duke of Suffolk. Then of course there was the brother she was probably closest to, Lord Leonard, born just two years before Elizabeth and executed in July 1541.

As for her sisters, Eleanor, the eldest (born c.1482) died at a young age in 1502. Her sister Mary also pre-deceased Elizabeth; she was born c.1491, just a year before Elizabeth and died in 1534. She is buried at St John the Baptist Church, Stowe by Charley. Her other three sisters may have outlived her but as with Elizabeth herself, details are sketchy. Cecily who was born c.1487 married John Sutton, 3rd Baron Dudley, a weak man and hugely careless with money, who left his family in financial dire straits later in life. It is thought she may have died sometime around 1554. Dorothy, born c.1488, died sometime after 1553 which is when she made her Will and little is known of the youngest, Margaret Grey who was likely born around c1494 but no details survive of when she died.

As for Elizabeth's children, her eldest son, Gerald, was accepted back at court by Edward VI and on 16 March 1551, the Privy Council awarded part of his father's inheritance to him 'to encourage him and his kin the better, and the more faithfully to serve'.[5] Later, on 13 May 1553, during Mary's reign, he was restored to all of his father's lands and title, becoming the 11th Earl of Kildare and Baron of Offaly with an annuity of 201.[6] With his title restored, he moved back to Maynooth but never managed to become the unofficial ruler of Ireland in the same way that his father and grandfather had been. An intelligent man, having spent much of his informative years in renaissance Europe, his interest in alchemy would earn him the nickname 'The Wizard Earl'. The man who accompanied him from childhood, his tutor, Leverous, also returned to Ireland and was awarded the position of Bishop of Kildare. Gerald would marry in 1554, a lady named Mabel Browne whom he reportedly met whilst dancing at a masked ball. Mabel was the daughter of Anthony Browne and stepdaughter of his sister, Elizabeth. Gerald remained in favour with the Crown and was particularly favoured by Queen Elizabeth I. Back in Ireland, as with previous Earls of Kildare before him, his enemies constantly tried to discredit him and he was imprisoned twice in Dublin. It was only the personal regard of Queen Elizabeth that saved him on occasion. He died in 1585 when the earldom of Kildare passed to his and Mabel's eldest son, Henry Fitzgerald and then later upon Henry's death in 1597 to their second son, William Fitzgerald.

Elizabeth's other son, Edward, bought up in the household of Prince Edward married Agnes Leigh, daughter of Sir John Leigh, who was a half-brother of Katherine Howard. He managed to forge a successful career from himself at court and was granted an annuity of £40 when his childhood playmate Edward became king, an annuity which was renewed by Mary. He retained his place under Elizabeth, receiving wages of £25 a quarter by 1584.[7] By 1563, he was a Member of Parliament for Great Grimsby. His wife was a substantial heiress with property in Dorset, Somerset, and Surrey and in 1581, he added to his estate by acquiring a lease of Twickenham Park. Yet when he died nine years later in 1590, he was practically ruined, most likely by the extravagance of his son and heir Gerald. Edward's son became the 14th earl after the death of his nephew, William Fitzgerald.

As for her daughter and namesake, Elizabeth, she became a young widow when her husband died in 1548. After her husband's death, she joined the household of Katherine Parr, residing with her at Chelsea Place and Sudeley Castle. Katherine had remarried quite quickly after King Henry's death, to a man she was reportedly in love with before her marriage to the king, Thomas Seymour, brother of Edward and Jane Seymour. Whilst serving in the dowager queen's household, Elizabeth Fitzgerald was able to continue her friendship with Princess Elizabeth, who lived with her stepmother for a while. She would also become acquainted with a relative of hers, a young Lady Jane Grey, the daughter of Henry Grey her cousin. Later, in 1552, Elizabeth also remarried – a gentleman named Edward Clinton – and the following year both she and her husband supported Jane Grey's ascension to the throne upon the death of King Edward. When Jane fell just nine days later, her previous close friendship with the Lady Mary thankfully gained her a pardon. During the reign of Elizabeth I, Lady Elizabeth Clinton was one of her closest friends and became an important part of her inner circle. When her brother Edward died in 1590, she was made a supervisor of his will, which was proved in May 1590. However, she was unlikely to have been unable to perform her duties as Elizabeth herself died in March 1590. She is buried in St George's Chapel, Windsor.

Nothing is known of the destinies of Elizabeth's other two daughters, Margaret and Cecily. If it was Cecily who married into the O'Carroll family, her life may have been even more turbulent than her mother's as the O'Carrolls were a fierce family, who often fought amongst themselves. Having supported Kildare's son Thomas during his rebellion, Fergenanym later called upon Lord Leonard Grey for his support and one of the accusations brought against Grey was that he had favoured the outrages committed by O'Carroll. Fergenanym himself was slain by one of his kinsmen in 1541 at Clonisk Castle.[8]

All of Elizabeth's five children were still alive in 1569 when they appealed to Queen Elizabeth to be restored to their family's blood and lineage. The petition in the Privy Acts reads:

> A restoration of the Earl of Kildare, his brothers and sisters, to their blood, anno 11 Regina Eliz. Petition of Gerald FitzGerald now Earl of Kildare, Edward Fitzgerald, brother to the said Earl, Margaret, Elizabeth and Cicely, sisters to the said Earl; to the Queen.
>
> At a Parliament holden at Dublin, 28 Hen. VIII., before Lord Leonard Grey, then Lord Deputy, Gerald FitzGerald, late Earl of Kildare, father to your suppliant, and Thomas Fitzgerald, son and heir to the said Earl, and elder brother to your suppliant, were attainted of high treason, by force of which act your suppliants are corrupted in their blood and lineage, and disabled to claim anything by descent from their said father and brother, or from any other collateral ancestors or cousins. After the said attainder your suppliant, the now Earl, being an infant and put in fear, travelled in the countries of strange and foreign potentates, till he was called home by Edward VI., who restored him to the greatest part of his father's lands; and afterwards Queen Mary gave our suppliant the title of Earl of Kildare. Of late, moreover, your Highness has restored your suppliant

to a portion of his living which hitherto was thought to be in some doubt. But your suppliant finds in himself a great defect, for that he is not restored to his blood. He therefore beseeches your Majesty that it may be enacted by this present Parliament, that your suppliants shall be restored to their blood and lineage; provided always, that this act shall not make void any grant or lease made by King Henry VIII., King Edward VI., Queen Mary, your Highness, or the said Gerald, now Earl, and his feoffees[9]

Had Elizabeth herself lived a few years longer, she would have received the news of the death of King Edward and the accession to the throne, albeit briefly, of one of her own.

In 1553, at the age of fifteen, King Edward had become ill. Never a strong boy anyway, it soon became clear that the young king was not going to recover. As Henry VIII had advanced from one wife to another, his daughters from his first two wives, the Princesses Mary and Elizabeth, had been barred from the succession and Henry had never re-installed them; he had hoped right to the end that he would father more sons with his last wife, Katherine Parr. The act of succession, therefore, stated that if the direct line from Henry was to fail (i.e. if his only son Edward were to die) then the crown should go to any heirs of his niece, Lady Frances, the daughter of his beloved sister Mary: 'to the heirs of the body of the Lady Frances our niece, eldest daughter to our late sister the French queen lawfully begotten; and for default of such issue of the crown … shall wholly remain and come to the heirs of the body of the Lady Eleanor, our niece, second daughter to our late sister the French queen'.[10] This plan had relied on the fact that Frances, who was married to Elizabeth's nephew Henry Grey, would produce a male heir. But she hadn't. Together Henry and Frances had three girls, Jane, Katherine and Mary Grey.

On 25 May 1553, at the age of sixteen, their eldest daughter, Jane Grey had been married to Guildford Dudley, a son of John Dudley, Duke of Northumberland. As King Edward's health declined, he had begun to think about the succession of his crown. As a Protestant king, Edward had made the decision to leave his strongly Catholic sister Mary out of the succession but he had the option of re-instating his half-sister Elizabeth, the daughter of Anne Boleyn, a Protestant like himself. But as he penned his will, he excluded both his sisters from taking the throne after him, instead making it clear that the crown was still to go to the heirs of his cousin Frances. Stating his instructions, he decreed that the crown was to be left 'to the Lady Frances's heirs male, for lack of such issue (before my death) to the Lady Janes heirs males'. If Frances had a son and he was underage at the time of Edward's death, Frances was to act as regent until he was old enough to rule. The only problem remained that Frances was the mother of three daughters and as yet no sons. This plan then relied on Lady Jane Grey having sons.

As it became clearer that Edward did not have long to live, the Duke of Northumberland, in his position as one of the leading men on the regency council and by then Jane's father-in-law, convinced the king to amend his will. The clause 'Lady Janes heirs males' was changed to 'Lady Jane and her heirs males'. The addition of this one simple word pushed Jane directly in line to succeed Edward upon his death. The reason Northumberland pushed for this was clear – once Jane was queen, his own son Guildford Dudley, as her new husband, would be ruling by her side.

On 6 July 1553, King Edward VI died and as per his amended will, Jane Grey, great-niece to Elizabeth Grey, suddenly found herself Queen of England. On 10 July, Jane was carried by barge along the Thames to the Tower of London where she was crowned. Seemingly Elizabeth's daughter, Elizabeth, Lady Clinton, supported her rise to the throne but although her transition to power had gone well, remaining there was going to be another matter. On the same day that Jane was crowned, Princess Mary wrote to the Privy Council asserting her 'right and title to the Crown and government of this realm'. Built in the mould of her mother, Katherine of Aragon, and utterly convinced of her right to be queen, Mary was not going to rest until she had taken her rightful place on the throne of England.

What Jane herself thought about her sudden propulsion to queenship is a bigger discussion than can be had here and is covered by some amazing authors recommended in the bibliography. It is supposed that she was a victim of those adults around her, who used her as a pawn in their games to gain power and this is probably in part true. But Jane did have a strength running through her and once she became queen, she quickly informed her father-in-law that Guildford Dudley would not serve as king beside her. The strength she showed in this decision may have served her well had she remained queen, but alas it was not to be. The Catholic Princes Mary was hugely popular with the people, who had taken Katherine of Aragon to their hearts and had done the same with her daughter, Mary. As she raised her army and set off from her base of Framlingham Castle in Norfolk, heading towards London, many of the nobility who had supported Jane initially began to retreat. In the end, there was no need for battle. On 19 July, the Earl of Pembroke rode into Cheapside to proclaim Mary as Queen of England and met with no resistance. All those who had supported Jane disappeared and Jane herself was moved from her royal apartments in the Tower to free them up for England's new queen. Jane had ruled England for nine days. She was housed in another set of rooms in the tower to await her fate. Her husband, Guildford Dudley was also captured and held in the tower.

In the days that followed Jane's mother, Frances, met with Queen Mary en route to the capital and begged for her family to be spared. Jane's father, Henry Grey, was pardoned but Jane was charged with treason. Queen Mary eventually arrived in London on 3 August and Jane's father-in-law, John Dudley, Earl of Northumberland, was executed for treason just under three weeks later. Mary also forgave her childhood companion, Elizabeth Clinton and her husband.

Jane herself wrote to Mary from the Tower and although she would not free her, Mary demonstrated some compassion and agreed she would spare her life. But a few months later, in early 1554, her foolish father, Henry Grey, led another rebellion. This time the rebels planned to remove Mary from the throne and replace her with her Protestant sister, Elizabeth. They failed in their task, and although his plan had not this time involved his daughter, Jane, Mary was persuaded by her councillors that allowing her to live would prove a continual threat to her queenship. On 12 February 1554, first Guildford and then Jane were led to the executioner's block. Carrying her prayer book, Jane gave a brave speech for a young girl who was just seventeen years old, and the executioner ended her short life. Henry Grey was executed eleven days later and all his properties and those that had belonged to Elizabeth and her family were confiscated by the state.

After Henry Grey's death, his wife Frances, mourning the loss of her husband and daughter, took up residence at Elizabeth's old home at Beaumanor, alternating between here and her home at Broughton

Astley. She married for a second time to her Master of the Horse, Adrian Stokes, and died in 1559. The manor house at Beaumanor remained in the possession of her second husband, before transferring into the possession of the Earl of Essex. The house eventually found its way into the Herrick family and today nothing remains of the Tudor mansion that Elizabeth and her family would have known.

And what of Elizabeth's marital home of Maynooth? Her son, Gerald, and his wife lived there as did subsequent Earls of Kildare. When Gerald died in 1585, his countess, Mabel Browne, continued to live at Maynooth for another fifty-two years, until her death in 1610 aged seventy-four.

The traveller Fynes Moryson, who was secretary to Lord Deputy Mountjoy, Governor of Ireland, recorded on the 10 January, 1600–1: 'We passed the Liflfey, and came to Milhussy, one Master Hussy's castle, passing by some pleasant villages, and by Menouth, a faire house belonging to the Earles of Kildare, now in the hands of the Countesse Mabel an old widdow'.[11] Future Earls of Kildare would continue to live there and the magnificent walls of Maynooth would once again find themselves under siege during the Irish rebellion of 1641. Much of the castle was destroyed and what remained gradually fell into ruins. In an account by Thomas Monk in his *Account of the County of Kildare*, Monk wrote: 'Maynooth, where is to be seen the remains of an ancient pile, venerable in its ruins, and which did partake of the hottest, and felt the fiercest malice of a revengefull enemie in the last rebellion'. Future Earls of Kildare would make Kilkea Castle and then Carton House their family seat.

After taking the throne in 1553, Mary reigned for just five years. A staunch Catholic, her burning of Protestants earned her the name of Bloody Mary. Having had a tumultuous childhood, her queenship was also blighted by her strict religious views and her love for her husband, Phillip of Spain, a passion that was seemingly one-sided and she died in a rather sad state aged just forty-two. So it was in 1558 that another Elizabeth took the throne of England. The great-granddaughter of Elizabeth Woodville, granddaughter of Elizabeth of York and a second cousin of Elizabeth Grey, she was not England's first female ruler, but undoubtedly was one of its greatest. The irony is not lost that her father, Henry VIII had literally moved heaven and earth (or at least Heaven's representative on earth – the Pope) to ensure that he had a male heir to continue the Tudor line, and yet it was his second daughter that proved herself his greatest successor. Predominantly Protestant, she famously claimed that she refused to make windows into men's souls. During her forty-five year reign, the arts flourished, and England saw the rise of playhouses, inspired by great writers such as Shakespeare and Marlowe. Men like Drake and Raleigh sailed the high seas bringing about an era of exploration and slowly but surely, as the country sailed into the seventeenth century, the England so familiar to our protagonists, slowly faded into the annals of history.

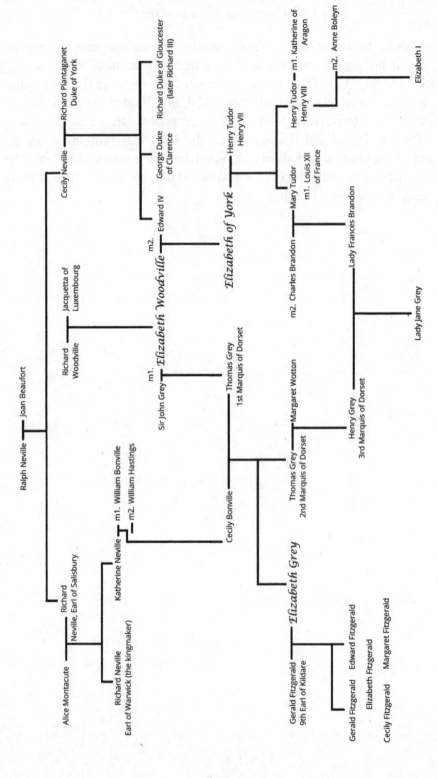

Author's Note

Our three Elizabeth's lived through just over 100 years of English history, during a time that saw the end of the great Plantagenet dynasty and the emergence of the Tudors. Between them, they witnessed the reign of six kings, beginning with the reign of Henry VI in the late 1430s when Elizabeth Woodville was born and with our last Elizabeth dying perhaps just two years before the reign of England's first independent queen, Mary I. By the time Elizabeth I ascended the throne, the world inhabited by our protagonists had changed dramatically and their lives would eventually disappear into the chronicles of time. I chose to write about these three women, connected by their name and their family relations to each other, because through their lives we too can journey through the fifteenth and sixteenth centuries. But not only that, their stories are inspiring. They lived in a different era, one that would be unrecognisable to us today; society was different, the rules were different and the choices available to them do not compare with our modern lives today. But ultimately the experience of being human is one that crosses the centuries and in the stories of Elizabeth Woodville, Elizabeth of York and Elizabeth Grey, we find courage, resilience, heartbreak, joy, laughter and family, themes that are still common to us all some 500 years later.

Bibliography

Bagwell, Richard, *Ireland under the Tudors, With a Succinct Account of the Earlier History*. Volume I (of II). Project Gutenberg, 2013.

Baldwin, David, *Elizabeth Woodville, Mother of the Princes in the Tower*. Sutton Publishing, 2002.

Baldwin, David, *The Kingmakers' Sisters*. The History Press, 2009.

Bell, Henry Nugent, *The Huntingdon Peerage (Comprising a Detailed Account of the Evidence and Proceedings Connected with the Recent Restoration of the Earldom ... to which is Prefixed a Genealogical and Biographical History of the Illustrious House of Hastings, Including a Memoir of the Present Earl and His Family*. Baldwin, Craddock and Joy, 1820.

Borman, Tracy, *The Private Lives of the Tudors*. Hodder & Stoughton, 2016.

Bridie, M.F., *The Story of Shute*. Shute School Ltd, Axminster, 1955.

Crossland, Margaret, *The Life and Legend of Jane Shore, The Mysterious Mistress*. Sutton Publishing, 2006.

Denny, Joanna, *Anne Boleyn*. Portrait, 2004.

Fitzgerald, Charles William (Duke of Leinster), *The Earls of Kildare, and Their Ancestors, from 1057 to 1773*. Hodges, Smith & Co., Dublin, 1858.

Gregory, Phillipa, *The Lady of The Rivers*. Simon & Schuster Ltd, 2012 (fiction).

Gregory, Phillipa, *The White Queen*. Simon & Schuster Ltd, 2012 (fiction).

Gregory, Phillipa; Baldwin, David and Jones, Michael, *The Women of the Cousin's War – the Duchess, the Queen and the King's Mother*. Simon & Schuster Ltd, 2012.

Harris, Barbara J., *English Aristocratic Women, 1450–1550: Marriage and Family, Property and Careers*. Oxford University Press, 2002.

Hicks, Michael, *The Family of Richard III*. Amberley Publishing, 2015.

Bibliography

Higginbotham, Susan, *The Woodvilles*. The History Press, 2013.

Hodder, Sarah J,. *Cecily Bonville-Grey, Marchioness of Dorset*. John Hunt Publishing, 2022.

Hodder, Sarah J., *The Queen's Sisters: The Lives of the Sisters of Elizabeth Woodville*, John Hunt Publishing, 2020.

Hodder, Sarah J., *The York Princesses*. John Hunt Publishing, 2021.

Jones, Dan, *The Hollow Crown: The Wars of the Roses and the Rise of the Tudors*. Faber & Faber, 2014.

Langley, Phillipa and Jones, Michael, *The Search for Richard III, The King's Grave*. John Murray, 2016.

Leyser, Henrietta, *Medieval Women: A Social History of Women in England 450–1500*. W&N, 2005.

Licence, Amy, *Anne Boleyn: Adultery, Heresy, Desire*. Amberley 2017.

Licence, Amy, *Edward IV and Elizabeth Woodville*. Amberley Publishing, 2016.

Licence, Amy, *Elizabeth of York – Forgotten Tudor Queen*. Amberley Publishing, 2013.

Licence, Amy, *The Field of the Cloth of Gold*. Amberley Publishing, 2020.

Lipscomb, Susannah. *The King is Dead*. Pegasus Books, 2016.

Lisle, Leanda de, *The Sisters Who Would Be Queen – The Tragedy of Mary, Katherine and Lady Jane Grey*. Harper Press, 2010.

Macgibbon, David, *Elizabeth Woodville – A Life: The Real Story of the White Queen*. 2013.

Moore, Thomas, *The History of Ireland:* Volume 3. Longman, Orme, Brown, Green and Longmans, 1846.

More, Thomas (Logan, George, ed.), *The History of King Richard III*. Indiana University Press, 2005.

Okerlund, Arlene, *Elizabeth: England's Slandered Queen*. The History Press, 2006.

Okerlund, Arlene, *Elizabeth of York*. Palgrave Macmillan, 2009.

Penn, Thomas, *The Brothers York: An English Tragedy*. Penguin Books, 2020.

Perry, Maria, *Sisters to the King*. Andre Deutsch, 2002.

Pisan, Christine, *The Treasure of the City of Ladies*. Penguin Books, 1985.

Plowden, Alison, *Lady Jane Grey: Nine Days Queen*. The History Press, 2004.

Sadlack, Erin A., *The French Queen's Letters*. Palgrave Macmillan, 2011.

Scofield, Cora L. *The Life and Reign of Edward IV, King of England and Lord of Ireland*. First published 1923. Ralph A Griffiths and Fonthill Media, 2016.

Steward, Desmond, *The Wars of the Roses*, Robinson, 2007.

Sutton, Anne and Visser-Fuch, Livia, *Royal Funerals of the House of York at Windsor*, Richard III Society, 2005.

Tallis, Nicola, *Crown of Blood: The Deadly Inheritance of Lady Jane Grey*. Michael O'Mara, 2017.

Thomas, Melita, *The House of Grey: Friends and Foes of Kings*, Amberley Publishing, 2019.

Watkins, Sarah Beth, *The Tudor Brandons*, Chronos Books, 2020.

Weir, Alison, *Lancaster and York*, Vintage, 2009.

Weir, Alison, *The Six Wives of Henry VIII*, Vintage, 2007.

Wroe, Anne, *Perkin*, Vintage, 2004.

References

Chapter 1: Before the Wars

1. Note of the Somerset Herald: Richard Erle Ryvers and Jaquett Duchesse of Bedford hath yssue Anthony Erle Ryvers, Richard, Elizabeth first wedded to Sir John Grey, after to Kinge Edward the fourth, Lowys, Richard Erle of Riueres, Sir John Wodeuille Knight, Jaquette lady Straunge of Knokyn, Anne first maryed to the Lord Bourchier sonne and heire to the Erle of Essex, after to the Erle of Kent, Mary wyf to William Erle of Huntingdon, John Woodville, Lyonell Bisshop of Sarum, Margaret Lady Maltravers, Jane Lady Grey of Ruthin, Sir Edward Woodville, Katherine Duchesse of Buckingham.
2. *Melusine; or the noble history of Lusignan* by Jean D'Arras. Translated by Donald Maddox. Intro by Sara Sturm Maddox. Pennsylvania State University, 2012.
3. Extract from Melusine poem. *Melusine and other poems* by Edward Yardley. Longmans, Green & Co, 1867.
4. Gregory, Phillipa; Baldwin, David; and Jones, Michael. *The Women of the Cousin's War – the Duchess, the Queen and the King's Mother*. Simon & Schuster Ltd, 2012.
5. De Monstrelet, Enguerrand. *The Chronicles of Enguerrand de Monstrelet, Containing an Account of the Cruel Civil Wars Between the Houses of Orleans and Burgundy; of the Possession of Paris and Normandy by the English; Their Expulsion Thence; and of Other Memorable Events that Happened in the Kingdom of France, as Well as in Other Countries*. Translated By Thomas Johnes, Esq. London, 1810.
6. www.britainexpress.com
7. Sidney, Philip. *The Countess of Pembroke's Arcadia*. Sampson, Low, Marston, 1893.
8. Harriss, G. Eleanor [née Eleanor Cobham], duchess of Gloucester (c. 1400–1452), alleged sorcerer. Oxford Dictionary of National Biography.

9. De Monstrelet, Enguerrand. *The Chronicles of Enguerrand de Monstrelet, Containing an Account of the Cruel Civil Wars Between the Houses of Orleans and Burgundy; of the Possession of Paris and Normandy by the English; Their Expulsion Thence; and of Other Memorable Events that Happened in the Kingdom of France, as Well as in Other Countries.* Translated By Thomas Johnes, Esq. London, 1810.
10. 'Grafton Regis', in *A History of the County of Northampton*: Volume 5, the Hundred of Cleley, ed. Philip Riden and Charles Insley (London, 2002), pp. 142–176. British History Online.
11. https://www.abbaye-de-grestain.fr/labbaye-fut-richement-dotee/
12. Published in *The History of Parliament: the House of Commons 1386–1421*, ed. J.S. Roskell, L. Clark, C. Rawcliffe, 1993.
13. 'Grafton Regis', in *A History of the County of Northampton*: Volume 5, the Hundred of Cleley, ed. Philip Riden and Charles Insley (London, 2002), pp. 142–176. British History Online.
14. Harriss, G. Eleanor [née Eleanor Cobham], duchess of Gloucester (c. 1400–1452), alleged sorcerer. Oxford Dictionary of National Biography.
15. Maurer, Helen E. *Margaret of Anjou Queenship and Power in Late Medieval England.* Boydell Press, 2005
16. *The Paston Letters A.D. 1422–1509*, Volume II. Project Gutenberg.
17. Calendar of Patent Rolls, Henry VI. PRO.
18. *www.groby.org.uk/history/greys-recent-findings.html*

Chapter 2: A Troubled Land

1. Thomas, Melita. *The House of Grey: Friends and Foes of Kings.* Amberley Publishing, 2019.
2. Pisan, Christine. *The Treasure of the City of Ladies.* Penguin Books, 1985.
3. Leyser, Henrietta. *Medieval Women – A Social History of Women in England 450–1500.* Weidenfeld and Nicholson, 1995.
4. Bryson, Sarah. *Childbirth in Medieval and Tudor Times.* The Tudor Society (*www.tudorsociety.com*), 2015.
5. Leyser, Henrietta. *Medieval Women – A Social History of Women in England 450–1500.* Weidenfeld and Nicholson, 1995.
6. Burley, Peter, Elliot, Michael and Watson, Harvey. *The Battles of St Albans.* Pen & Sword, 2013.

7. *The Paston Letters A.D. 1422–1509*. Volume III. Project Gutenberg.

8. Burley, Peter, Elliot, Michael and Watson, Harvey. *The Battles of St Albans*. Pen & Sword, 2013.

9. Baldwin, David. *Elizabeth Woodville: Mother of the Princes in the Tower*. The History Press, 2010.

10. 'The Full Itinerary of Edward IV' by John Ashdown-Hill. Available to download in pdf format from Amberley Books.

11. National Archives Chancery records: Grey v Fylding. Ref: C 1/27/268.

12. National Archives Chancery records: Wydevyle v. Bourchier. Ref: C 1/27/269.

13. Hodder, Sarah. *The Queen's Sisters*. John Hunt Publishing (Chronos Books), 2020.

14. Baldwin, David. *Elizabeth Woodville: Mother of the Princes in the Tower*. The History Press, 2010.

15. Thomas, Melita. *The House of Grey: Friends and Foes of Kings*. Amberley Publishing, 2019.

16. Visser-Fuchs, Livia. *English Events in Caspar Weinreich's Danzig Chronicle, 1461–1495*. The Ricardian Online.

17. Hall, Edward. *Hall's Chronicle, Containing the History of England During the Reign of Henry IV and the Succeeding Monarchs to the End of the Reign of Henry VIII*. Edited by Sir Henry Ellis, London, 1809.

18. Fabyan, Robert. *The new chronicles of England and France, in two parts. Reprinted from Pynson's edition of 1516*. By Fabyan, Robert (d. 1513) and Ellis, Henry, Sir, 1811.

19. De Monstrelet, Enguerrand. *The Chronicles of Enguerrand de Monstrelet, Containing an Account of the Cruel Civil Wars Between the Houses of Orleans and Burgundy; of the Possession of Paris and Normandy by the English; Their Expulsion Thence; and of Other Memorable Events that Happened in the Kingdom of France, as Well as in Other Countries*. Translated By Thomas Johnes, Esq. London, 1810.

20. Warkworth, John. *A Chronicle of the first thirteen years of the reign of King Edward IV*. Camden Society, London, 1839.

21. 'Houses of Austin Canons: The hermitage of Grafton Regis', in *A History of the County of Northampton*: Volume 2, ed. R M Serjeantson and W R D Adkins (London, 1906), p. 137. British History Online.

22. 'Grafton Regis', in *A History of the County of Northampton*: Volume 5, the Hundred of Cleley, ed. Philip Riden and Charles Insley (London, 2002), pp. 142–176. British History Online.

23. Fabyan, Robert. *The new chronicles of England and France, in two parts. Reprinted from Pynson's edition of 1516*. By Fabyan, Robert (d. 1513) and Ellis, Henry, Sir, 1811.

24. 'The Full Itinerary of Edward IV' by John Ashdown-Hill, Available to download in pdf format from Amberley Publishing.

Chapter 3: Elizabeth the Queen, Elizabeth the Princess

1. Visser-Fuchs, Livia. *English Events in Caspar Weinreich's Danzig Chronicle, 1461–1495*. The Ricardian Online.

2. De Monstrelet, Enguerrand. *The Chronicles of Enguerrand de Monstrelet, Containing an Account of the Cruel Civil Wars Between the Houses of Orleans and Burgundy; of the Possession of Paris and Normandy by the English; Their Expulsion Thence; and of Other Memorable Events that Happened in the Kingdom of France, as Well as in Other Countries*. Translated By Thomas Johnes, Esq. London, 1810.

3. *Letters and Papers Illustrative of the Reigns of Richard III and Henry VII*. Edited by James Gardner. Longman, Green, Longman & Roberts, 1861.

4. Hodder, Sarah J. *The Queen's Sisters*. John Hunt Publishing (Chronos Books), 2020.

5. English Heritage: www.english-heritage.org.uk/visit/places/eltham-palace-and-gardens/history

6. Beattie, William. *The Castles and Abbeys of England*, from the National Records, Early Chronicles and Other Standard Authors ... Illustrated by Upwards of Two Hundred Engravings: Volume 1. George Virtue, 1842.

7. Scofield, Cora L. *The Life and Reign of Edward IV, King of England and Lord of Ireland*. First Published 1923. Ralph A Griffiths and Fonthill Media, 2016.

8. De Monstrelet, Enguerrand. *The Chronicles of Enguerrand de Monstrelet, Containing an Account of the Cruel Civil Wars Between the Houses of Orleans and Burgundy; of the Possession of Paris and Normandy by the English; Their Expulsion Thence; and of Other Memorable Events that Happened in the Kingdom of France, as Well as in Other Countries*. Translated By Thomas Johnes, Esq. London, 1810.

9. Sutton, Anne F., and Visser-Fuchs, Livia. *The Entry of Queen Elizabeth Woodville over London Bridge*, 24 May 1465. The Ricardian Online.
10. Ibid.
11. William Ballard, King of Arms. *Account of the coronation of Elizabeth Woodville as Queen of Edward IV on 26th March 1465*. Bodleian Libraries, University of Oxford.
12. Okerlund, Arlene. Elizabeth: *England's Slandered Queen*. The History Press, 2006.
13. Ibid.
14. Myers, AR. *The household of Queen Elizabeth Woodville, 1466–7*: II Bulletin of the John Rylands Library. 1968;50(2):443–481.
15. Ibid.
16. Scofield, Cora L. *The Life and Reign of Edward IV, King of England and Lord of Ireland*. First Published 1923. Ralph A Griffiths and Fonthill Media, 2016.
17. 'The Full Itinerary of Edward IV' by John Ashdown-Hill. Available to download in pdf format from Amberley Books.
18. Scofield, Cora L. *The Life and Reign of Edward IV, King of England and Lord of Ireland*. First Published 1923. Ralph A Griffiths and Fonthill Media, 2016.
19. Strickland, Agnes. *Memoirs of the Queens of Henry VIII and of his mother, Elizabeth of York*. 1873.
20. Scofield, Cora L. *The Life and Reign of Edward IV, King of England and Lord of Ireland*. First Published 1923. Ralph A Griffiths and Fonthill Media, 2016.
21. Myers, A.R. (ed.). *The Household of Edward IV, The Black Book and the Ordinance of 1478*. Manchester University Press, 1959.
22. Holinshed, Raphael. *The Chronicles of England, Scotland and Ireland*. First printed 1577. Project Gutenberg, 2014.
23. Licence, Amy. *Edward IV and Elizabeth Woodville: A True Romance*. Amberley Publishing, 2016.
24. *The Paston Letters A.D. 1422–1509*. Vol. V. Project Gutenberg.
25. Okerlund, Arlene. *Elizabeth: England's Slandered Queen*. The History Press, 2006.
26. Strickland, Agnes. *Lives of the Princesses of England from the Norman Conquest*. Cambridge University Press, 2010.
27. Licence, Amy. *Edward IV and Elizabeth Woodville: A True Romance*. Amberley Publishing, 2016.

28. Walter Thornbury, 'Westminster Abbey: The sanctuary and almonry', in *Old and New London*: Volume 3 (London, 1878), pp. 483–491. British History Online.
29. Scofield, Cora L. *The Life and Reign of Edward IV, King of England and Lord of Ireland*. First Published 1923. Ralph A Griffiths and Fonthill Media, 2016.

Chapter 4: All's Well that ends Well

1. Strickland, Agnes and Strickland, Elizabeth. *Lives of the Queens of England from the Norman Conquest*. Cambridge University Press, 2010.
2. Philippe de Commynes, Jean de Roye. *The Memoirs of Philip de Commines, Lord of Argenton: Containing the Histories of Louis XI, and Charles VIII, Kings of France, and of Charles the Bold, Duke of Burgundy. To which is Added the Scandalous Chronicle, Or, Secret History of Louis XI*, Volume 1. H.G. Bohn, January 1855.
3. Ibid.
4. Ibid.
5. Seward, Desmond. *The Wars of the Roses*. Robinson, 2007.
6. Strickland, Agnes and Strickland, Elizabeth. *Lives of the Queens of England from the Norman Conquest*. Cambridge University Press, 2010.
7. Licence, Amy. *Edward IV and Elizabeth Woodville: A True Romance*, Amberley Publishing, 2016.
8. *The Paston Letters A.D. 1422–1509*. Vol. V. Project Gutenberg.
9. Seward, Desmond. *The Wars of the Roses*. Robinson, 2007.
10. Weir, Alison. *Elizabeth of York: The First Tudor Queen*. Vintage, 2014.
11. Hodder, Sarah J. *Cecily Bonville-Grey, Marchioness of Dorset*. John Hunt Publishing (Chronos Books), 2022.
12. More, Thomas (Logan, George Ed.). *The History of King Richard III*. Indiana University Press, 2005.
13. Philippe de Commynes, Jean de Roye. *The Memoirs of Philip de Commines, Lord of Argenton: Containing the Histories of Louis XI, and Charles VIII, Kings of France, and of Charles the Bold, Duke of Burgundy. To which is Added the Scandalous Chronicle, Or, Secret History of Louis XI*, Volume 1. H.G. Bohn, January 1855.

14. Crossland, Margaret. *The Life and Legend of Jane Shore, The Mysterious Mistress*. Sutton Publishing, 2006.
15. Pisan, Christine. *The Treasure of the City of Ladies*. Penguin Books, 1985.
16. Myers, A. R. *The Household of Edward IV; the Black Book and the Ordinance of 1478*. Manchester University Press, 1959.
17. Weir, Alison. *Elizabeth of York: The First Tudor Queen*. Vintage, 2014.
18. Sutton, Anne F. and Visser-Fuchs, Livia. *The Prophecy of G*. The Ricardian, September 1990.
19. Holinshed, Ralph. *Chronicles of England, Scotland and Ireland*. Project Gutenberg, May 2014.
20. Sutton, Anne F. and Visser-Fuchs, Livia. *Royal Funerals of the House of York at Windsor*, Richard III Society, 2005.
21. Dean, Kristie. *On The Trail of the Yorks*. Amberley Publishing, 2016.
22. Ibid.
23. "F.M.," "Christening of the Princess Bridget, 1480." *Gentleman's Magazine*, January 1831.

Chapter 5: The World Falls Apart

1. More, Thomas (Logan, George Ed.). *The History of King Richard III*. Indiana University Press, 2005.
2. Strickland, Agnes and Strickland, Elizabeth. *Lives of the Queens of England from the Norman Conquest*. Vol.2, Cambridge University Press, 2010.
3. Croyland Chronicle (second continuation).
4. Vergil, Polydore (Ellis, Sir Henry Ed.). *Three books of Polydore Vergil's English history, comprising the reigns of Henry VI., Edward IV., and Richard III. from an early translation, preserved among the mss. of the old royal library in the British museum. Printed for the Camden Society, JB Nichols & Sons, 1844.*
5. Sutton, Anne F. and Visser-Fuchs, Livia. *Royal Funerals of the House of York at Windsor*, Richard III Society, 2005.
6. Ibid.
7. Jones, Dan. *The Hollow Crown: The Wars of The Roses and the Rise of the Tudors*. Faber & Faber, 2015.

8. Strickland, Agnes and Strickland, Elizabeth. *Lives of the Queens of England from the Norman Conquest.* Vol.2, Cambridge University Press, 2010.
9. Ibid.
10. Jones, Dan. *The Hollow Crown: The Wars of The Roses and the Rise of the Tudors.* Faber & Faber, 2015.
11. *Croyland Chronicle* (second continuation).
12. Crossland, Margaret. *The Life and Legend of Jane Shore, The Mysterious Mistress.* Sutton Publishing, 2006.
13. Okerlund, A. *Elizabeth of York*, Palgrave Macmillan, 2009.
14. Vergil, Polydore (Sir Henry Ellis K.H. ed). *Three Books of Polydore Vergil's English History: Comprising the Reigns of Henry VI, Edward IV and Richard III.* Camden Society, 1844.
15. Weir, Alison. *Elizabeth of York: The First Tudor Queen*, Vintage, 2014.
16. Vergil, Polydore (Sir Henry Ellis K.H. ed). *Three Books of Polydore Vergil's English History: Comprising the Reigns of Henry VI, Edward IV and Richard III.* Camden Society, 1844.

Chapter 6: And then there were two Queens

1. Bacon, Francis. *History of the Reign of King Henry VII*: With Notes by J. Rawson Lumby. (Written in 1622 during the reign of James I). University Press, 1889.
2. Bacon, Francis. *History of the Reign of King Henry VII*: With Notes by J. Rawson Lumby. (Written in 1622 during the reign of James I). University Press, 1889.
3. *www.richardIII.net*. (Titulus Regius).
4. Ibid.
5. Ibid.
6. *Croyland Chronicle* (second continuation).
7. Weir, Alison. *Elizabeth of York, the First Tudor Queen.* Jonathan Cape, 2013.
8. Ibid.
9. Andre, Bernard. *The Life of Henry VII.* Translated and introduced by Daniel Hobbins. Italica Press, 2011.
10. Bacon, Francis. *History of the Reign of King Henry VII*: With Notes by J. Rawson Lumby. (Written in 1622 during the reign of James I). University Press, 1889.

11. Andre, Bernard. *The Life of Henry VII*. Translated and introduced by Daniel Hobbins. Italica Press, 2011.
12. Borman, Tracy. *The Private Lives of the Tudors*. Hodder & Stoughton, 2016.
13. Leland, *Joannis Lelandi Antiquarii de rebus Britannicis Collectanea (Vol. 5)*. Thomas Hearne, 1770.
14. Ibid.
15. Bacon, Francis. *History of the Reign of King Henry VII*: With Notes by J. Rawson Lumby. *(*Written in 1622 during the reign of James I). University Press, 1889.
16. Ibid.
17. Ibid.
18. Weir, Alison. *Elizabeth of York, the First Tudor Queen*. Jonathan Cape, 2013.
19. Bacon, Francis. *History of the Reign of King Henry VII*: With Notes by J. Rawson Lumby. *(*Written in 1622 during the reign of James I). University Press, 1889.
20. Hall, Edward. *Hall's Chronicle, Containing the History of England During the Reign of Henry IV and the Succeeding Monarchs to the End of the Reign of Henry VIII*. Edited by Sir Henry Ellis, London, 1809.
21. Weir, Alison. *Elizabeth of York, the First Tudor Queen*. Jonathan Cape, 2013.
22. Leland, *Joannis Lelandi Antiquarii de rebus Britannicis Collectanea (Vol. 5)*, Thomas Hearne, 1770.
23. Strickland, Agnes. *Lives of the Queens of England from the Norman Conquest*, Lea and Blanchard, 1852.
24. Weir, Alison. *Elizabeth of York: The First Tudor Queen*. Vintage, 2014.
25. Strickland, Agnes. *Henry VIII*, Lea and Blanchard, 1852.
26. Hodder, Sarah J. *The Queen's Sisters*. John Hunt Publishing (Chronos Books), 2020.

Chapter 7: An End and a Beginning

1. Sutton, Anne F. and Visser-Fuchs, Livia. *Royal Funerals of the House of York at Windsor*. Richard III Society, 2005.

2. Bacon, Francis. *History of the Reign of King Henry VII*: With Notes by J. Rawson Lumby. *(*Written in 1622 during the reign of James I). University Press, 1889.

3. https://www.westminster-abbey.org/abbey-commemorations/ royals/elizabeth-daughter-of-henry-vii

4. Moore, Thomas. *The History of Ireland: Volume 3*. Longman, Orme, Brown, Green and Longmans, January 1846.

5. Ibid.

6. Fitzgerald, Charles William (Duke of Leinster). *The Earls of Kildare, and Their Ancestors, from 1057 to 1773*. Hodges, Smith & Co., Dublin 1858.

7. 'Spain: 1493', in *Calendar of State Papers, Spain*, Volume 1, 1485–1509, ed. G A Bergenroth (London, 1862), pp. 43–51. British History Online.

8. Fitzgerald, Charles William (Duke of Leinster). *The Earls of Kildare, and Their Ancestors, from 1057 to 1773*. Hodges, Smith & Co., Dublin 1858.

9. Moore, Thomas. *The History of Ireland:* Volume 3. Longman, Orme, Brown, Green and Longmans, January 1846.

10. Fitzgerald, Charles William (Duke of Leinster). *The Earls of Kildare, and Their Ancestors, from 1057 to 1773*. Hodges, Smith & Co., Dublin 1858.

11. A P Baggs, W J Blair, Eleanor Chance, Christina Colvin, Janet Cooper, C J Day, Nesta Selwyn and S C Townley, 'Blenheim: The King's houses', in *A History of the County of Oxford*: Volume 12, Wootton Hundred (South) Including Woodstock, ed. Alan Crossley and C R Elrington (London, 1990), pp. 435–439. British History Online.

12. BHO: 'Venice: 1497', in *Calendar of State Papers Relating To English Affairs in the Archives of Venice*, Volume 1, 1202–1509, ed. Rawdon Brown (London, 1864), pp. 252–266. British History Online.

13. Hall, Edward. *Hall's Chronicle, Containing the History of England During the Reign of Henry IV and the Succeeding Monarchs to the End of the Reign of Henry VIII*. Edited by Sir Henry Ellis, London, 1809.

14. Ibid.

15. Green, Mary Anne Everett. *Letters of Royal and Illustrious Ladies of Great Britain: From the Commencement of the Twelfth Century to the Close of the Reign of Queen Mary*. Volume 1. H. Colburn, 1846.

16. Licence, Amy. *Elizabeth of York, the Forgotten Tudor Queen.* Amberley Publishing 2014.
17. 'Spain: 1501', in *Calendar of State Papers, Spain*, Volume 1, 1485–1509, ed. G A Bergenroth (London, 1862), pp. 253–265. British History Online.
18. Borman, Tracy. *The Private Lives of the Tudors.* Hodder & Stoughton, 2016.
19. 'Spain: 1501', in *Calendar of State Papers, Spain*, Volume 1, 1485–1509, ed. G A Bergenroth (London, 1862), pp. 253–265. British History Online.
20. 'Spain: 1501', in *Calendar of State Papers, Spain*, Volume 1, 1485–1509, ed. G A Bergenroth (London, 1862), pp. 253–265. British History Online.
21. Ibid. 304. Henry VII. to the Archbishop of Santiago and the Count de Cabra.
22. Strickland, Agnes. *Lives of the Queens of England: From the Norman Conquest.* Volumes 4–5. Lea and Blanchard, 1847.
23. Ibid.
24. Hall, Edward. *Hall's Chronicle, Containing the History of England During the Reign of Henry IV and the Succeeding Monarchs to the End of the Reign of Henry VIII.* Edited by Sir Henry Ellis, London, 1809.
25. Ibid.
26. Ibid.
27. Strickland, Agnes. *Lives of the Queens of England: From the Norman Conquest.* Volumes 4–5. Lea and Blanchard, 1847.
28. Spain: 1501', in *Calendar of State Papers, Spain*, Volume 1, 1485–1509, ed. G A Bergenroth (London, 1862), pp. 253–265. British History Online.
29. Ibid
30. Leland, *Joannis Lelandi Antiquarii de rebus Britannicis Collectanea (vol. 5)*, Thomas Hearne, 1770.
31. Nicolas, Sir Nicholas Harris. *Privy purse expenses of Elizabeth of York; Wardrobe Accounts of Edward the Fourth. With a memoir of Elizabeth of York.* Sir Nicholas Harris. William Pickering, 1830.
32. Saint Claire Byrne, Muriel (ed.) *The Lisle Letters – an Abridgement*, University of Chicago Press, 1983.

33. Nicolas, Sir Nicholas Harris. *Privy purse expenses of Elizabeth of York; Wardrobe Accounts of Edward the Fourth. With a memoir of Elizabeth of York.* Sir Nicholas Harris. William Pickering, 1830.
34. Ibid.
35. Ibid.

Chapter 8: Taken Too Soon

1. Nicolas, Sir Nicholas Harris. *Privy purse expenses of Elizabeth of York; Wardrobe Accounts of Edward the Fourth. With a memoir of Elizabeth of York.* Sir Nicholas Harris. William Pickering, 1830.
2. Ibid.
3. Borman, Tracy. *The Private Lives of the Tudors.* Hodder & Stoughton, 2016.
4. Nicolas, Sir Nicholas Harris. *Privy purse expenses of Elizabeth of York; Wardrobe Accounts of Edward the Fourth. With a memoir of Elizabeth of York.* Sir Nicholas Harris. William Pickering, 1830.
5. https://www.library.wales/discover/digital-gallery/manuscripts/the-middle-ages/the-vaux-passional
6. *Sadlack, Erin A.* The French Queen's Letters. *Palgrave Macmillan, 2011.*
7. Hall, Edward. *Hall's Chronicle, Containing the History of England During the Reign of Henry IV and the Succeeding Monarchs to the End of the Reign of Henry VIII.* Edited by Sir Henry Ellis, London, 1809.
8. Weir, Alison. *Elizabeth of York: The First Tudor Queen.* Vintage, 2014.
9. Ibid.
10. Evans, Thomas. *Old Ballads, Historical and Narrative, With Some of Modern Date;* Collected with Some Rare Copies and Mss.
11. CCR Henry VII vol.2 Sealed 4 Dec., 20 Henry VII. English. (Ref: 478).
12. Turpyn, Richard (editor). *The Chronicle of Calais: In the Reigns of Henry VII. and Henry VIII. to the Year 1540.* Edited from a Mss. in the British Museum. Camden Society, January 1846.
13. Hall, Edward. *Hall's Chronicle, Containing the History of England During the Reign of Henry IV and the Succeeding Monarchs to the End of the Reign of Henry VIII.* Edited by Sir Henry Ellis, London, 1809.

14. Turpyn, Richard (editor). *The Chronicle of Calais: In the Reigns of Henry VII. and Henry VIII. to the Year 1540*. Edited from a Mss. in the British Museum. Camden Society, January 1846.
15. 'Venice: October 1514', in *Calendar of State Papers Relating To English Affairs in the Archives of Venice*, Volume 2, 1509–1519, ed. Rawdon Brown (London, 1867), pp. 193–202. British History Online.
16. Perry, Maria. *Sisters to the King*. Andre Deutsch, 2002.
17. 'Venice: October 1514', in *Calendar of State Papers Relating To English Affairs in the Archives of Venice*, Volume 2, 1509–1519, ed. Rawdon Brown (London, 1867), pp. 193–202. British History Online.
18. S.P. Hen. VIII., 9, f. 136. R.O.
19. Sadlack, Erin A. *The French Queen's Letters*. Palgrave Macmillan, 2011.
20. Ibid.
21. Ibid.
22. Perry, Maria. *Sisters to the King*. Andre Deutsch, 2002.
23. Ibid.
24. Sadlack, Erin A. *The French Queen's Letters*. Palgrave Macmillan, 2011.
25. Perry, Maria. *Sisters to the King*. Andre Deutsch, 2002.
26. Sadlack, Erin A. *The French Queen's Letters*. Palgrave Macmillan, 2011.
27. Spinelly To [Henry VIII.] 13 Feb. L&P.
28. Watkins, Sarah-Beth. *The Tudor Brandons*. John Hunt Publishing (Chronos Books), 2020.
29. Perry, Maria. *Sisters to the King*. Andre Deutsch, 2002.
30. https://www.bloischambord.co.uk/explore/the-chateaux/the-royal-chateau-de-blois
31. Licence, Amy. *Anne Boleyn: Adultery, Heresy, Desire*. Amberley 2017.
32. Sadlack, Erin A. *The French Queen's Letters*. Palgrave Macmillan, 2011.
33. Ibid.
34. 'Henry VIII: July 1517, 1–10', in *Letters and Papers, Foreign and Domestic, Henry VIII*, Volume 2, 1515–1518, ed. J S Brewer (London, 1864), pp. 1092–1102. British History Online.
35. Oxford DNB: Fitzgerald [née Grey], Elizabeth, countess of Kildare fl. 1514–1548) Steven G. Ellis, 23 September 2004.

36. 'Henry VIII: July 1517, 11–20', in *Letters and Papers, Foreign and Domestic, Henry VIII*, Volume 2, 1515–1518, ed. J S Brewer (London, 1864), pp. 1102–1114. British History Online.
37. Licence, Amy. *The Field of the Cloth of Gold*. Amberley Publishing, 2020.
38. Moore, Thomas. *The History of Ireland:* Volume 3. Longman, Orme, Brown, Green and Longmans, 1846.
39. Moore, Thomas. *The History of Ireland:* Volume 3. Longman, Orme, Brown, Green and Longmans, 1846.
40. Bell, Doyne C. *Notices of the historic persons buried in the Chapel of St Peter Ad Vincula in the Tower of London (with an account of the discovery of the supposed remains of Queen Anne Boleyn).* John Murray, London, 1877.
41. 'Henry VIII: September 1520', in *Letters and Papers, Foreign and Domestic, Henry VIII*, Volume 3, 1519–1523, ed. J S Brewer (London, 1867), pp. 356–369. British History Online.

Chapter 9: The wilds of Ireland and the wives of England

1. Harris, *English Aristocratic Women, 1450–1550: Marriage and Family, Property and Careers*. Oxford University Press, 2002.
2. Oxford DNB: Fitzgerald [née Grey], Elizabeth, countess of Kildare (fl. 1514–1548) Steven G. Ellis.
3. Hore, Herbert Francis. *The Rental Book of Gerald, Ninth Earl of Kildare, A. D. 1518.* Source: The Journal of the Kilkenny and South-East of Ireland Archaeological Society, 1866, New Series, Vol. 5, No. 3 (1866), pp. 501–518, 525–546 Published by: Royal Society of Antiquaries of Ireland.
4. Holinshed, Raphael. *The Chronicles of England, Scotland and Ireland*. First printed 1577. Project Gutenberg, 2014.
5. Peil, James and the Knight of Glin. *Irish Furniture*. Yale University Press, 2007.
6. 'Venice: November 1531', in *Calendar of State Papers Relating To English Affairs in the Archives of Venice*, Volume 4, 1527–1533, ed. Rawdon Brown (London, 1871), pp. 291–307. 694. Report of England, made to the Senate by Lodovico Falier.
7. Oxford DNB: Fitzgerald [née Grey], Elizabeth, countess of Kildare (fl. 1514–1548) Steven G. Ellis.

References

8. Green. Mary Anne Everett. *Letters of Royal and Illustrious Ladies of Great Britain: From the Commencement of the Twelfth Century to the Close of the Reign of Queen Mary*. Volume 1. H. Colburn, 1846. Elizabeth Countess of Kildare to Cardinal Wolsey . A.D. 1523.

9. Fitzgerald, Charles William (Duke of Leinster). *The Earls of Kildare, and Their Ancestors, from 1057 to 1773*. Hodges, Smith & Co., Dublin 1858.

10. Henry VIII: August 1526, 11–20', in *Letters and Papers, Foreign and Domestic, Henry VIII*, Volume 4, 1524–1530, ed. J S Brewer (London, 1875), pp. 1066–1081. British History Online.

11. Bagwell, Richard. *Ireland under the Tudors*, Volume I (of II). With a Succinct Account of the Earlier History. Project Gutenberg, 2013.

12. Ibid.

13. Harris, *English Aristocratic Women, 1450–1550: Marriage and Family, Property and Careers*. Oxford University Press, 2002.

14. Bagwell, Richard. *Ireland under the Tudors*, Volume I (of II). With a Succinct Account of the Earlier History. Project Gutenberg, 2013.

15. Green. Mary Anne Everett. *Letters of Royal and Illustrious Ladies of Great Britain: From the Commencement of the Twelfth Century to the Close of the Reign of Queen Mary*. Volume 1. H. Colburn, 1846.

16. Harris, Sir Nicholas. *The privy purse expenses of king Henry the eighth, from November mdxxix, to December mdxxxii: with introduction, remarks and illustrations*. Notes by N.H. Nicholas. W. Pickering, 1827.

17. Given under the Privy Seal and sign manual at Colyweston, 16 July, 18 Henry VII. English. Close Rolls, Henry VII: 1502–1503', in *Calendar of Close Rolls, Henry VII*: Volume 2, 1500–1509, ed. R A Latham (London, 1963), pp. 89–95. British History Online.

18. Bagwell, Richard. *Ireland under the Tudors*, Volume I (of II). With a Succinct Account of the Earlier History. Project Gutenberg, 2013.

19. Du Bellay To Francis I. 22nd June 1529. 'Henry VIII: June 1529, 2`1–25', in *Letters and Papers, Foreign and Domestic, Henry VIII*, Volume 4, 1524–1530, ed. J S Brewer (London, 1875), pp. 2523–2531. British History Online.

20. 'Venice: November 1531', in *Calendar of State Papers Relating To English Affairs in the Archives of Venice*, Volume 4, 1527–1533, ed. Rawdon Brown (London, 1871), pp. 291–307. British History Online.

21. Ibid.

22. Bagwell, Richard. *Ireland under the Tudors*, Volume I (of II). With a Succinct Account of the Earlier History. Project Gutenberg, 2013.

23. Ref: 'Henry VIII: June 1533, 21–25', in *Letters and Papers, Foreign and Domestic, Henry VIII*, Volume 6, 1533, ed. James Gairdner (London, 1882), pp. 306–313. British History Online.

24. 'Henry VIII: July 1534, 6–10', in *Letters and Papers, Foreign and Domestic, Henry VIII*, Volume 7, 1534, ed. James Gairdner (London, 1883), pp. 363–373. British History Online.

25. Chapuys to Charles V on 7th July 1534. 'Henry VIII: July 1534, 6–10', in *Letters and Papers, Foreign and Domestic, Henry VIII*, Volume 7, 1534, ed. James Gairdner (London, 1883), pp. 363–373. British History Online.

26. Bagwell, Richard. *Ireland under the Tudors*, Volume I (of II). With a Succinct Account of the Earlier History. Project Gutenberg, 2013.

27. Bell, Doyne C. *Notices of the historic persons buried in the Chapel of St Peter Ad Vincula in the Tower of London (with an account of the discovery of the supposed remains of Queen Anne Boleyn*. John Murray, London, 1877.

28. Ibid.

Chapter 10: A widow in England as Maynooth burned

1. 'Henry VIII: March 1535, 11–20', in *Letters and Papers, Foreign and Domestic, Henry VIII*, Volume 8, January–July 1535, ed. James Gairdner (London, 1885), pp. 149–161. British History Online.

2. 'Henry VIII: May 1535, 26–31', in *Letters and Papers, Foreign and Domestic, Henry VIII*, Volume 8, January–July 1535, ed. James Gairdner (London, 1885), pp. 287–305. British History Online.

3. Bagwell, Richard. *Ireland under the Tudors*, Volume I (of II). With a Succinct Account of the Earlier History. Project Gutenberg, 2013.

4. *Calendar of the Carew Manuscripts: 1515–1574*. Longmans, Green, Reader & Dyer, 1867.

5. Bagwell, Richard. *Ireland under the Tudors*, Volume I (of II). With a Succinct Account of the Earlier History. Project Gutenberg, 2013.

6. Ballad by JC Mangan, published by the Kildare Archaeological Society, Dublin, 1908.

7. *Calendar of the Carew Manuscripts: 1515–1574.* Longmans, Green, Reader & Dyer, 1867.

8. Fitzgerald, Charles William (Duke of Leinster). *The Earls of Kildare, and Their Ancestors, from 1057 to 1773.* Hodges, Smith & Co., Dublin 1858.

9. The itinerary of John Leland in or about the years 1535–1543. Edited by Lucy Toulmin Smith. London, G. Bell 1907.

10. Burke, Bernard. *The Historic Lands of England,* Volume 2. E. Churton, 1849.

11. Fitzgerald, Charles William (Duke of Leinster). *The Earls of Kildare, and Their Ancestors, from 1057 to 1773.* Hodges, Smith & Co., Dublin 1858.

12. *Calendar of the Carew Manuscripts: 1515–1574.* Longmans, Green, Reader & Dyer, 1867.

13. 'Henry VIII: July 1536, 16–20', in *Letters and Papers, Foreign and Domestic, Henry VIII*, Volume 11, July–December 1536, ed. James Gairdner (London, 1888), pp. 46–54. British History Online.

14. Bagwell, Richard. *Ireland under the Tudors,* Volume I (of II). With a Succinct Account of the Earlier History. Project Gutenberg, 2013.

15. Green. Mary Anne Everett. *Letters of Royal and Illustrious Ladies of Great Britain: From the Commencement of the Twelfth Century to the Close of the Reign of Queen Mary.* H. Colburn, 1846.

16. REF: 'Henry VIII: June 1538, 1–10', in *Letters and Papers, Foreign and Domestic, Henry VIII*, Volume 13 Part 1, January–July 1538, ed. James Gairdner (London, 1892), pp. 416–435. British History Online.

17. 'Henry VIII: December 1537, 26–31', in *Letters and Papers, Foreign and Domestic, Henry VIII*, Volume 12 Part 2, June–December 1537, ed. James Gairdner (London, 1891), pp. 443–481. British History Online.

18. 'Letters and Papers: Miscellaneous, 1539', in *Letters and Papers, Foreign and Domestic, Henry VIII*, Volume 14 Part 2, August–December 1539, ed. James Gairdner and R H Brodie (London, 1895), pp. 303–358. British History Online.

19. Howard, Henry (Earl of Surrey). *The Poems of Henry Howard, Earl of Surrey.* Bell and Daldy, 1831.

20. 'Henry VIII: June 1540, 21–30', in *Letters and Papers, Foreign and Domestic, Henry VIII*, Volume 15, 1540, ed. James Gairdner and R H Brodie (London, 1896), pp. 376–412. British History Online.

21. 'Henry VIII: July 1541, 1–10', in *Letters and Papers, Foreign and Domestic, Henry VIII*, Volume 16, 1540–1541, ed. James Gairdner and R H Brodie (London, 1898), pp. 465–477. British History Online.
22. Madden, Frederick. *Privy purse expenses of the Princess Mary, daughter of King Henry the Eighth, afterwards Queen Mary: with a memoir of the princess, and notes*. London, W. Pickering, 1831
23. 'Henry VIII: December 1545, 21–25', in *Letters and Papers, Foreign and Domestic, Henry VIII*, Volume 20 Part 2, August–December 1545, ed. James Gairdner and R H Brodie (London, 1907), pp. 504–518. British History Online.
24. *The household of Queen Katherine Parr* by Dakota L. Hamilton. Masters Thesis. https://scholarworks.calstate.edu/concern/theses/0p096922j
25. 'Henry VIII: August 1546, 26–31', in *Letters and Papers, Foreign and Domestic, Henry VIII*, Volume 21 Part 1, January–August 1546, ed. James Gairdner and R H Brodie (London, 1908), pp. 749–785. British History Online.
26. 'Henry VIII: November 1546, 11–20', in *Letters and Papers, Foreign and Domestic, Henry VIII*, Volume 21 Part 2, September 1546–January 1547, ed. James Gairdner and R H Brodie (London, 1910), pp. 188–203. British History Online.

Chapter 11: An End always signals a new Beginning

1. Everett Green, Mary-Anne. *Letters of Royal and Illustrious Ladies of Great Britain: From the Commencement of the Twelfth Century to the Close of the Reign of Queen Mary*, Volume 3. H. Colburn, 1846.
2. 'Pages 426–451', in *Acts of the Privy Council of England*, Volume 2, 1547–1550, ed. John Roche Dasent (London, 1890), pp. 426–436. British History Online.
3. 'Pages 26–51', in *Acts of the Privy Council of England*, Volume 3, 1550–1552, ed. John Roche Dasent (London, 1891), pp. 26–50. British History Online.
4. Hodder, Sarah J. *Cecily Bonville-Grey, Marchioness of Dorset*. John Hunt Publishing, 2022.
5. Bagwell, Richard. *Ireland under the Tudors*, Volume I (of II). With a Succinct Account of the Earlier History. Project Gutenberg, 2013.

References

6. *Calendar of the Carew Manuscripts: 1515–1574.* Longmans, Green, Reader & Dyer, 1867.

7. Hasler, P. W. (ed.) *The History of Parliament: the House of Commons 1558–1603.* Boydell and Brewer, 1981.

8. Cooke, Thomas Lalor. *The Early History of the Town of Birr, Or Parsonstown: With the Particulars of Remarkable Events There in More Recent Times; Also the Towns of Nenagh, Roscrea, Banagher, Tullamore, Philipstown, Frankford, Shinrone, Kinnetty and Ballyboy, and the Ancient Septs, Princes, and Celebrated Places of the Surrounding Country.* Robertson & Company, 1875.

9. *Calendar of the Carew Manuscripts: 1515–1574.* Longmans, Green, Reader & Dyer, 1867.

10. Thomas, Melita. *The House of Grey: Friends and Foes of Kings.* Amberley Publishing, 2019.

11. Hore, Herbert Francis. *The Rental Book of Gerald, Ninth Earl of Kildare, A. D. 1518.* Source: The Journal of the Kilkenny and South-East of Ireland Archaeological Society, 1866, New Series, Vol. 5, No. 3 (1866), pp. 501–518, 525–546 Published by: Royal Society of Antiquaries of Ireland.

Index